Archaic Instruments in Modern West Java

Archaic Instruments in Modern West Java: Bamboo Murmurs explores how current residents of Bandung, Indonesia, have (re-)adopted bamboo musical instruments to forge meaningful bridges between their past and present—between traditional and modern values. Although it focuses specifically on Bandung, the cosmopolitan capital city of West Java, the book grapples with ongoing issues of global significance, including musical environmentalism, heavy metal music, the effects of first-world hegemonies on developing countries, and cultural "authenticity." Bamboo music's association with the Sundanese landscape, old agricultural ceremonies, and participatory music making, as well as its adaptability to modern society, make it a fertile site for an ecomusicological study.

Henry Spiller is Professor in the Department of Music at University of California, Davis and the author of several books, including *FOCUS: Gamelan Music of Indonesia.*

SOAS Studies in Music
Series Editors:
Rachel Harris, SOAS, University of London, UK
Rowan Pease, SOAS, University of London, UK

Board Members:
Angela Impey (SOAS, University of London)
Henry Spiller (University California)
Kwasi Ampene (University of Michigan)
Linda Barwick (University of Sydney)
Martin Stokes (Kings College London)
Moshe Morad (Tel Aviv University)
Noriko Manabe (Temple University)
Richard Widdess (SOAS, University of London)
Suzel Reily (Universidade Estadual de Campinas)
Travis A. Jackson (University of Chicago)

SOAS Studies in Music is today one of the world's leading series in the discipline of ethnomusicology. Our core mission is to produce high-quality, ethnographically rich studies of music-making in the world's diverse musical cultures. We publish monographs and edited volumes that explore musical repertories and performance practice, critical issues in ethnomusicology, sound studies, historical and analytical approaches to music across the globe. We recognize the value of applied, interdisciplinary and collaborative research, and our authors draw on current approaches in musicology and anthropology, psychology, media and gender studies. We welcome monographs that investigate global contemporary, classical and popular musics, the effects of digital mediation and transnational flows.

Archaic Instruments in Modern West Java
Bamboo Murmurs
Henry Spiller

Musical Collaboration Between Indigenous and Non-Indigenous People in Australia
Exchanges in The Third Space
Edited by Katelyn Barney

For more information about this series, please visit: www.routledge.com/music/series/SOASMS

Archaic Instruments in Modern West Java

Bamboo Murmurs

Henry Spiller

NEW YORK AND LONDON

Cover image: Bamboo surrounding a waterfall at the foot of Mt. Arjuno-Welirang near Malang, East Java. Photo: Febry Reviansyach Dewandra, via Wiki Commons. Licensed under the Creative Commons Attribution-Share Alike 4.0

First published 2023
by Routledge
605 Third Avenue, New York, NY 10158

and by Routledge
4 Park Square, Milton Park, Abingdon, Oxon, OX14 4RN

Routledge is an imprint of the Taylor & Francis Group, an informa business

© 2023 Henry Spiller

The right of Henry Spiller to be identified as author of this work has been asserted in accordance with sections 77 and 78 of the Copyright, Designs and Patents Act 1988.

All rights reserved. No part of this book may be reprinted or reproduced or utilised in any form or by any electronic, mechanical, or other means, now known or hereafter invented, including photocopying and recording, or in any information storage or retrieval system, without permission in writing from the publishers.

Trademark notice: Product or corporate names may be trademarks or registered trademarks, and are used only for identification and explanation without intent to infringe.

ISBN: 978-1-032-29934-1 (hbk)
ISBN: 978-1-032-29935-8 (pbk)
ISBN: 978-1-003-30279-7 (ebk)

DOI: 10.4324/9781003302797

Typeset in Times New Roman
by Newgen Publishing UK

Contents

List of Figures		vi
Notes and Acknowledgments		viii
	Introduction	1
1	Bamboo Murmurs	12
2	When in Bandung ...	33
3	Bamboo Wisdom	64
4	Roots Values	85
5	Entanglements	116
	References	139
	Index	153

Figures

1.1	Java in the fourteenth century	13
1.2	a. Topographic map of Java. b. View from the train of flat expanses in Central Java. c. View from the train in West Java	16
1.3	*kujang* (left) vs *keris* (right)	19
1.4	Aeolian bamboo poles in the "Java Village," World's Columbian Exposition, Chicago, 1893	22
1.5	Irma Noerhaty demonstrates how to hold an angklung. The parts are labelled	23
1.6	Hypothetical angklung ostinatos. a. aligned. b. interlocking	25
1.7	Parts of a Sundanese suling	27
1.8	*Tembang Sunda*. Instruments in the back row (l to r): *kacapi indung* (Matt Ashworth), *suling* (Lili Rochili), *kacapi rincik* (Dadang); singers (l to r): Hendrawati, Arif Budiman	28
1.9	Sundanese *gamelan salendro*. Back row: *kenong* (player not visible), *pasinden* (female singer), *goong* and *kempul* (hanging from the same frame), *kendang* (drums), *bonang* (gong chime). Front row: *rebab*, *peking* (no player), *saron*, *saron*	29
2.1	A *tampian* (rustic bathing hut)	34
2.2	Gedung Merdeka in 2018, Bandung	36
2.3a	"Hallo-Hallo Bandung" (Ismail Marzuki) arranged by Daeng Soetigna	43
2.3b	Transnotation of Daeng's arrangement of "Hallo-Hallo Bandung"	44
2.4	First line of "Hallo-Hallo Bandung"; the note "5" is highlighted in to demonstrate that it is part of three distinct "voices" in the texture, even though it is played by a single individual	45
2.5	The afternoon show at SAU	50
2.6	Chromatic angklung toel	56
3.1	Bandung and the Cikapundung River	65
3.2	Galengan Sora Awi performs at the Cikapundung Hiking Orienteering Games (CIHOG), March 30, 2013	66

Figures vii

3.3	GSA rehearsing in the lobby area of Taman Budaya, Bandung	67
3.4	Akim playing one of his celempung with the various parts labelled.	70
3.5	Akim makes a celempung. a. bamboo culm; b. separating strings; c. adding the bridges; d. adding the weight	71
3.6	Akim's celempung renteng	72
3.7	Goong awi	73
3.8	a. Otong Rasta's cross-section sketch of the hollow inside a kendang (pc, June 12, 1981); b. kendang	74
3.9	Ujang (a.k.a. Handi Purnaman) plays Akim's baragbag (a.k.a. kendang awi)	75
3.10	Gambang awi	76
3.11	Tarompet (l) and suling (r) flanked by two gambang awi	78
4.1	Tangkuban Perahu, viewed from northern Bandung	86
4.2	The author at the Bandung holy spring, now in the basement of a bank	87
4.3	Teddy Kusmayadi plays *karinding*	88
4.4	Parts of a Karinding, according to Kubarsah (1996, 51), Abah Olot, and Oyon Naroharjo	89
4.5	Ki Amenk and Wisnu play karinding with Karinding Attack; note the bamboo microphone stands for the karinding	91
4.6	Karinding as a fashion item	95
4.7	Formal and riff analysis for "Refuse/Resist" (Sepultura)	104
4.8	Formal and riff analysis for "Refuse/Resist" (Karinding Attack)	106
4.9	"Maaf" motifs: a. Rhythmic motif for second section of "Maaf." b. Melody for third section of "Maaf."	109
5.1	Suling. a. Ismet Ruchimat plays suling panjang. b. Mang Toto measures the halfway point to drill the first hole in a suling he's making. c. arrangement of holes on a suling panjang into two groups of three equidistant holes.	118
5.2	A display of bamboo flutes from all over the Indonesian archipelago, most with equidistant fingerholes, on display at the Sri Baduga Museum, Bandung	119
5.3	Keeping the middle holes of each of a suling's three-hole groups closed to simulate four equidistant holes for salendro	120
5.4	Covering suling holes to create pelog degung's small and large intervals	121
5.5	A collection of Endo Suanda's musical instruments made from boards of laminated bamboo. From top to bottom: kacapi indung; *gambus*; guitar; *tarawangsa*	131
5.6	One of Asep Nata's karinding toél	135

Notes and Acknowledgments

Notes on Names and Orthography

This book cites consultants and texts whose original language was English, Dutch, Indonesian, or Sundanese. Although English and Dutch orthographies have undergone various reforms and modifications over the decades, they do not require explanation here. Indonesian and Sundanese approaches to orthography, however, are sometimes confusing for readers of English and other European languages, as are the conventions of personal names and appellations.

Regarding spelling: it is customary to convey both Indonesian and Sundanese languages using the Roman alphabet, although in the past, Sundanese intellectuals have used other systems as well (e.g., *aksara Sunda* and the Arabic alphabet). In the current system, adopted in 1972, most consonants and vowels are pronounced as in Spanish or Italian; the exception is that the letter 'c' is always pronounced 'ch.' The vowel 'e' can be pronounced in a number of ways: some sources differentiate 'è,' 'e,' and 'é' while others provide no diacritical marks and assume that readers will know which vowel to pronounce.

Under Dutch colonial control, the official spelling for Indonesian followed Dutch-language conventions: 'oe' was pronounced as 'u,' 'j' was pronounced as 'y,' 'tj' as 'ch,' and 'dj' as 'j'; it is important to note the date of publications in Indonesian or Sundanese to determine proper pronunciation. Official changes in orthography did not necessarily apply to personal names, however, and many individuals still spell their names using the old Dutch orthography. It is my understanding that Indonesia's first president, Sukarno, for example, preferred to cast off the Dutch spelling of his name ("Soekarno"), while Indonesia's second president, Soeharto, preferred the conservative connotations (if not necessarily the Dutch associations!) of the 'oe' spelling. It is my policy to honor individuals' personal preferences when spelling their names; when directly quoting other sources, however, I use the original spelling.

Beyond spelling, Indonesian and Sundanese personal names present a variety of additional challenges to the "given-name surname" conventions of Europe and North America. (I am always amused, when reading very

Notes and Acknowledgments   ix

short journalistic accounts of current events in Indonesia, by the proportion of the total verbiage that is devoted to quoting eye-witnesses: "*So-and-so*, who like many Indonesians goes by only one name, reports that ... .")

Most Sundanese individuals use at least two names, but these do not necessarily represent the exact equivalents of given names and surnames. Sundanese parents typically give their children a formal name (or several) at birth. People with aristocratic roots often bestow flowery, Sanskrit-derived names. But these are rarely used. Instead, individuals are commonly addressed throughout their lives by a nickname, which may or may not be derived from their formal name.

More importantly: in everyday discourse, people take care to define their relationships with the individuals they address by prefacing their name—usually their most familiar name—with an appropriate honorific. It is instructive to interpret these conventions by examining how my interlocutors address me in different contexts. During my field work, I was introduced as Om ("[Dutch] Uncle") Henry to the young people in my karinding class, which consisted of teenage boys (see Chapter 4); presumably, my introducers wanted to minimize any status difference between me and my fellow karinding acolytes, despite our obvious age and status difference. University students, however, addressed me as "Prof Henry" (as far as I can tell, Prof is a relatively new honorific), to acknowledge my academic status. Most other people called me "Pa Henry"—"Pa" (short for "bapa" [father]), recognizing my advanced age. Notable exceptions: fellow academics, even much younger ones, typically called me "Kang Henry" ("kang" is an honorific that literally means "elder brother," but actually implies a relationship of equals [comparable to "Mas" in Central Java]); by using this title, these individuals respectfully assert their equal status.

In this book, I sometimes include (hopefully) appropriate honorifics when discussing my interlocutors. For the most part, however, it is more expeditious (if not necessarily comfortable) to provide only their familiar name, without any honorific; in doing so, I intend no disrespect. When citing published works by Indonesian authors, I treat Indonesian names as any Western bibliographer would—as if the final name in their moniker were the surname by which the source is alphabetized.

Acknowledgments

Much of the first-hand information for this study was gathered during five months of field work in Bandung (March–August 2013) conducted with the support of a Fulbright Senior Scholar grant. I am grateful not only to the Fulbright commission for their financial support, but to the American Indonesian Exchange Foundation (AMINEF) for their practical support in Indonesia. The AMINEF staff in Jakarta— executive director Michael McCoy, program officers Ceacelia Dewitha, M. Rizqi Arifuddin, Astrid Lim, and especially Nellie Paliama—all deserve my special thanks.

x *Notes and Acknowledgments*

Prof. Yudi Sukmayadi at the Universitas Pendidikan Indonesia (UPI) Bandung agreed to be my research sponsor, and I am grateful for his generosity and friendship. Yudi convened a team of like-minded UPI scholars for me to consult with, including Rita Milyartini, Uus Karwati, Suwardi Kurmawardi, and Iwan Gunawan, and I thank them for their helpful input to my research. Juju Masunah, currently on the UPI faculty, was extremely helpful to me in many ways before, during, and after my trip to Indonesia.

I am also grateful for academic support and fellowship to the faculty of the Bandung branch of the institution known as Sekolah Tinggi Seni Indonesia (STSI) during my 2013 field work, currently known as Institut Seni Budaya Indonesian (ISBI). Rektor Endang Caturwati, and the then assistant rector (now the current rector) Een Herdiani continue to be generous and gregarious colleagues. I also thank the faculty of ISBI's Program Studi Musik Bambu, including Deni Hermawan, Ismet Ruchimat, Komarudin, Dinda Satya Upaja Budi, Abun Somawijaya, and Iyon Supiono, for their help. My interactions with Asep Nata, an independent scholar, musician, and instrument builder, were always informative, thought-provoking, and fun.

While in Bandung in 2013, my fieldwork focused on three musical organizations pursuing different approaches to bamboo music: (1) Angklung Web Institute (whose acronym, "AWI," is the Sundanese word for bamboo), an independent organization dedicated to the promulgation of diatonic *angklung* music using the tools and methods of the internet age; (2) Galengan Sora Awi, a neighborhood-based group of musicians who play a variety of traditional Sundanese musical styles on bamboo instruments of their own invention; and (3) Karinding Attack, a group of heavy metal musicians who play their metal-inspired compositions on obsolete bamboo instruments adapted for their purposes. I also investigated related organizations, such as the famous Saung Angklung Udjo (SAU), which presents daily traditional and modern *angklung* performances to tourists, and the newly formed bamboo music program at ISBI, as well as influential individuals in the Sundanese bamboo scene, including Endo Suanda and Asep Nata.

AWI's prime mover, Budi Supardiman (see Chapter 2), is a selfless advocate for angklung, and was generous to a fault to me as I pursued this project. Pa Budi allowed me to intrude on his life in many ways as he introduced me to many important figures in the angklung world. I also owe a debt of gratitude to Irma Noerhaty, who was the instructor for the angklung teaching course I took under AWI's auspices.

The members of Galengan Sora Awi (GSA, see Chapter 3) were also generous with their friendship, time, and experience. I would like to thank especially Asep Bobeng (GSA's "impresario," who took pains to keep me apprised of GSA's activities, answer my questions, and hang out), as well as one of GSA's prime advocates, the late Agus I. P. Wiryapraja. And of course GSA's members: Lia, Irma (Novianti), Deny (Firmansyah), Ujang,

Akim, Teddy, Restu, Dadang, and Gofar, who all welcomed me to their rehearsals, performances, and ancillary social activities.

The members of Karinding Attack (see Chapter 4) were similarly welcoming: Kimung; Man Jasad; Amenk; Ari; Mang Hendra; and Jimbot (a.k.a. Iman Rohman), among others. Gustaff H. Iskandar, of Common Room (an open platform for arts, culture, and media in Bandung), and the various other denizens of Common Room all were very supportive of my efforts as well.

Over the decades I have developed a network of Bandung-based friends and associates—scholars and performers who are unfailingly generous with practical, emotional, and material support for my own studies of Sundanese performing arts, especially: Endo and Marjie Suanda; Andy Bouchard, Rina Oesman, and family; Matt Ashworth, Hendrawati and family; and Irawati Durban Ardjo and Mas Durban. During my 2013 stay, my Dago landlords Ahadiat and Rini often acted as consultants and friends as well. I'd also like to acknowledge my fellow Fulbright grantee (and, it turned out, close neighbor in Dago), Doug Singleton, along with his wife Si and their son Denali. I was fortunate to meet Palmer Keen (who became the purveyor of the eye-opening website, Aural Archipelago) in Bandung in 2013. My interactions with him (and his wife, Sinta), are always stimulating.

A network of like-minded colleagues has long nourished my involvement with Sundanese music in various ways. Andrew Weintraub, Sean Williams, Rae Ann Stahl, Richard North, and Luigi Monteanni are always ready to respond to my data and ideas, or just to have a little fun. The many individuals who play music with me in the Bay Area gamelan groups Sari Raras (based in Berkeley, led by Midiyanto and Ben Brinner) and Pusaka Sunda (based in San Jose, led by Burhan Sukarma and Rae Ann Stahl) help to keep my interest in gamelan music grounded in actual performance.

At UC Davis, I am fortunately to have a large group of very supportive colleagues; I am especially grateful to Beth Levy, Anna Maria Busse Berger, Katherine Lee, and Juan Diego Díaz for their helpful feedback on this project at various stages. A series of small grants from the UC Davis Faculty Senate provided additional funding for this project. Bill and Susi Haworth (faithful patrons of the UC Davis music department) were instrumental in connecting me to the angklung community in the USA.

The Netherlands Institute for Advanced Study in the Humanities and Social Sciences (NIAS) awarded me a residential fellowship in Amsterdam to work on this project in the fall of 2019. This semester at NIAS provided welcome time and space to focus on writing up the results. In addition, the rich, collaborative environment provided many new ideas and approaches. I am especially grateful to my NIAS cohort, including Nilgun Bayraktar, Hanne Marlene Dahl, Wilco van Dijk, Michiel van Elk, Robert Glas, Herbert van Hoijtink, Susanne Klausen, Maarten Kleinhans, Jana Krause, Kristine Krause, Mirjam Künkler, James Mark, Sabah Mofidi, Rudolf

xii *Notes and Acknowledgments*

Mrazek, Basile Ndjio, Hagar Peeters, Yolanda Plumley, Bart Ramakers, Nadim Rouhana, Ellen Rutten, Vineet Thakur, Jaap Tielbeke, Simona-Luiza Țigriș, Tiia Tulviste, Natasha Veldhorst, Liesbeth van Vliet, and Şebnem Yardımcı-Geyikçi, as well as the NIAS staff, including Jan Willem Duyvendak, Fenneke Wekker, Kahliya Ronde, and Astrid Schulein. Other simpatico Dutch scholars have been very supportive as well, including Wim van Zanten, Barbara Titus, and Ben Arps. Jennifer Post read an earlier version of this manuscript, and her many helpful suggestions have strengthened the current iteration. I thank Patrick Liddell for his beautiful typesetting of the various staff notation examples. Constance Ditzel of Routledge was, as always, a supportive and generous editor. Constance assembled a responsive team to bring the book into its finished form, including editorial assistant Kaushikee Sharma, project manager Jayashree Thirumaran, and copy editor Robert Wilkinson, and I am grateful to them all.

I am fortunate to have had the opportunity to study Sundanese (and Javanese) music with some remarkable teachers over the decades. I thank especially my teachers who are based in the USA: Undang Sumarna, Burhan Sukarma, and Midiyanto. I am grateful for their ongoing (indeed, sometimes constant) contributions to my research—and my life—as time goes on. I spent hour after hour in *latihan* (lessons) over the past decades with many other teachers as well. I treasure the many fond memories I have of teachers who have died, especially Otong Rasta, Abay Subardja, Enoch Atmadibrata, Sujana Arja, Nugraha Sudiredja, Nano S., Entis Sutisna, and Hardja Susilo. It is my hope that my ongoing work honors their legacies.

As always, I owe my partner Michael Seth Orland an overwhelming debt of gratitude. His excellent ear for music, his skill and precision in writing, and his willingness to think through sometimes capricious theories all exert positive influences on my research. He is generous in putting up with absences—sometimes literal (when I go abroad for months at time), sometimes figurative (when I tune out the everyday world). And equally generous with active emotional, moral, and practical support. Thanks, Michael.

Introduction

From a global perspective, Indonesian music is all but synonymous with gamelan, the bronze-dominated percussion orchestras from Java and Bali. Since their initial appearances in the Western world at the late nineteenth-century great world expositions, awareness of gamelan has spread far beyond Indonesia. But there is another strain of musical traditions in Indonesia which has attracted less attention from international audiences and scholars, even though it involves far more people: musical practices that make use of bamboo. In West Java, bamboo music's long association with a distinctly Sundanese landscape, with pre-modern agricultural ceremonies, and with the aesthetics of participatory music making, as well as its adaptability to modern West Javanese society, make it a fertile site for investigating how musical meaning commingles with environment and culture.

This book focuses on a very specific time (the present) and place (Bandung, the cosmopolitan capital city of Indonesia's West Java province and the center of Sundanese culture). The pressing issues that modern residents of Bandung face, however—climate change and environmental crises, the continuing effects of first-world hegemonies on developing countries, cultural "authenticity" and ownership, and even the effects of UNESCO's "Representative List of Intangible Cultural Heritage"—are widespread. An understanding how the residents of Bandung deploy bamboo music-making to respond to these globally pressing issues is relevant all over the planet.

Bamboo

Bamboo grows like a weed in the warm, wet climate of West Java. Culms of bamboo shoot up in dense clumps; when a breeze blows, they sway gracefully together in the wind to create a pleasing visual effect. Because the hollow stalks are sonorous, any movement also creates a melodious murmuring. The Sundanese people who dominate West Java manifest these qualities in the proverb that lends this book its title metaphor: "kawas awi sumear di pasir"—"like bamboo murmuring on the hill." According to some, this aphorism adjures individuals to create harmony by working

DOI: 10.4324/9781003302797-1

2 Introduction

closely with their neighbors; in any case, it drives home the notion that bamboo, the landscape, and Sundanese values are inextricably intertwined (Rusnandar 2009).

Nadia Bystriakova et al. estimate that there are nearly 1,000 species of bamboo in the entire Asia-Pacific region, with more that 1,500 documented uses (2003a, 7–8). In Southeast Asia, "most significant uses ... are for building material, for making various types of baskets, ... as a vegetable ... as a source of raw material for making paper, for musical instruments and handicrafts" (Dransfield and Widjaja 1995, 19). Indonesia is home to a relatively modest number of indigenous bamboo species— fifty-six, according to Bystriakova et al. (2003a,10)—supplemented by a large number of imported species. There is no question that bamboo is an important resource for Indonesians—and for Sundanese.

Herry Dim provides a list of more than forty uniquely Sundanese bamboo items that continue to be useful in everyday life (2017). Marah Maradjo et al. (1976, 10–27) describe a few species of bamboo that have proven to be especially useful in West Java in making such items. Some varieties, for example, *bambu talang* (*Schiostachyum brachycladium*, called *awi buluh* in Sundanese) and *bambu perling*, with thin walls that are easy to split, are especially good for fine weaving (for walls, baskets, and kitchen implements). *Bambu betung* (*Dendrocalamus asper*) and *bambu gombong* (*Gigantochloa verticillate*) are large and strong and make excellent building material.

Not surprisingly, given bamboo's sonorous qualities and ready avail- ability, the sounds of bamboo have been a fundamental source for Sundanese music for centuries. Maradjo et al. also describe some bamboo varieties that are especially good for making musical instruments. *Bambu tamiang* (*Schiostachyum blumei*; called *awi tamiang* or *awi bunan* in Sundanese), with its thin walls and long segments (up to one meter) between nodes, is suitable for making *suling* (bamboo flutes; see Chapters 1 and 5) and other instruments. *Bambu ater* (*Gigantochloa atter*, called *awi temen* in Sundanese) and *bambu hitam* (*Gigantochloa atroviolacea*, *awi hideung* in Sundanese), with relatively large diameters (up to 13 cm) are useful for making percussion instruments, such as *angklung* (see Chapters 1 and 2), *calung*, and *gambang* (see Chapter 3).[1]

Bamboo music's intimate connections with the Sundanese landscape and Sundanese culture extend well beyond the sounds that bamboo can make, however. Pre-modern agricultural ceremonies to honor the rice goddess, Nyi Pohaci (also known as Dewi Sri), typically featured bamboo rattles called angklung. Participants, each playing a single rattle, performed intricately interlocking parts—thus rooting an aesthetic manifestation of the kind of close cooperation that brought success to their agricultural season in bamboo technology (see Chapter 1). Traditional bamboo music, then, united the aesthetics of musical style with aspects of the physical environment, available materials and technologies, and principles of social interaction to create complex, multifaceted, and rich human experience.

Introduction 3

In the twentieth century, Indonesians, like other colonial subjects, aligned themselves with modern Europeans by distancing themselves from their own Asian past either by erasing local history completely or finding ways to reconceive the past in ways consistent with modern European values. The so-called "New Order" government of Indonesia's authoritarian second president, Soeharto (1966–1998), promoted what Jeremy Wallach calls a "'top-down' culture of timidity, fear, and docility." The fall of Soeharto, in 1998, ushered in the era of *reformasi* (reformation), in which the "top-down" timidity was rapidly replaced by a "cacophony of unruly voices competing in a thriving democratic public sphere" (Wallach 2005, 17).

At least some of those unruly voices are echoes of Sundanese ancestors. In a wide-ranging essay, the Indonesian journalist Herry Dim identifies many modern problems that can be mitigated by paying attention to Sundanese ancestors' experiences ("pengalaman leluhur") with bamboo (Dim 2017). He points out that traditional rice growing practices relied on the presence of a small bamboo forest, called *geger*, in or near the rice fields, which complemented the intensive cultivation of rice by providing a habitat for various animals that could control the pest population and foliage that could absorb and store water (Dim 2017). Traditional knowledge of bamboo and its roles in premodern Sundanese life, Dim argues, can speak to contemporary environmental concerns as well as provide potential solutions to socio-economic problems (Dim 2017).

Various bottom-up approaches to music, including locally inflected underground metal scenes, also contributed to the cacophony Wallach describes. Some Sundanese musicians also turned their eyes and ears to bamboo for inspiration. Embracing bamboo is a way to reconfirm a relationship of Sundanese culture to the landscape of West Java. The musical qualities of bamboo recall a sense of Sundaneseness, even among the thoroughly modern residents of Bandung in the reformasi period.

Since the beginning of reformasi, one hears more and more bamboo murmurs throughout West Java's capital city. Genteel groups of middle-class Indonesians perform arrangements of international easy-listening standards on *angklung padaeng* (diatonically tuned choirs of bamboo rattles). A multi-generation group of musicians from a local neighborhood plays well-known traditional songs on homemade bamboo xylophones, usually for environmentally themed events. Death metal rockers adapt their underground music to rural bamboo instruments, such as *karinding* (mouth-resonated lamellophone) and *celempung* (idiochord tube zither). These and other bamboo music activities represent a dramatic about-face for the predominantly ethnic Sundanese residents of Bandung, who until recently eschewed bamboo music as irrelevant to modern life.

About Bandung, West Java, and Indonesia

Like every locale, Bandung represents a unique and complicated nexus of geographies, histories, natural resources, and human relationships. The city

4 Introduction

occupies a high-elevation river basin (768 m), surrounded by high volcanic peaks, in the interior of the western part of the island of Java. Its relatively cool climate (cool by Indonesian standards, anyway) and its natural defensibility (provided by the high mountains) made it attractive as a new capital for the Dutch colonial administration in the early twentieth century. But plans to move the capital from Batavia (modern-day Jakarta) were derailed by the Great Depression (pc, Budi Supardiman, May 7, 2013), then World War II, and finally Indonesian independence. (It's interesting to note that twenty-first-century plans are proceeding to move the capital of Indonesia, this time to Kalimantan [Westfall 2022].)

That cool climate also made Bandung a popular vacation destination for Dutch expatriates living on Java in the first part of the twentieth century, and for Indonesian tourists after independence. The burgeoning art gallery and café scene in the city's northern Dago neighborhood, the thriving fashion and outlet store culture of the Cipaganti area (known as "jeans street," which also features the Ciwalk open-air mall), and the massive shopping center, Paris van Java (PVJ),[2] are testaments to Bandung's ongoing appeal for visitors from other parts of Indonesia and beyond (the location of these landmarks are visible on the map in Figure 3.1 in Chapter 3).

Although Bandung is a relatively new city (see Chapter 4), and eminently cosmopolitan, it is also thoroughly Sundanese. "Sundanese" refers to the ethnic identity of most of the region's original inhabitants, who speak a language also called Sundanese. The Sundanese are the second largest ethnic group in modern-day Indonesia (after the Javanese); about 40 million people speak Sundanese as their first (or at least as a heritage) language.

English-language accounts of Sundanese culture sometimes use the term "Sunda" as a place name. In the Sundanese language, however, Sunda is not a proper name for a geographic area, but rather an adjective that describes the culture of communities living in the interior, high-elevation parts of western Java (Eringa 1984, 724). Thus, *urang Sunda* means "Sundanese people," and *basa Sunda* means "Sundanese language." Historical names for the region—Parahyangan, Priangan, Preanger, Pasundan—are rarely used in modern geographical discourse. Although the present-day Indonesian province of Jawa Barat (West Java) is roughly coterminous with some of these historical territories, it does not precisely correspond to something that could be characterized as a Sundanese region.

Modern Sundanese look back nostalgically to the medieval Pajajaran kingdom as the foundation of Sundanese culture. As Chapter 1 will relate in detail, however, Pajajaran fell to Javanese conquest in the sixteenth century, and the Sundanese homeland has endured governance by outside authorities—Javanese, Dutch, and finally Indonesian—ever since. Typically, these outside authorities relied on the native Sundanese aristocracy—the *menak*—to govern, which helped to develop and maintain a unique Sundanese culture over the centuries.

Today, Bandung is the provincial capital and the center of regional government for West Java, which is one of thirty-four provinces in the modern Republik Indonesia (Republic of Indonesia). The boundaries of modern Indonesia are roughly the same as those of the Dutch colony called Nederlands-Indië (in English, Dutch [East] Indies), as consolidated in the twentieth century. It is anachronistic, of course, to use terms such as Indonesia or West Java when discussing matters that predate Indonesian independence in 1945; it is often more expedient, however, than expecting readers to memorize the various historically precise place names.

Bandung and Me

For me, the year 2021 (as I write these words) marks four decades of engagement with the Sundanese people, culture, and performing arts of Bandung. I first became aware of Bandung when I happened into the Sundanese gamelan ensemble course at University of California, Santa Cruz, in 1976. My gamelan teacher, Undang Sumarna, was a Bandung native and spoke often of the city and the various artistic activities that went on there. At the time, like many other Americans, I was completely unaware of the existence of a city called Bandung, even though, with a population of 1,452,000 (in 1980), Bandung ranked as the 125th largest city in the world.[3] Indeed, I was only dimly aware of Indonesia, which was the world's fifth most populous nation at the time (after the breakup of the Soviet Union ten year later, it moved into fourth place).

When I expressed an interest in studying Sundanese music and dance in Bandung, Pa Undang put me in contact with Enoch Atmadibrata (1927–2011), a luminary in the Bandung arts scene who, among many other activities (see Rosidi 2003, 150), operated a government-supported project to promote Sundanese performing arts (Proyek Penunjang Peningkatan Kebudayaan Nasional Daerah Jawa Barat) and who had provided support for other Americans hoping to learn about Sundanese music and dance in Bandung. I arrived in Bandung for the first time in April of 1981 (along with fellow student and traveler, Michael Ewing, now Associate Professor of Indonesian at the University of Melbourne).

It is unlikely I would have been able to navigate Bandung, or even find evidence of its elusive arts scene, without the help of Pa Enoch and the various individuals to whom he introduced me: in particular, the dancer Abay Subardja and his family (who arranged for a room and board for me and Michael Ewing), and the *dalang* (puppet master) and musician Otong Rasta, who spent three long afternoons each week tutoring me in gamelan and drumming.

Before my trip, another American who was under the wing of Pa Enoch sent me a copious list of tips about how to cope with everyday activities in Bandung, compiled during a two-year stay in the city, including medical care, personal safety, food, drinking water, local businesses, the immigration office, and money changing. I had rarely given much thought to such

6   *Introduction*

quotidian matters in my daily life, but this account of Bandung made it all sound extremely complicated. For example, my associate provided notes on a dizzying array of public transportation options, and which ones to use in different situations. Despite this excellent advice, I frequently got lost riding the *kol* (Colts, small vans) and *honda* (even smaller vans) that followed fixed, yet bewildering, routes through the mazes of Bandung's one-way streets; and I ran into many other unfamiliar situations and circumstances. Once I had spent some time in Bandung, I came to understand my correspondent's contradictory feelings about the place: "As I told you before, I loved being there. I can't understand why I have so many things to warn you about" (pc, March 17, 1981).

I dwell on these personal details to drive home the point that Bandung, at least in the early 1980s, was not yet the cosmopolitan place I saw it become in the following decades. Except for faint echoes of the famous 1955 Bandung Asia-Africa Conference (see Chapter 2), at the outset of the 1980s Bandung was, in essence, a provincial city. Each of many subsequent visits contributed to a growing sense that Bandung was not only an increasingly cosmopolitan city, but in fact a trendsetting place—truly a vanguard for technological and social advancements. It was in Bandung in the late 1980s that I first encountered individual plastic bottles of water (Aqua brand)—a dubious marker of progress in retrospect, to be sure, but one that immeasurably improved health and hygiene for Indonesians. I acquired my first cell phone there, too (in 1998), long before my American friends universally embraced them. (Telephones were a rare commodity for ordinary citizens on previous visits, in part because the wiring infrastructure was not well developed; cellular technology leapfrogged such limitations.) In the 2000s, I discovered that ATM cards worked quite easily in many Bandung bank machines, and that a variety of pay-as-you-go satellite internet options were readily available.

Following up on my 1980s transportation woes: by the late 1980s I was able to buy a published map and guide to the public transportation system (by then consisting of small vans called *angkot*, short for *angkutan kota* [city transport]), and then in 2013 to come across a web page that would calculate a viable *angkot* route between any two addresses. I assume there is a whizzy angkot app out there by now, but on recent trips I have elected to use the ride-hailing app Grab for casual transportation. Construction of a high-speed rail link between Bandung and Jakarta is underway, as are plans for a rail-based rapid transit system to speed up intracity transportation in Bandung (Clark 2021).

On the cultural front, Bandung also is well known as a center for experimental art, for heavy metal music (see Chapter 4), for fusion restaurants, and for grassroots movements to empower the poor through artistic activities (e.g., the audacious projects of Harry Roesli [1951–2004]; see Purwanti and Widiastuti 2015). In 2015, Bandung was added to UNESCO's "Creative Cities Network"; a designation that indicates a desire on the part of Bandung's business community to enhance the city's "brand" as

Introduction 7

culturally rich and inventive, to attract investment to the city, to foster a sense of civic pride among residents, and to encourage local development and international interchange (Gathen, Skogen, and Gavlin 2021).

I was inspired to write this book by what I observed to be a revival of archaic bamboo musical instruments against this backdrop of global cosmopolitanism. Having studied the available literature on Sundanese music, I was aware that bamboo instruments such as karinding and celempung were part of Sundanese music history. Jaap Kunst's accounts of karinding (1921) and celempung (1921; 1973) were intriguing, but Kunst made them sound already obsolete, even in the early twentieth century. I was fascinated, too, by the wooden celempung Iim Junaedi took with him on a tour of Japan, as documented in Koizumi et al. (1977, 147–148). I had never actually encountered these instruments in person (except in museums) as I researched Sundanese music over the decades, however; I was led to believe that they were no longer played.

My first real-life encounters with these obsolete instruments came via Ismet Ruchimat, founder of the group Sambasunda (and currently *dosen* [professor] of bamboo music at Institut Seni Budaya Indonesia [ISBI]). Since the late 1990s, Ismet and Sambasunda have promulgated wildly successful fusions of global pop and Sundanese music. Among their innovations was the inclusion of various bamboo percussion instruments to supplement their core instrumentation of guitar, bass, keyboards, violin, and drums (on the global side) and kacapi, suling, and kendang (on the Sundanese side). Sometime in the late 2000s, Ismet handed me a couple of bamboo karinding to fool around with, and I noticed that Sambasunda was including them in their performances as well. My interest in the topic only grew as I became aware of other cases of apparent revivals in other contexts in Bandung. With these examples in mind, I developed a research plan, and (with the support of a Fulbright senior scholar grant) arrived in Bandung in March 2013 to conduct field research.

When a group of college students from Universitas Pasundan (UNPAS), who were visiting Common Room (see Chapter 4) during one of my visits there, asked me about my research, I told them I chose bamboo music as a topic because of this recent revival. The students attributed bamboo's current popularity not to any deliberate connections to Sundanese tradition, or to any contemporary social or political movements. They didn't know or care about tradition or traditional music, they told me, but rather about that which seems relevant to their own lives. "We care about what's modern and cool, and some musicians have made bamboo cool" (pc, May 22, 2013).

That bamboo has become "cool" is doubtless the case; this book attempts, however, to delve a little more deeply. I argue that the resurgence of interest in bamboo musical instruments represents an alternative approach to modernity in which Sundanese communities fashion uniquely Sundanese histories against which to articulate a coherent Sundanese modernity instead of adopting disdain of their own past as the primitive

8 *Introduction*

"other" against which (a European-tinged) modernity is constructed. Twentieth-century European views of Asia tend to see a timeless, backward place, whose residents are "people without history," as Eric R. Wolf famously wrote (1982). Indonesians who were eager to embrace European modernity aligned themselves with modern Europeans by distancing themselves from their own "backward" Asian past either by erasing the local past or finding ways to reconceive the past in ways consistent with modern European values. Initial forays toward modernity forced Indonesians to adopt European conflations of the European past with the Asian present and to disregard their own history. For musicians, becoming modern meant abandoning bamboo instruments, whose simple technology and rustic appearance were not compatible with modernist European values.

In contrast, establishing alternative modernities for musicians in a post-colonial, reformasi-era Indonesia requires constructing music histories that root contemporary values in a distinctly local (rather than European) past. For Sundanese people, sounds made with bamboo are a sensual manifestation of the relationship between bamboo and the land. Bamboo's capacity to produce sounds without human intervention—those murmurs on the hill (see Chapter 1)—makes this symbolism especially potent. For these new modernities, bamboo's status as an emblem of Sundanese places and cultural values, coupled with its musical versatility, provide potent means for constructing, evoking, and sustaining uniquely Sundanese histories, modernities, and identities.

My use of the plural "modernities" here is intended to be more than simply trendy: the plural conveys the many different approaches that contemporary Sundanese musicians take to reviving bamboo instruments. Those musicians perfecting their renditions of international standards on diatonic bamboo rattles have a much different sense of what it means to be modern and Sundanese than the rockers who adapt their death metal repertory to bamboo instruments. And neither group shares much (beyond bamboo) with musicians who are trying to render traditional Sundanese repertories using bamboo instruments of their own design. Indeed, twenty-first-century engagements with bamboo music in Bandung resonate with a variety of contemporary movements and concerns among Sundanese communities. What they share, however, is an understanding that bamboo provides a medium for grounding a variety of contemporary concerns firmly in a uniquely Sundanese past.

One concern that many Bandung residents share is a growing awareness of planet Earth's fragility, and that wholesale adoption of Western approaches to agriculture, hygiene, and consumerism have accelerated the degradation of Bandung and its surrounding communities. Bamboo, as a renewable resource, fits well into the international green movement, which promotes renewable resources and conservation and cleanup of urban environments. Bamboo, which can be fashioned into a variety of useful products with relatively simple technologies, also resonates with the embrace of a global "do-it-yourself" (DIY) ethos by some counter-culture

Introduction 9

groups, who reject modern, sterile, mass-produced products in favor of local, hand-made items. Because it is difficult to erase bamboo's distinctive visual and auditory signatures—consider the look and feel of modern bamboo laminate flooring, which retains bamboo's distinctive grain and node patterns—bamboo lends its unmistakably Sundanese qualities even to the globally popular musical styles and genres that Sundanese musicians choose to "cover" with bamboo (see Spiller 2018). By integrating bamboo into musical expressions, as a soundmark, as a cover, and as a political statement, modern Sundanese musicians assert an instinctive understanding of how bamboo can transform the space of Bandung into localized and meaningful musical places. All these forces combine, I suggest, to make bamboo "cool."

Chapter Outlines

It is hardly surprising, given the importance to Sundanese lifeways of the many varieties of bamboo that grow in their West Javanese homeland, that bamboo looms large in many Sundanese proverbs. Nandang Rusnandar identifies quite a few such adages in a 2003 blog post.[4] Readers are already familiar with at least one proverb that cites bamboo's sonorous qualities: "Kawas awi sumear di pasir"—"like bamboo murmuring on the hill"—evokes the sight and sound of stalks of bamboo swaying mellifluously in the wind. Rusnandar's interpretation locates basic Sundanese values—mutual cooperation, acting in harmony, and recognition of individual contributions to the whole—in the proverb, as well (Rusnandar 2009). Others, however, interpret the metaphor in a more negative light—"making noise for no good reason" (Eringa 1984, 41; pc, Burhan Sukarma).[5]

The proverb "Kudu kawas awi jeung gawirna" ("we should be like bamboo and its cliff"), on the other hand, indubitably exhorts people to stick together to resist threats (Rusnandar 2009). It equates Sundanese solidarity with the landscape by referencing the fact that bamboo quite literally holds West Java together: the root systems of bamboo groves prevent soil erosion on the mountainous slopes of the region (Christanty et al. 1996; Masunah et al. 2003, 1; Iskandar 2003, 15; Dim 2017).

But those tangly roots themselves can be a threat, however, if not treated carefully: "Tamiang meulit ka bitis" literally means "tamiang (a variety of bamboo) entangles your legs," and has a sense similar to the English "hoist with one's own petard." Bamboo's flexibility as a material is at the heart of another adage—"leuleus jeujeur liat tali" (flexible bamboo fishing rod, tough fishing line). It suggests that wisdom requires a combination of freedom of interpretation and close adherence to basic values. Flexibility of a different sort is implied by "pindah cai pindah tampian"—literally, "moving to a new river requires changing one's bamboo bathing hut"— which encourages people to adjust themselves to the local customs of a new place (à la "when in Rome, do as the Romans do").

10   *Introduction*

Each of these proverbs provides a loose focus for one of the following chapters. Inspired by the image of the quiet but omnipresent rustling of "bamboo murmuring on the hill," Chapter 1 examines how bamboo "murmurs" have pervaded Sundanese music and soundscapes since time immemorial by introducing two perennial Sundanese musical instruments: *angklung* (shaken bamboo rattle) and *suling* (end-blown bamboo flute).

In Chapter 2, the rural angklung ensemble's transformation into a medium for all sorts of western-derived diatonic/chromatic music that mirrors different socio-economic ideologies (such as indigenous gotong-royong, socialism, and global neoliberalism) is a case study of "pindah cai, pindah tampian"—conforming to new norms and values. The chapter addresses the twenty-first-century diatonic angklung scene in Bandung, which has been continuous since the 1940s. The bamboo revival, how-ever, has given its proponents new energy, and angklung enthusiasts have embraced all sorts of new technology to promote diatonic angklung music.

Chapter 3 develops a musical interpretation of the adage, "flexible bamboo fishing rod, tough fishing line," by examining how Galengan Sora Awi (a neighborhood musical group) exploits bamboo's flexibility as a raw material for musical instruments to provide accompaniments for diverse genres of traditional Sundanese music, including *jaipongan*, *pop Sunda*, Sundanese children's songs, and *dangdut*, demonstrating the music's durability. This group of musicians and friends from the North Bandung neighborhood of Dago, inspired in part by a grassroots environ-mental movement in Bandung, created an ensemble of homemade bamboo instruments with an idiosyncratic blend of diatonic and *salendro/pelog* tunings. They frequently appear at events associated in some way with the green movement, including "No Car Day" and orienteering events.

Chapter 4's account of the renaissance of the *karinding* (bamboo guimbarde), whose sound serves as an icon for rooted Sundanese values as they find footing in the modern world, is an exemplar of how to "be like bamboo and its cliff." It focuses on a group of heavy metal musicians who became intrigued by the sound of karinding as made and played by a musician from a village east of Bandung. Calling themselves Karinding Attack, they exploited parallels between the aesthetics of heavy metal, such as distortion and repeated ostinatos, and the sounds of karinding. They pioneered using these "old" instruments to play metal-inspired music that appealed to a growing demographic of urban youth who wanted to embrace their Sundanese roots. Their young Bandung fans emulated them, leading to an explosion of making and playing karinding in a variety of contexts.

To conclude, Chapter 5 explores the "entangled" ways (following Ian Hodder's notion of Engtanglement [2012]) in which other artists have taken bamboo music in very different directions. The lavish "Grand Symphony Angklung" production manages to recontextualize angklung as promoting neoliberal economics. Endo Suanda's bamboo luthiery is com-parable to GSA's approach in that it finds ways to use bamboo in all kinds

Introduction 11

of music-making. And Asep Nata's experiments in transforming karinding into a melodic instrument suggests different ways to bring the karinding's symbolic power into the twenty-first century.

It is worth noting that each of these chapters also engages with Bandung's unique history and geography in some way, revealing the myriad ways that bamboo, Sundanese culture, and the local Sundanese environment intertwine. Chapter 1 recounts the history of Sundanese tension with their Javanese neighbors over the past centuries; Chapter 2 discusses Bandung's role as the host to the 1955 Konperensi Asia-Afrika; Chapter 3 addresses twenty-first-century approaches to environmentalism; and Chapter 4 engages with the founding of Bandung and its relationship to the city's waterways, especially the Cikapundung river.

Bamboo is the common link that binds these very different musical excursions to the same font of Sundanese culture. In effect, the exploitation of bamboo brands these different approaches to music as modern while still retaining a core of Sundaneseness. Incorporating bamboo soundmarks also provides a means to integrate these various genres—including traditional Sundanese, heavy metal, and sentimental pop—into a truly modern, yet uniquely Sundanese, culture. This reflorescence of bamboo music goes hand in hand with other "modern" Sundanese expressions, such as styles of dress (especially head-cloths and carry-bags), in empowering people to forge a tangible connection to the local landscape while marching boldly into the global twenty-first century.

Notes

1 Dransfield and Widjaja corroborate Maradjo et al.:

> species of the genus *Schizostachyum* are the most suitable for making aerophones (like "kan" or "sompotan"), because of small diameter culms, long internodes and thin walls. The main species used for making idiophones (e.g. "angklung") and chordophones are *Gigantochloa atroviolacea, G. atter, G. levis, G. pseudoarundinacea* and *G. robusta;* sometimes *Dendrocalamus asper* and *Gigantochloa apus* are also used. The large-diameter culms of *G.atroviolacea* are used for making bass drums and bass horns.
>
> (1995, 21)

2 The name of this mall riffs on the colonial era Dutch designation of Bandung as the "Parijs van Java" (Paris of Java).
3 According to the data in United Nations, Department of Economic and Social Affairs, Population Division (2018). World Urbanization Prospects: The 2018 Revision, Online Edition. "File 12: Population of Urban Agglomerations with 300,000 Inhabitants or More in 2018, by country, 1950–2035 (thousands)," https://population.un.org/wup/Download/Files/WUP2018-F12-Cities_Over_300K.xls. According to the same data set, in 2020 Bandung's population was 2,580,000, 200th largest in world.
4 http://sundasamanggaran.blogspot.com/2009_11_01_archive.html
5 See also http://jasoenda.blogspot.com/2011/07/babasaan.html; www.peribah asa.net/peribahasa-sunda.php?page=11).

1 Bamboo Murmurs

Bamboo Murmurs is fundamentally rooted in the notion that the look, sounds, and feel of bamboo have long been, and continue to be, powerful emblems of place in the Sundanese imaginary. Since long before the beginning of recorded history in West Java, Sundanese people have performed their relationship to the land and with each other with bamboo technology, including cooperative music-making using bamboo instruments. This chapter introduces two formative Sundanese bamboo instruments, namely *angklung* (rattle) and *suling* (flute), and how the texture that results from their distinctive sounds and playing techniques constitutes a fundamental soundmark for Sundanese music. But, to begin to understand the musical significance of bamboo, as well as the recent revitalization of music made with bamboo instruments in the Sundanese city of Bandung in the twenty-first century, a little historical and geographical context is in order.

A Very Selective History

This selective account begins in the fourteenth century, when, according to several old texts,[1] Lingga Buana, the ruler of the West Javanese kingdom of Pajajaran, agreed to the marriage of his daughter, Princess Dyah Pitaloka Ratna Citraresmi, to Hayam Wuruk, sovereign of the powerful rival Majapahit kingdom in East Java (see Figure 1.1). Hayam Wuruk's prime minister, Gajah Mada, however, was intent on implementing an ambitious plan to unite the entire archipelago—including Lingga Buana's kingdom—under a united Majapahit rule. Gajah Mada convinced Hayam Wuruk to insist that the princess was not a bride, but rather a concubine. Lingga Buana resisted the notion that his royal daughter was merely tribute from a vassal kingdom, and the bloody Battle of Bubat ensued, which left most of the Sundanese delegation, including the king and the princess, dead.

In the twentieth century, Indonesian nationalists, such as the country's first president, Sukarno, cast Gajah Mada as a national hero because of his early vision of a unified Indonesia.[2] In most Indonesian cities, there are streets named after the Javanese heroes of the Bubat war—Hayam Wuruk and Gajah Mada. But not in the capital of West Java, Bandung—at least not until 2018, when the naming of two streets "Jalan Majapahit" and "Jalan

DOI: 10.4324/9781003302797-2

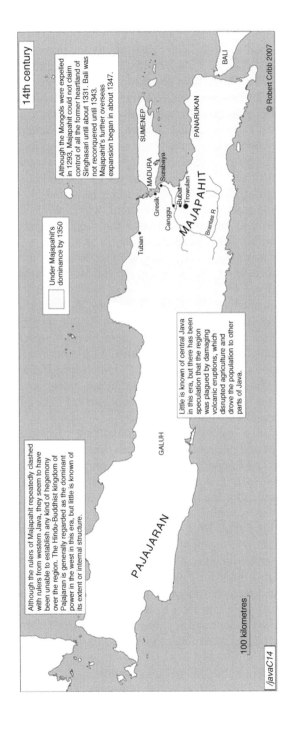

Figure 1.1 Java in the fourteenth century.
Source: From Robert Cribb, *Digital Atlas of Indonesian History* (Copenhagen: NIAS Press, 2010), reproduced with permission.

14 *Bamboo Murmurs*

Hayam Wuruk" warranted national news stories about a breakthrough in the centuries-old rivalry between the Sundanese, Indonesia's second-largest ethnolinguistic group (about 42 million, 15.5% of Indonesia's population of about 271 million in 2019), who constitute the majority of West Java's population, and the Javanese, the country's largest ethnolinguistic group (about 40%, or 108 million), who dominate most of the rest of the island of Java.[3] The Sundanese look back to Lingga Buana and his successors as their ancestors, while the Javanese regard the rulers of Majapahit as theirs. Despite any recent rapprochement, however, for most Sundanese, Gajah Mada remains a villain who insulted their sovereignty and murdered their king. Mikihiro Moriyama asserts that "most Sundanese were familiar with this tale, and they remembered the incident with anger and rage" (2005, 9). Literary critic Taufiq Hanafi describes Yoseph Iskandar's 1991 romantic novelization of the story, *Sang Mokten Bubat*, which paints Gajah Mada and Hayam Wuruk as the antagonists to the noble Lingga Buana, for example, as "nuanced with Sundanese grudge" (2014, 1).

Indeed, Sundanese people resent the Javanese domination that has colored their existence for centuries. Although the West Javanese kingdom of Pajajaran endured for 200 years following the defeat at Bubat, it was completely vanquished in the sixteenth century by Banten (an Islamic kingdom to the west) in alliance with Cirebon (to the north) and ultimately by Mataram, a powerful Central Javanese Islamic kingdom, by 1620. Mataram eventually ceded control of both Central and West Java to the Vereenigde Oostindische Compagnie (VOC; Dutch East India Company), a consortium of Dutch trading companies that was managing Dutch colonial activities in the archipelago (Herlina et al. 2019, 1522), but continued to maintain cultural influence over the area.

For administrative reasons, Dutch colonial rulers isolated West Java from Central Java and encouraged the Sundanese to maintain an identity distinct from the Javanese, in part to take advantage of West Java's aristocratic structure—which, in contrast with the polities in Central Java, was decentralized, likely allowing the Dutch to avoid opposition from a single, powerful leader in managing their considerable agricultural interests in the area (see Herlina et al. 2019, 1518). During the struggle for independence, in 1947, the former regent of Garut, R.A.A. Musa Suriakartalegawa, proclaimed the establishment of a semi-independent Negara Pasundan (Sundanese Nation), with the reluctant endorsement of the Dutch, who would clearly have preferred maintaining control through a loose federation of such small polities in their East Indies colony over the completely independent, united Indonesian republic that finally took form under the leadership of the Javanese-born Sukarno (Frakking 2017; Moriyama 2005, 259n23).

After independence, the Republic of Indonesia adopted a motto— *Bhinneka Tunggal Ika* ("Unity in Diversity")—that promised a multicultural approach to an Indonesian national identity. The motto is taken from a poem, which, ironically, is not in the Indonesian language (the Malay variant associated with "unity" in the archipelago), but rather in the Old Javanese language—a poem that was written under the patronage of none other than Hayam Wuruk of Majapahit. This pedigree belies an ongoing hegemonic Javanese bias permeating even Indonesian national culture and constitutes yet another source of Sundanese resentment of the Javanese. Both Sukarno and his successor, President Soeharto (who overthrew Sukarno in 1965 and governed until his own deposition in 1998), promulgated cultural policies that upheld courtly Javanese culture as an ideal, to the detriment of local cultures throughout the nation (Lippit 2016, 17; Muljadji 2016). In modern Indonesia, however, this resentment has rarely seen any overt political expression, but rather has only been "addressed at the level of popular culture (and football hooliganism)" (James and Walsh 2015, 29).

West Java's Geography

The eight-hour train ride from Yogyakarta in Central Java to Bandung dramatizes the differences between the ecologies that nurtured the cultures of the Javanese and Sundanese and kept them separated. As the train moves west, Central Java's flat expanses of rice fields, interrupted occasionally by volcanic peaks, give way to long expanses of dramatic mountainous scenery, with forests of various palms, bananas, trees … and magnificent stands of bamboo (see Figure 1.2). According to Nadia Bystriakova et al., who have compiled voluminous data about bamboo in the Asia-Pacific region,

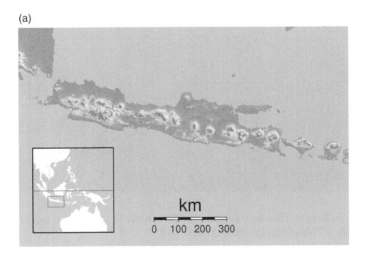

(b)

(c)

Figure 1.2 a. Topographic map of Java. b. View from the train of flat expanses in Central Java. c. View from the train in West Java.

Note: https://commons.wikimedia.org/wiki/File:Java_Locator_Topography.png#/media/File:Java_Locator_Topography.png

Source: Sadalmelik, Public domain, via Wikimedia Commons; photos: Henry Spiller.

"detailed, transparent, and comprehensive estimates of bamboo resources are lacking for nearly all Asian countries" (Bystriakova et al. 2003b, 1834). They report that there are fifty-six species indigenous to Indonesia, and that five other Asian countries (China, India, Japan, Myanmar, and Vietnam) have more (2003a,10). The journalist Herry Dim, however, takes into account the many imported species that thrive in Indonesia (and on Java in particular) to assert that Indonesia is the second-richest country in terms of the number of bamboo species (2017).

The sheer majesty of West Java's rugged landscape may have inspired the Sundanese residents of this mountainous region to call it "Parahyangan"— the land of the gods. It comprises two high plateaus (about 730 m above sea level), surrounded by volcanic peaks (some more than 3000 m high). When Mataram seized control in the early seventeenth century (Herlina Lubis 2000, 77), they shortened the name to "Priangan," which the Dutch in turn rendered as the "Preanger."

The rugged landscape likely limited the power and reach of early Hindu kingdoms in the region, which were smaller and less influential than the powerful kingdoms of Central Java and Sumatra. Even Pajajaran, the culmination of centuries of political development, was, according to Heather Sutherland, basically "networks of villages grouped together under ruling families" (Sutherland 1975, 63). The Mataram rulers gave the top aristocrat in each *kabupaten* (administrative district) the title *bupati*. Under Mataram's influence, Sundanese aristocrats consolidated their power by adopting many of their Mataram overlords' courtly practices (Heins 1977, 35), but also, according to Sutherland, maintained "their own specialities and dialects" (1975, 63). The Dutch adopted Mataram's system of aristocrats and districts, but applied a Dutch title—"regent"—to the *bupati*.

Although modern residents do not adhere strictly to conventions of the stratified society that is a consequence of such a social organization, there are, even in modern Bandung, traces of two very different social classes: the rural Sundanese *rakyat* (common people) and the refined *menak* (aristocrats) of Sundanese royal courts. There is often evidence in an individual's name: those from rakyat families may have only a single name, while those with menak blood, regardless of their current financial circumstances, often bestow graceful Sanskrit-derived names to their children, even hereditary titles (e.g., *raden* for a close male relative of a ruler). In daily life, however, most rakyat individuals go by two names, often a familiar nickname followed by their given name, while most descendants of menak eschew their titles and flowery names and adopt monikers more like their rakyat compatriots.

Among the trappings of Central Javanese royalty adopted by the Sundanese menak was bronze technology, including bronze musical instruments. Medieval aristocrats on Java equated the metal's rich color, durability, and malleability with both political and cosmic power. Commissioning bronze implements demonstrated power

18 *Bamboo Murmurs*

through the earthly mobilization of considerable financial and human resources, as well as through a supernatural alchemy combining the physical elements (earth, wind, fire, water). And the music played on bronze instruments—with its relentless periodic rhythmic structures—metaphorically captured the cycles of the Indic cosmos and translated them into a humanly perceptible form (cf. Spiller 2004, 5–11; Becker 1979; 1988; Hoffman 1978).

"The Death of Citraresmi"

This historical and geographical background helps to make sense of the 2013 presentation in Bandung of an ambitious *dramatari* (dance-drama) based on the Battle of Bubat. It can be seen as a political statement that expressed ongoing resistance to the Javanese hegemony that many Sundanese have endured for centuries and as a vehicle for highlighting the Bandung population's assertion of a unique local/regional Sundanese identity. "Citraresmi Labuh Pati" ("The Death of Citraresmi"),[4] with only a few lines of dialogue, relies on costumes, gesture, music, cultural symbols, and theatrics to recount the broad outlines of the Battle of Bubat.

The dancers playing Majapahit roles—Hayam Wuruk, his advisors, and his soldiers—wore costumes characterized by fabrics generally recognized as belonging to Central Javanese courts. The bare-chested Javanese soldiers wore the brown-and-white *parang* (diagonal stripes in the shape of a knife blade) batik associated with court culture, folded in half to provide freedom for leg movement and to reveal black trousers underneath, and black *blankon* (Javanese-style head-coverings). The rank-and-file soldiers wielded shields and *trisula*, three-prong spears associated with Hinduism. The high-ranking aristocratic advisors, also bare-chested, wore the bird-inspired pattern generically called *semen*, which was once restricted for use only by the Sultan and his kin (Bennett 2019, 171), over red velvet trousers with gold trimming.

The Sundanese soldiers, in contrast, wore no batik at all—just red cloth over their black trousers—and simple tied black *iket* (Sundanese-style headcloths). They wielded *golok*, the long, heavy knife associated with West Java in general and more specifically with the Sundanese martial arts (*penca silat*). The Sundanese aristocrats, as well as the king himself, wore batik, but patterns not associated with Central Javanese court culture.

The Majapahit aristocrats and the king each bore a *keris*, the Javanese ceremonial dagger usually with a wavy blade. The Sundanese king and his high-ranking associates, in contrast, were armed with *kujang*, a distinctly Sundanese weapon whose shape is an icon of Sundanese identity. At several points in the *dramatari*, dancers posed with these two very different blades in opposition to one another—often with lighting that rendered the weapons' shapes in stark silhouette (see Figure 1.3).

Figure 1.3 kujang (left) vs *keris* (right).
Source: Henry Spiller; Kujang image from https://commons.wikimedia.org/wiki/File:Kujang.png licensed under https://creativecommons.org/licenses/by-sa/4.0/deed.en (creator Yusup Ramdani); Keris image from https://commons.wikimedia.org/wiki/File:Semar_Kris_(no_background).png licensed under https://creativecommons.org/licenses/by-sa/3.0/deed.en

The Javanese characters' dance gestures were marked by the two-dimensional quality that characterizes Javanese court dance and the characteristic straight-extended-leg stepping of *gagah* (strong masculine) dance idioms. Sonically, their scenes were accompanied with loud, bronze-dominated gamelan music (albeit in Sundanese, not Javanese, style). The Sundanese aristocratic characters danced with movement vocabulary drawn primarily from the *ibing keurseus* repertory associated with Sundanese aristocratic men's dancing (see Spiller 2010), while the soldiers drew upon Sundanese penca silat for their movement vocabulary.

For the most part, the Sundanese characters, like the Javanese characters, danced to the accompaniment of gamelan music. A completely different soundtrack, however, set the tone for the scene set in a Sundanese village, in which the dancers wore the simple clothing of Sundanese farmers and mimicked rice farming activities and Sundanese games. The musicians switched to a variety of bamboo percussion instruments and the characteristic Sundanese bamboo flute called (like similar flutes in many parts of Indonesia) *suling*. In later scenes, reprises of bamboo sounds shifted the audience's focus quickly from the outward violence of the Javanese, with their clangorous gamelan music, to the inner anguish of their Sundanese victims, when the gamelan suddenly went silent, replaced by the mournful sound of a solo suling.

In this dramatari, the contrast between bamboo sounds and bronze sounds, in essence, delineated two nesting binary contrasts: (1) the ethnic rivalry between the Sundanese and their Javanese antagonists, and (2) the class differences between the Sundanese peasants (rakyat), and the Sundanese aristocrats (menak), who long ago adapted some of the trappings of Javanese aristocracy, including bronze gamelan music. Simply put: for Sundanese listeners, the sounds of bamboo—like the shape of the kujang—immediately and effectively index uniquely Sundanese locales, histories, and identities.

Bamboo vs Bronze

As Anthony Reid (1988) and Robert Wessing (1998), among others, have noted, bamboo technology is by no means unique to West Java—indeed, it is a hallmark of societies and cultures throughout Southeast Asia (and beyond). In contrast to bronze technology—which was imported by outside invaders, is difficult to master, and materially endures for eons—bamboo is entrenched in the oldest strata of Indonesia's human history, is easily worked, and is ephemeral.

Despite its ubiquity in Southeast Asia, the Sundanese population that makes up the majority of Indonesians in the province of West Java identify especially strongly with bamboo. The journalist Yenti Aprianti titled her 2007 article about bamboo and the Sundanese people, published in the popular Indonesian national newspaper, *Kompas*, "Dari kelahiran hingga kematian urang Sunda" (from the birth to the death of Sundanese persons)—a sort of "cradle-to-grave" metaphor (Aprianti 2007). The father of diatonic angklung, Daeng Soetigna (see Chapter 2), summed up this way of thinking as follows in an address to an English-speaking audience:

> Indonesians ... build their houses of bamboo, even the floors and walls. Also furniture and kitchen utensils are often made of bamboo. They even sleep on beds made of the same material. Bamboo is also eaten; young bamboo shoots, in Indonesian called "rebung," constitute an essential ingredient in many delicious dishes. And when Indonesians die, their mortal remains are carried forth in bamboo contraptions and buried in bamboo groves. ... Indonesians are also good at making music, using ... bamboo.
>
> (Quoted in Sjamsuddin and Winitasasmita 1986, 67)

I've come across comparable statements in newspaper and journal articles, in blogs, in conversations with my bamboo music consultants, and even in off-hand comments from taxi drivers.[5]

The Voice of Bamboo (*Sora Awi*)

Even after considerable technological manipulation, bamboo's "natural" state shines through. All bamboo varieties generally have a culm (the hollow stem), which is segmented with nodes (a solid joint). Bamboo's uneven color and texture are the result of the different densities and qualities of these two components. The look of bamboo helps to visually define places as Sundanese—all restaurants that specialize in Sundanese food, for example, advertise the fact with rustic bamboo walls, tables, and chairs.

Bamboo asserts its bamboo-ness in sonic dimensions, too. Bamboo—stirred by the breeze—can produce musical sounds even without any human intervention. Sir Thomas Stamford Raffles, in his 1817 *The History of Java*, states that "Javans say the first music of which they have an idea was produced by the accidental admission of the air into a bámbu tube, which was left hanging on a tree" (1817v1, 472). Douglas Kahn notes that the wind "can blow through a bamboo stand and produce wind music or can break bamboo and then blow across it like a flute" (Kahn 2013, 41). Thus, the wind can elicit both the percussive sounds of bamboo stalks hitting one another as well as various kinds of whistling sounds that emerge when either the stalks themselves vibrate (like a string on an Aeolian harp) or create a vibrating column of air inside a broken bamboo stalk (like a panpipe). These bamboo sounds are an integral component of the Sundanese environment and explain how bamboo has the capacity to elide any conceptual separation between "nature" (the physical environment) and "culture" (meanings inscribed by humans). Sounds made with bamboo are a sensual manifestation of the relationship between Sundanese people and their environment.

This relationship is manifest in many Sundanese place names. Nandang Rusnandar points out that the names of many Sundanese locales memorialize a species of bamboo that grows locally. For example, appellations such as Cicalengka, Cigombong, Ciater, Cihaur, Citamiang, and Ciawi are derived from the common name for a species of bamboo combined with the prefix "Ci," which means "water," and suggests that there were springs in the area as well. Other places names, for example, Gombong, Rangkasbitung, Gegerbitung, Haurpugur, Haurpancuh, and Kedungwuluh simply incorporate the names of different kinds of bamboo (Rusnandar 2009).

Over the centuries, Sundanese people have developed ways to encourage Aeolian bamboo sounds with small technological interventions. Throughout the Malay world, there was once a custom of placing tall bamboo poles, with slits made in the tops of the bamboo, in the rice fields; the wind makes the bamboo whistle to entertain the spirit of the rice (Wilken 1912:40; Kurz 1876, 233–234; see also Wahl n.d.). Various wind- and water-driven bamboo chimes, too, provide means to keep the air filled with percussive, yet melodious, bamboo murmurs.

A nineteenth-century Sundanese excursion to the United States illustrates the significance of these (semi-)environmental sounds to a Sundanese sense of well-being. One of the exhibits at the 1893 World's Columbian Exposition in Chicago, Illinois, was the "Java Village." A Dutch coffee and tea syndicate transported 125 Sundanese villagers to live in a recreated village in the Midway Plaisance (the Exposition's amusement area; see Spiller 2015, 29). The villagers wasted no time in installing familiar passive bamboo sound devices to help them feel at home by reproducing a Sundanese soundscape. Even before the exhibition opened, fairgoers heard "weird, wondrously melodious" sounds of tall bamboo stalks erected inside the village walls ("On the Midway Plaisance" 1893, 173– 174; see Figure 1.4). The villagers also transformed an unglamorous water pipe into a whimsical bamboo chime powered by a water wheel (see Spiller 2015, 33).

STREET SCENE IN THE JAVA VILLAGE.

Figure 1.4 Aeolian bamboo poles in the "Java Village," World's Columbian Exposition, Chicago, 1893.
Source: Drawing from Rogers, W. A. 1894. "The Little People from Java." *St. Nicholas: An Illustrated Magazine for Young Folks* 21:275–278, p. 275.

Several chroniclers of the Exposition note how these quasi-environmental sounds helped to make the villagers comfortable in the alien Chicago environment. For example:

> A lyre, high in the air, gave forth sweet, weird sounds, from voices of the breezes, and a bamboo water wheel played a musical jingle. The [Sundanese residents] would have been lonely without these, which were so familiar a sound to them when at home.
> (Stevens 1895, 91)

Bamboo and Sundanese Music

Bamboo's innate sounds—the "voice" of the Sundanese landscape—are heard in two basic forms: the distinctly pitched percussive sound of bamboo hitting bamboo, and the whistling sound of air blowing into it.[6] The transformation of these natural sounds into musical instruments involves more than simply initiating sonic vibrations through human actions. Various technological interventions interacted with social and cultural process to create musical instruments that not only imitate the voice of the Sundanese landscape but domesticate these voices to express Sundanese social values as well. The following discussion considers two bamboo instruments: *angklung* and *suling* (N.B. angklung will be discussed further in Chapter 2). The invention of angklung (bamboo rattles) was likely inspired by the observation of the melodious percussive qualities of bamboo shaking in the wind. Similarly, aeolian bamboo whistles might have provided the inspiration for suling, the bamboo whistle flute that is emblematic of Sundanese music.

Angklung

Processions featuring marching angklung ensembles have long been associated with small-scale, egalitarian Sundanese agricultural communities (Masunah et al. 2003, 3–4). Such communities, whether they practiced dry- (*huma* or *ladang*) or wet-rice (*sawah*) agriculture, conceived their rice-growing activities as a part of a much larger cosmological whole, with various practices, rituals, and ceremonies to keep everything in proper synchronization. Although the details of ceremonial angklung music varied from location to location, reverence for the rice goddess, Nyi Pohaci (a.k.a. Dewi Sri), whose death and rebirth miraculously provide humans with sustenance, was essentially universal in West Java.

Two or three individual bamboo tubes (*tabung*), each with one end closed by a node, are mounted in a frame to make a single *angklung* (see Figure 1.5). The node end of each tube rests in notches in the base of the frame (*tabung soko* or *tabung dasar*), which is constructed of bamboo and rattan, and the other end attached to the upper part of the frame, so that the tubes have only a limited range of motion. The open ends of the tubes can be trimmed and tuned so that the tube sounds a particular pitch (see

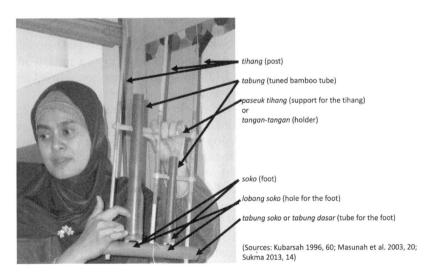

Figure 1.5 Irma Noerhaty demonstrates how to hold an angklung. The parts are labelled.
Source: photo: Henry Spiller.

24   Bamboo Murmurs

Zainal et al. 2009). When a player shakes the frame, each of the tubes hits the frame to produce a pitched tone. Skilled players can modulate their motions to create different sound articulations; the most characteristic *angklung* sound involves producing a steady tremolo to sustain a single note. The individual tubes in a single *angklung* are usually tuned in octaves, so that each *angklung* sounds a single pitch with a timbre rich in overtones.

Angklung makers use several bamboo species to make angklung.[7] *Awi hideung* (*Gigantochloa atroviolacea*), also known by a second Sundanese name, *awi wulung* (Maradjo et al. 1976, 17), in Indonesian as *bambu hitam*, and in English as black bamboo, is a popular choice for the tabung. It is especially suitable for this purpose because of its "straight stem, long culms, and perfectly round tube shape" ("berbatang lurus, berbuluh panjang, dan bentuk tabungnya bulat sempurna"; Sukma 2013, 35). Masunah et al. also mention *bambu kuning* (*Bambusa vulgaris*) in this role (2003, 18), but Zainal et al. report that it is rarely used for angklung anymore (2009, 24). The tabung soko (also known as tabung dasar) provides the main support for the other instrument components. *Awi temen* (*Gigantochloa atter*) and *awi gombong* (*Gigantochloa verticillate*) are common choices. *Awi tali* (*Gigantochloa apus*), as well as awi temen and awi gombong, are appropriate choices for the *tihang* (the rods that form the framework that supports the tabung).

Bamboo for angklung should have been growing for about three or four years, "not too old, not too young" ("tidak terlampau tua, juga tidak terlampau muda"; Masunah et al. 2003, 18; see also Sukma 2013, 36). Bamboo that is too young will shrink, changing its pitch and timbre (Sukma 2013, 61). Old bamboo is liable to break or crack. The bamboo should be at its driest when it is cut. The dry season is best, and some experts advise harvesting in the morning, when the bamboo's moisture content is lowest (Masunah et al. 2003, 18–19; Sukma 2013, 36). The bamboo is left standing in the forest after it is cut until the leaves dry up and fall off (Masunah et al. 2003, 19; Sukma 2013, 37). Then the bamboo is dried for several more months in the sun before it is used.

According to Masunah et al., the whole culm is usable. The thicker, bottom parts are for the non-sounding frame parts; the thinner, upper parts for the sound tubes. The selection process happens while the bamboo is drying (2003, 19). The timbre of the angklung depend on thickness of the bamboo; thicker bamboo makes the sound "soft and round" ("lunak dan bulat"), while thinner is more "hard and shrill" ("keras dan cempreng"; Sukma 2013, 60).

Handiman Diratmasasmita (b. 1939) is a highly regarded angklung maker who maintains a workshop on Jalan Surapati in the heart of Bandung. Most Bandung angklung enthusiasts acknowledge his instruments are exceptionally fine. This is in part, Budi Supardiman told me (pc, May 17, 2013), because Handiman maintains tight control over the whole process. Unlike other angklung makers, who purchase bamboo from middlemen, Handiman travels to bamboo forests to choose the bamboo, and oversees the cutting and drying of the raw materials. Handiman stressed to me the importance of this care and control: "You can't make an angklung in a day. The bamboo has to be left to cure. Given a voice. Left to rest again. And then tuned several times." "I make angklung myself from the bamboo forest. I choose the bamboo while it's still growing. This is not the case with other makers. I was lucky to learn how to choose bamboo, how to cut bamboo, and how to dry it" (pc, May 17, 2013). Handiman told me that he uses three different varieties of bamboo: awi gombong for the tabung soko (base), awi tali for the tihang (frame), and awi wulung for the tabung (tone tubes). Handiman sources his awi wulung (black bamboo) for the tabung from the Garut area near West Java's southern coast;[8] the other bamboo varieties are available near Bandung (pc, May 17, 2013; for more information about Handiman, see Chapter 2).

The way angklung are played models the cooperation that residents of small farming communities need to achieve a successful harvest, in which individuals coordinate their efforts to create a result that is greater than the sum of its parts. To mirror this cooperation, each individual *angklung* is easy to play. Each angklung, and each player, represents only a single musical event (or pitch) in the overall texture, in the same way that each agricultural worker contributes only a small part of the work required to produce a crop. The composite of their short, single-pitch ostinatos, carefully coordinated to interlock, is a melody—an audible analog to the fruits of the cooperative agricultural endeavors they celebrate.

A hypothetical example: four different angklung players, each with an angklung of a different pitch, can play different one-pitch ostinatos, each with its own density, over an 8-beat cycle. Angklung #1 and #4 play once every 8 beats (once per cycle). Angklung #2 plays once every 4 beats (twice per cycle), and angklung #3 once every 2 beats (four times per cycle; see Figure 1.6a).

beat/pitch	1	2	3	4	5	6	7	8
1/g	x							
2/e	x		x		x		x	
3/d	x				x			
4/c	x							

(a)

beat/pitch	1	2	3	4	5	6	7	8
1/g					x			
2/e		x		x		x		x
3/d			x			x		
4/c	x							

(b)

Figure 1.6 Hypothetical angklung ostinatos. a. aligned. b. interlocking.

26   *Bamboo Murmurs*

Now, suppose these ostinatos are offset so that no two *angklung* sound at the same time (see Figure 1.6b); a melody emerges from the interlocking ostinatos (c e d e g e d e); when repeated, it becomes a catchy tune. Thus, an *angklung* ensemble's cooperative approach to music-making performs the sociality of small-scale village agriculture; bamboo's close association with the landscape further reinforce the connections that Sundanese farmers forge between community, agriculture, and the environment.

Sundanese philosophers do not consider only musical style when analyzing angklung's association with Sundanese values of cooperation. For them, the presence of several bamboo tubes on each angklung suggests the social nature of humans because a single angklung is made up of several components that complete one another. Furthermore, the presence of tubes of various sizes is thought by some to represent the obligation of more powerful individuals (the larger tubes) to stand with and protect the less powerful (smaller tubes; Tryana 2011). In sum, angklung—both as an object and as a practice—is a powerful index of the fundamental values of the Sundanese rakyat.

Suling

One instrument that has remained relatively unchanged from its earliest models is the suling—the simple bamboo whistle flute that has become emblematic of Sundanese culture. A suling is fashioned from a piece of bamboo of the tamiang variety (*Schiostachyum blumei*), which has long, straight internodes and thin walls (Dransfield and Widjaja 1995, 21; see also Chapter 5). According to Kubarsah, the bamboo stock is first soaked in water for a month, then allowed to dry out in a warm place (Kubarsah 1996, 39). The suling maker cuts a notch (*sogatan*) across the node (*sirah*) that also creates a small hole in the bamboo (*liang tiup*, i.e., blowing hole), then wraps a rattan ring (*sumber*) around the node so that blowing on the notch in the node sets the column of air inside the tube vibrating (see Figure 1.7). The maker completes the suling by cutting the stock to tune the suling to a desired fundamental, and then drills fingerholes (usually four or six for Sundanese suling; see Chapter 5).[9]

In contrast to Central Javanese music, in which the suling's role is peripheral, and its idiom limited to short, formulaic ornamental phrases (see Brinner 1993), the virtuosic, extended melodies of Sundanese suling-playing are in the foreground of several iconic genres of Sundanese music. The sound of a suling evokes intense feelings of nostalgia in Sundanese listeners. The suling owes its modern prominence in large part to its vital role in a nineteenth-century aristocratic genre of sung poetry. The genre was originally cultivated in the courts of the bupati (regent) of the area called Cianjur, and so became known as *Cianjuran*.

Raden Adipati Aria (R.A.A.) Kusumaningrat, a.k.a. Dalem Pancaniti, who was regent 1834–63, adapted a regional sung narrative tradition, *pantun* (see Weintraub 1990; 1993; 1994/1995), in which a solo bard

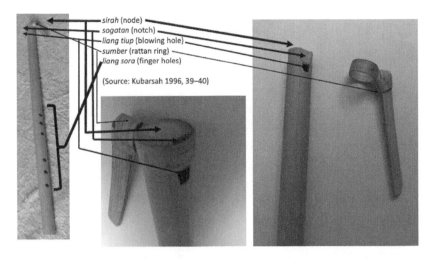

Figure 1.7 Parts of a Sundanese suling.
Source: photos: Henry Spiller.

recounted the legends of medieval Sundanese kingdoms, usually accompanying himself with a zither called *kacapi* (Wiradiredja 2012). Male and female aristocrats alike cultivated singing the florid, sophisticated melodies and expressing the deep poetry. They were accompanied by professional musicians on kacapi (elegantly upgraded to be suitable in the court) and, eventually, suling. The suling player's role was to make their employers' singing sound even better, so they learned to play the same complex, florid melodies in a way that subtly reminded the singers what was coming next (see Zanten 1989; Williams 2001).

Cianjuran itself acquired new relevance in post-independence West Java because of its focus on articulating a Sundanese regional identity by perpetuating legends and impressions of medieval Sundanese kingdoms and by deemphasizing its aristocratic roots. In this more democratic form, it acquired the name *tembang Sunda* and became known all over Sundanese-speaking areas (see Williams 2001). In the 1960s and 1970s, an instrumental version of tembang Sunda called *kacapi-suling* (because it featured both instruments) became popular on the radio, providing a forum for musicians—especially emerging suling players such as Burhan Sukarma—to develop astonishing skill and ingenuity, transforming the suling into a vehicle for true virtuosity (see Figure 1.8).

Soundmarks

The two different kinds of bamboo sounds—murmuring and whistling in their natural forms—along with their respective cultural representations

Figure 1.8 Tembang Sunda. Instruments in the back row (l to r): *kacapi indung* (Matt Ashworth), *suling* (Lili Rochili), *kacapi rincik* (Dadang); singers (l to r): Hendrawati, Arif Budiman.
Source: photo: Henry Spiller.

in the angklung's percussive interlocking ostinatos and the suling's lyrical melodies, are important *soundmarks*, to use R. Murray Schafer's terminology (1977). These soundmarks identify and unify characteristically Sundanese landscapes, soundscapes, and social values.

West Java's history is rife with invasions by foreign empires— Srivijaya, Majapahit, Mataram, and various European powers—as well as outside philosophies—Hinduism, Buddhism, Islam, modernism, capitalism. These hegemonies promoted imported technologies, ideas, and even musical sounds, while relegating indigenous bamboo technologies to the background. Elite outsiders devalued bamboo music, first in favor of the ostentatious display of bronze gamelan, and more recently in favor of Western-, Malay-, and Indian-style pop music and musical instruments.

These newer musical forms nevertheless display bamboo soundmarks, deployed in very specific ways, resulting in musical textures characterized by the simultaneous presentation of two contrasting approaches to melody and rhythm: (1) accompaniments that consist of multiple interlocking ostinatos, sometimes (but not always) with repetitive, rhythmically regular tunes that emerge as a side-effect or composite of the individual ostinato patterns, reminiscent of the angklung ensembles associated with agricultural ceremonies; and (2) lyrical, melismatic, quasi-free-rhythm melodies, of the sort that is idiomatic for the suling.

For example, Sundanese aristocrats eagerly adopted imported bronze gamelan ensembles. And Sundanese gamelan ensembles, while physically similar to their Central Javanese antecedents, exhibit a Sundanese aesthetic preference for a combination of two bamboo-derived musical characteristics: (1) an accompaniment, provided by fixed-pitch instruments (i.e., instruments that produce only certain pitches, with no provision for portamentos, vibrato, etc.), typically presented with regular, steady, duple rhythms, and (2) lyrical melodies with relatively free rhythm. Gamelan music usually features a set of interlocking ostinatos played on gongs of various sizes (the large hanging gong called *goong*, the smaller hanging gong called *kempul*, the large horizontal gong chimes *kenong* and/or *jengglong*, and optional addition small horizontal gongs), reminiscent of interlocking bamboo ostinatos (see Spiller 2004). Kunst called such structures *colotomic* because the different sounds marked off subperiods of a long cycle (from the Greek *colon* [in rhetoric, a grammatically complete unit] and *-tomic* [a suffix indicating that something is cut or divided into sections]). In contrast to Central Javanese court gamelan music, which often involves very long colotomic forms, Sundanese gamelan music tends to have much shorter cycles, perhaps hearkening back to the more rustic ostinatos of angklung music. In Sundanese gamelan music, a singer (usually female) and the player of the *rebab* (a two-string spike fiddle) provide the florid, quasi-free-rhythm parts (see Figure 1.9).

Figure 1.9 Sundanese *gamelan salendro*. Back row: *kenong* (player not visible), *pasinden* (female singer), *goong* and *kempul* (hanging from the same frame), *kendang* (drums), *bonang* (gong chime). Front row: *rebab*, *peking* (no player), *saron*, *saron*.

Source: photo: Henry Spiller.

30   *Bamboo Murmurs*

Sundanese musicians tuned their Javanese-style gamelan to the *salendro* tuning system (which the Javanese also knew). But they also created a new uniquely Sundanese kind of gamelan ensemble, called *degung*, which was tuned to the uniquely Sundanese pentatonic *pelog degung* scale, and eventually came to feature *suling* as its primary melodic instrument. (See Chapter 5 for more information about these tunings' possible roots in bamboo technologies.)

Tembang Sunda, too, reflects a bamboo-derived texture with fixed-pitch/regular-rhythm accompaniment and lyrical, free-rhythm melodies. The accompaniments played on the *kacapi indung* (large, "mother" kacapi) feature three-pitch ostinatos in regular rhythm in the right-hand part, which recall the kinds of interlocking ostinatos performed in angklung ensembles. These patterns provide a predictable tonal and rhythmic framework for the singer's and suling player's melismatic melodies that slip and slide around the edges of the ostinato accompaniment.[10]

It is a stretch to suggest that Sundanese listeners think "bamboo" when they hear these soundmarks, or that they make a conscious connection between these musical elements and the landscape of West Java. It is not an exaggeration, however, to assert that music-makers and listeners alike turn to such soundmarks when they want to evoke or experience a sense of a uniquely Sundanese identity.

A case in point: Rhoma Irama's *dangdut* hit from the 1980s, "Kuda Lumping," made popular by the singer Elvy Sukaesih, which has become one of the genre's golden oldies and continues to be performed frequently. Dangdut is Indonesia's most popular music (Weintraub 2006: 412). This combination of Malay, Arabic, Indian, and Western musical elements was initially embraced primarily by the underclasses in Indonesia's capital city of Jakarta, where its hybrid musical style and Indonesian language texts suited the multicultural urban population. By the 1990s, dangdut's appeal extended across the Indonesian nation, and to middle class and elite audiences as well. One of dangdut's attractions is its contribution to the capacity of these audiences to attain a pleasurable altered state of consciousness.

The song "Kuda Lumping" describes the Sundanese rural trance ritual of the same name, in which men dance on *kuda lumping* (hobby horses) to angklung accompaniment in order to enter a trance state. The song's verses relate the basic facts: there's an activity called kuda lumping in which the participants *lupa diri* (literally, "forget themselves," i.e., enter a trance state) and exhibit horse-like behaviors such as eating straw, whinnying and panting, and trotting around (see also Foley 1985; Kartomi 1973a; Kartomi 1973b). The chorus switches gears—it repeats the words "kuda lumping" several times to create a suddenly agitated rhythmic gesture. This rhythmic hook catches the listeners off-guard, reawakens the associations of rhythm with movement that urbanites may have forgotten but which nevertheless incite them to react by moving—in effect, to "forget themselves." The song's lyrics, then, encourage modern listeners, whether they're

Bamboo Murmurs 31

Sundanese or not, to relate modern, urban dangdut to old-fashioned Sundanese trance rituals.

Rhoma Irama makes this connection explicit by opening the song with a melodic motif, played on electric guitar, which is the sort of melody that could be played by a group of angklung players—in fact, it is the very melody illustrated earlier in the chapter, in Figure 1.6. The rhythmically regular composite of ostinatos is then answered by a more lyrical motif, played with some rhythmic elasticity on *bangsing* (sometimes called *suling bangsing*), which is the transverse bamboo flute associated with dangdut ensembles, and/or synthesizer. By referencing these Sundanese bamboo soundmarks—the timbre and idiom of the suling, the interlocking nature of the ostinato, and the contrast of rhythmically regular parts with rhythmically free elements—at the beginning of the song, Rhoma Irama immediately invokes a sense of rural Sundanese identity among his listeners.[11]

Conclusion

The Sundanese denizens of West Java have long cultivated a unique identity, rooted in the region's unique history and geography, in which bamboo sounds play a central role. In its natural state, bamboo affords two very different kinds of sounds: a pleasing pitched percussive sound as the culms hit one another in the wind, and more sustained whistle sounds as the wind blows through (or across) individual stalks. These two different sounds likely provided the inspiration for two very different Sundanese musical instruments: angklung and suling. A combination of these two sounds also can be considered the precursors of a texture that dominates Sundanese traditional music: the superimposition of rhythmically regular, interlocking patterns with lyrical melodies performed with elastic rhythms.

As it always has, bamboo provides local solutions to many different problems. The revival of bamboo music over the past decade has a number of root causes, all of which mutually reinforce one another, and contribute to the ongoing creation and maintenance of a uniquely Sundanese cultural identity in a modern world.

Notes

1 The *Nagarakĕrtagama*, an epic poem from fourteenth-century Majapahit in praise of Hayam Wuruk, provides one account (from the Majapahit point of view; see Hall 1985, 267). The *Pararaton*, probably composed in the fifteenth century in Majapahit, provides an account more sympathetic to the Sundanese side of the story (Hall 2001, 95). *Kidung Sunda* and *Kidung Sundayana* are later (likely from the sixteenth century), romanticized versions, apparently of Balinese provenance (Hall 2001, 99), that also show a more Sundanese bias.

2 For example, in 1949, the nascent Indonesian government named the first state university, in Yogyakarta, "Universiteit Negeri Gadjah Mada" (now Universitas Gadjah Mada) as a way to afford a purely local historical precedent

32 *Bamboo Murmurs*

to the notion of a modern Indonesian state, rather than accede to the supposition that Indonesia's boundaries were an artefact of Dutch colonialism.

3 see Kompas.com, "Kini ada Jalan Majapahit dan Hayam Wuruk di Kota Bandung," May 11 2018 https://regional.kompas.com/read/2018/05/11/18322 431/kini-ada-jalan-majapahit-dan-hayam-wuruk-di-kota-bandung; Tempo. com, "Kini ada Jalan Majapahit dan Hayam Wuruk di Kota Bandung," May 11 2018. https://nasional.tempo.co/read/1088002/kini-ada-jalan-majapahit-dan-jalan-hayam-wuruk-di-bandung/full&view=ok; and many others. Population figures are from http://worldpopulationreview.com/countries/indonesia-pop ulation/.

4 I saw the production on May 31, 2013, at the Teater Tertutup (indoor theatre) at Taman Budaya Jawa Barat (West Java's government-supported regional cultural center, located in Bandung on the site of the historic Dago Thee Huis [Dago Tea House]). It was a joint production presented by Universitas Pendidikan Indonesia (UPI) Bandung and Sekolah Tinggi Seni Indonesia (STSI, currently operating under the name Institut Seni Budaya Indonesia [ISBI]). UPI students had mounted a similar production in 2010, of which there is video available on YouTube: www.youtube.com/watch?v=NpuJgHI-CWg and www.youtube. com/watch?v=-lq26nVW6Rg.

5 Other examples include Faisal and Kinasih 2010, 334; Dim 2017; Rusnandar 2009; Rosyadi 2012, 29–31; and others.

6 Or, more technically, the sound that emerges when a sharp edge of bamboo splits a stream of air and causes the column of air inside the bamboo's tube to vibrate in a periodic manner that human ears and brains perceive as a steady pitch.

7 This summary of bamboo varieties for angklung making is derived from interviews with angklung makers, as well as published sources, including Kubarsah 1996; Majid 2013; Maradjo et al. 1976; Masunah et al. 2003; Sukma 2013; and Zainal et al. 2009.

8 Masunah et al. (2003, 18) corroborate that black bamboo comes from the southern coast of West Java.

9 documentary film by Gigi Priadji and M. Reza, showing the suling maker, Toto Suling (see Chapter 5), performing all these steps to make a suling is available at www.youtube.com/watch?v=AvQ6Ki9WxAs. The film also features Iman Jimbot (see Chapter 5) playing the suling.

10 See www.youtube.com/watch?v=FOdE1nrPdyM for representative video of tembang Sunda.

11 recent "Kuda Lumping" performance by Elvy Sukaesih (www.youtube.com/ watch?v=nVwXOlzT6MQ), includes young men on stage dancing with hobby horses. The motif I associate with angklung is at 0:13–0:18, while the flute motif is at 0:18–0:24. The chorus begins at 0:54. Elvy Sukaesih is joined by the male contestants in MNCTV's "Kontes Dangdut Indonesia (KDI)" ("Indonesia-wide dangdut contest") for a similar rendition (www.youtube.com/watch?v= QHygpgJO7LU). The song's lyrics and an English translation can be found at the bottom of the blog post at https://seethatmyblogiskeptclean.wordpress. com/2012/08/31/unknown-artist-kuda-lumping/, which also includes a link to a version performed by street musicians.

2 When in Bandung ...

Pindah cai, pindah tampian
"A new stream, a new bathhouse"
("When moving, follow the customs of the new location")
("When in Rome, do as the Romans do")

Both the *celempung* (idiochord bamboo tube zither), introduced in Chapter 3, and the *karinding* (bamboo guimbarde), which will be covered in Chapter 4, experienced their renaissances rather recently. Sundanese *angklung* (bamboo rattles), however, underwent a revival—really more of a reinvention as an instrument for rendering Western music—in the 1930s, and played a prominent role in the emergence of Indonesia as an independent nation in the twentieth century.

As outlined in Chapter 1, angklung music is inherently cooperative. But social cooperation can take on many forms in different economic systems (egalitarianism, colonialism, capitalism, communism, socialism, neoliberalism, and globalism), and angklung music has proven to be relevant to any—indeed, to all—of them. In this way, it epitomizes the Sundanese proverb, "pindah cai, pindah tampian." A *tampian* is a rustic shelter, typically fashioned from bamboo and rattan, on a river or stream that creates a modicum of privacy for bathing and toilet activities (see Figure 2.1). Maintaining privacy under such conditions requires adhering to a set of protocols. "Pindah cai, pindah tampian" literally means "move river, move bathhouse"; more figuratively, it suggests that one must get accustomed to a new tampian and its associated privacy protocols when one moves to a new community ("when in Rome ..."). This chapter will examine the ways in which diatonic angklung music is able to model—indeed, to performatively express—the nuances of different economic/political ideologies in Indonesian history.

Konperensi Asia-Afrika

This account starts neither at the beginning of angklung's modern journey, nor in the present, but in the middle—in 1955. Between April 18–24 of that year, Indonesia hosted representatives from twenty-nine African

DOI: 10.4324/9781003302797-3

34 *When in Bandung ...*

Figure 2.1 A *tampian* (rustic bathing hut).
Source: Wikimedia Commons via the National Museum of World Cultures.

and Asian nations in Bandung. Many of the nations, like Indonesia, were newly independent in the aftermath of World War II. Known in Indonesian as the *Konperensi Asia-Afrika* (KAA), and in English as the "Bandung Conference" or the "Afro-Asian Conference," the meeting marks an important milestone in the so-called non-aligned movement, in which newly emerging countries in the Global South jockeyed to establish a modern presence that did not rely on either of the dominant post-war superpowers (i.e., the United States and the Soviet Union).

Following Japan's surrender to the Allies at the end of World War II, Indonesian republicans, under the leadership of President Sukarno, declared an independent Indonesia, and then struggled for four years to throw off the yoke of Dutch colonial rule once and for all, finally succeeding in 1949. It was six short years later that delegates to the KAA met in Bandung to promote cooperation among emerging African and Asian nations, coordinate strategies for decolonization, and discuss options for navigating alternative paths through the opposing ideologies of the US and the USSR.

At that time, Sukarno believed that submitting to either American imperialism or Soviet socialism/communism could only perpetuate the European colonial exploitation of Third World countries. In his own nation building, he looked to values he believed were shared among a variety of Indonesian peoples—first, a decision-making process in small communities that emphasizes democratic consensus under the guidance of respected elders, rather than majority votes, and second, *gotong royong* (spirit of mutual cooperation)—as alternative approaches to achieving equality and freedom in the modern world. He advocated a loose alliance between African and Asian nations, rooted in such non-Western values, that avoided siding with either the USA or the USSR, but which instead relied on sharing resources, knowledge, and cultural exchange between the emerging nations of Africa and Asia.

Sukarno's leadership in these matters is apparent in the ten resolutions (*dasasila Bandung*), adopted by the KAA delegates, which focused on safeguarding the sovereignty of independent nation-states, protecting the rights of individuals and minorities, and prohibiting hegemonic actions by large countries. Although these principles were aligned with the UN Charter, and rooted in many ways in Western philosophical pretexts, they carry the Sanskrit name *dasasila*—a designation familiar to many Buddhists as guiding principles for various religious activities—thus lending a deliberately non-Western flavor. Sukarno's advocacy eventually culminated in the (ultimately short-lived) non-aligned movement in the 1960s, as well as to his "guided democracy" approach to governing Indonesia, which came to an end in 1965 with the overthrow of Sukarno's regime and its replacement with Soeharto's *Orde Baru* ("New Order"). Although the New Order continued to promote collective values, it was much more favorable toward Western neoliberal/capitalist policies.

It was no accident—indeed it was an intentional symbolic repudiation of Dutch colonial domination—that the Indonesians repurposed Dutch colonial infrastructures (roads, hotels, and meeting halls) to host the conference (Shimazu 2014, 235). The grand old Sociëteit Concordia headquarters, a premier gathering spot for the Dutch elite in colonial times, originally built in 1895 and remodeled with a spectacular art deco façade in 1926, was freshened up and rechristened "Gedung Merdeka" ("Freedom Building") for the occasion (see Figure 2.2).[1] The street in front of Gedung Merdeka, once the *postweg* around which the city of Bandung was founded (see Chapter 4), was rechristened "Jalan Asia-Afrika." And the upscale hotels in the area—the Savoy Homann, the Preanger (which Sukarno himself, in his earlier days an architectural assistant to Charles Prosper Wolff Schoemaker, assisted in refurbishing), and others—provided international-standard lodging for the diplomats.

In a similar vein, angklung played a small, but important, role in these diplomatic machinations. Sukarno recognized that diatonic angklung ensembles, as pioneered by Daeng Soetigna in the 1930s and 1940s, were a powerful metaphor of *gotong royong* because they were fundamentally cooperative; each musician controlled a single note, so only together could they create harmonious sounds (see Chapter 1). Furthermore, diatonic angklung ensembles "covered" Western tunes and songs with the unmistakably Indonesian sound of shaken bamboo, thus repurposing Western technologies and infrastructures in "native" Indonesian ways—in much the

Figure 2.2 Gedung Merdeka in 2018, Bandung.
Source: photo: Henry Spiller.

same way that Gedung Merdeka, the Preanger Hotel, and other Dutch monuments were repurposed. Throughout his rule, Sukarno frequently deployed diatonic angklung ensembles at international events as a *"maskot kesenian"* (arts mascot), as Tatang Sumarsono and Erna Garnasih Pirous put it (2007, 141).[2]

An evening concert on April 18, 1955, which capped off the opening day of the KAA, held at the governor's office, featured Sundanese music and dance, including angklung and Sundanese "classical" dance.[3] The angklung group featured approximately 25 female schoolteachers, dressed in simple non-matching *kain* and *kabaya* (traditional skirt and blouse), each holding a single angklung. Although the angklung group was associated with Daeng Soetigna, Daeng himself was in Australia during the KAA (Sumarsono and Pirous 2007, 141). Several young female dancers performed "Tari Kukupu" (Butterfly Dance)—a favorite of Sukarno's—recently choreographed by R. Tjetje Somantri (Imran, Malik et al. 2011, 84).

Angklung appeared in other contexts during the conference as well (Sumarsono and Pirous 2007, 292).[4] According to a placard in the museum of the KAA, which now occupies Gedung Merdeka, "Indonesian women demonstrated how to play the 'angklung', one of the activities in the ladies programme." It also appears that the assembled diplomats and their entourages may have participated in an angklung workshop sometime during the conference (pc, Budi Supardiman, August 7, 2013); certainly such workshops were a mainstay of later diplomatic events. The movement of the delegations from the hotels to Gedung Merdeka provided the Bandung populace with moments of political theatre (Shimazu 2014), and at least one source suggests that marching angklung groups at times accompanied the delegates as they moved from place to place. "Just imagine," said General Dr. H.C. Mashudi in 2005, stressing the KAA's peaceful and open atmosphere, "when heads of state walked from the Hotel Savoy Homann to the Gedung Merdeka, they were accompanied by nothing more than a single policeman and an angklung ensemble" (Roberts and Faulcher 2016, 224; Surono 2005, 89).[5]

Angklung in West Java

Recapitulating Chapter 1's brief introduction to angklung construction and basic playing techniques: a single angklung consists of two or three tuned bamboo tubes mounted in frame in such a way that, when shaken, produce a pleasing musical sound. An ensemble consists of a set of angklung, each tuned to a different pitch. Each player holds one angklung, shaking their instrument only when its particular pitch is called for in the musical composition. This cooperative approach to playing is a manifestation of gotong royong (mutual cooperation), the same social principle that guided the communal cultivation and harvest of rice in egalitarian rural communities.

Scholars generally agree that bamboo musical instruments in the Indonesian archipelago predate the Hindu period. Artur Simon identifies "duct end blown and transverse flutes, jew's harps of the Southeast Asian type, and idiochord tube zithers made of bamboo" as Neolithic Malay instruments (2010, 25). Some scholars, such as Curt Sachs (2006 [1940], 233) and Isaac Groneman and Jan Pieter Nicolaas Land (1890, 4), have included angklung in particular as an instrument that predates the onset of Indian influence in Java; but there is no clear evidence for this assertion, and many scholars are more cautious. Obby Wiramihardja, for example, cites depictions of bamboo xylophones in the stone carvings of the eighth-century Hindu monument, Prambanan, and the ninth-century Buddhist Borobudur temple, but is careful to point out that nothing resembling an angklung appears there (2007).

Wiramihardja suggests that the first clear historical record of angklung is in the *Serat Centhini*, a massive twelve-volume compendium of Javanese philosophy and stories, promulgated in 1814 under the patronage of the individual who eventually was crowned Pakubuwana V (Susuhunan of Surakarta 1820–1823). The *Serat Centhini* is set in the early seventeenth century in the Mataram kingdom (the antecedent of Pakubuwana's kingdom) and purports to describe events and customs of that time. In verse 321,

38   *When in Bandung ...*

one of the main characters, Mas Cebolang, entertains a nobleman with a musical ensemble that includes angklung (Kusnadi 2006, 145; Anderson 2018, 271, 284).

Around the same time as the composition of the *Serat Centhini*, Sir Thomas Stamford Raffles describes angklung in his 1817 *The History of Java*, emphasizing that the instrument is especially common in "the Súnda districts" (1817, 472). Although his verbal descriptions are mostly consistent with modern versions of the instrument, the drawing he included with the book (on the plate between pp. 168 and 169) is rather strange, as Wim van Zanten points out (2021, 145); Raffles's angklung includes five sounding tubes (most modern instruments have only two or three), which are not very different in size. In any case, by the early nineteenth century it appears that angklung were widely distributed. It may not be possible to ascertain many details of its history before then, however.

Earlier twentieth-century sources, such as Kunst and Wiratanakoesoema (1921, 241–243), give tantalizing detail of a variety of angklung traditions in different locales. Individual West Javanese rice-growing communities maintained distinctive local angklung styles and repertories that helped mark annual growing cycles and align agricultural practices with cosmological concerns. Not many agricultural angklung traditions have survived into the present, however. Perhaps not surprisingly, the famously conservative Baduy/Kanekes communities sometimes perform angklung music for rice-related ceremonies (see Wessing 1977; Zanten 1995 and 2021; Ekadjati 1995, 100–101; Atmadibrata et al. 2006, 4–6; Masunah 2003, 25–27; Nugraha 2015, 12–17). More recently, some self-consciously traditional *kasepuhan* ("adhering to the old") communities have revived ceremonial angklung music (Satya Upaja Budi 2015).

Masunah et al. describe several of these angklung traditions as they exist in the present day in considerable detail, and document how each tradition has proved its "sustainability" (*berkesinambungan*) by changing according to the local geography and history (2003, 25–89). According to Masunah et al., in each locale, angklung "undergoes changes in line with changes in the supporting community." ("angklung di setiap daerah mengalami perubahan sejalan dengan perubahan masyarakat pendukungnya"; 2003, 89).

Some traditions, such as those in Baduy communities (see also Zanten 2021), as well as *dogdog lojor* (from the Sukabumi area), continue to be centered around ancestral animistic belief systems, in which angklung performance is a ritual honoring the rice goddess. These communities also see their angklung activities as a way to maintain a connection to their perceived roots in the medieval Pajajaran kingdom. These communities are effectively isolated in many ways from modern Sundanese life (2003, 89–90).

In contrast, angklung practices from areas that are closer to Bandung have minimized such associations. *Angklung badeng* (from the village of Sanding [near Garut], for example), has developed strong Islamic associations. The performers of *angklung buncis* (from Cipurut, east of Bandung; see also Baier 1985) have minimized religious connections to focus more on the entertainment value of angklung performance (Masunah et al. 2003, 63); *angklung Badud* from Ciamis, *angklung badeng*, *angklung bungko* from the village Bungko (near Cirebon), and *angklung gubrag* from Cipining (near Bogor) are other examples (Masunah et al. 2003; Hermawan et al. 2012). Masunah et al.'s final case study, Saung Angklung Udjo (discussed in more detail later in this chapter), likewise develops angklung music's entertainment value in the service of economic development (2003, 90).

The decline of angklung in ceremonial contexts might be attributable to changes in agricultural practices in the nineteenth and twentieth centuries, mostly linked to Dutch colonial practices (e.g., increased reliance on wet-rice [*sawah*] cultivation, Dutch *cultuurstelsel* policies, and [later] the introduction of high-yielding "green revolution" rice varieties [see Bolman 2006, 16–21]), which disrupted the traditional agricultural cycles marked by rituals including angklung.

Recent research suggests that the Dutch colonial administration actively suppressed angklung music because of concerns that it might foment anti-Dutch sentiments and actions among rural Sundanese, who were poorly treated under the cultuurstelsel system (Sumarsono and Pirous 2007, xxvii; Caturwati 2017, 7; Wiramihardja 2007). Perhaps it was precisely angklung's fundamentally cooperative nature that spooked the Dutch (pc, Budi Supardiman, August 7, 2013). Some writers assert that the Dutch bans did not apply to beggars (Pasmandas 2011; Rosyadi 2012, 37), so that by the turn of the twentieth century, angklung was a decidedly unprestigious musical instrument, associated primarily with panhandling.

The Rise of Diatonic Angklung

Indeed, it was an angklung played by a beggar that inspired Daeng Soetigna (1908–1984) to redeem and refashion angklung as a Sundanese musical instrument for the modern era. As a child, Daeng learned about Sundanese aristocratic arts, including music, poetry, and handicrafts, from his mother (Sumarsono and Pirous 2007, 11). Because his father was a member of the *santana* class—a Dutch social innovation that rewarded talented and hard-working non-aristocratic Sundanese individuals with responsible positions in the colonial administration (see Lubis 1998, 68–69)—Daeng was eligible for a Dutch-language education at the Hollandsch-Inlandsche School (HIS) in his hometown of Garut (Sumarsono and Pirous 2007, 59). He later earned teaching qualifications at the Kweekschool (KS) in Bandung and began his teaching career in Cianjur (Sumarsono and Pirous 2007, 89), later moving to Kuningan, just south of Cirebon. There, he cultivated his personal interest in music by learning to play the violin and began to give his students some basic instruction in Western music (Sumarsono and Pirous 2007, 103).

40   When in Bandung ...

By the mid-1930s, Daeng also became involved in the scouting movement, which was already well-established in the Indies since its inception there in 1912 by P.J. Smith and Major de Jager (Semedi 2011, 21). As a scout leader, Daeng's mission was to foster good character and teamwork, and to these ends he engaged his scouts in musical activities as well. When the angklung-playing beggar caught his ear, he became captivated by its sound and bought the instrument from the beggar. He eventually located an angklung craftsman (named Djaja) from whom he learned to make the instruments himself (Rosyadi 2012, 36; Sjamsuddin and Winitasasmita 1986, 30).[6] But first, according to his biographers, he had to convince Djaja that his goal wasn't to teach children how to beg! (Sumarsono and Pirous 2007, 101; 106–107; pc, Budi Supardiman, August 7, 2013.)

Daeng's notion to make angklung that were tuned to the Western diatonic/chromatic scale was audacious at the time—people unconsciously assumed that the worlds of traditional Sundanese music and modern Western music were not compatible. Although orientalist composers, such as Paul J. Seelig, Constant van de Wall, Charles T. Griffes, and others, adapted Indonesian music for Western voices and instruments (see Dijk 2007; Spiller 2009), attempts to render Western music on Indonesian instruments, or for non-Europeans to attempt such experiments, were unheard of. Nevertheless, by 1938, after considerable trial and error, Daeng completed a set of angklung that was based on the range of his violin: thirty rattles, which he numbered 1 to 30, comprising chromatic pitches from g3 to c5. He debuted the angklung as a team-building activity for his scouts. Daeng arranged *kroncong* and Dutch melodies with simple harmonization and wrote notation on a poster-sized piece of paper (*partitur*) that everybody could see (Sumarsono and Pirous 2007, 210–214).[7] Diatonic angklung ensembles became popular at scout events, and reportedly became an indispensable accessory around scout campfires (Haas 1964, 5; Sjamsuddin and Winitasasmita 1986, 70).

It was a fellow scout leader who suggested that diatonic angklung might help solve some of Daeng's problems teaching music in school. Some of the students were too shy to sing, for example, but it was difficult and expensive to obtain standard Western musical instruments. Angklung were producible from local materials, inexpensive, and easy to play (Sumarsono and Pirous 2007, 111, 103).

Daeng maintained his angklung activities during the Japanese occupation of Java (1942–1945), although he adjusted the repertory to include Japanese songs. The Japanese administration approved of angklung, likely because of its clear Asian progenitors and the Japanese regard for bamboo as a material (Sumarsono and Pirous 2007, xxvii, 124; Sjamsuddin and Winitasasmita 1986, 31). Daeng's group performed frequently for the Japanese occupiers (Rosyadi 2012, 38), but also earned praise from Sundanese nationalists who approved of his approach to modernizing local traditions (Sumarsono and Pirous 2007, 117).

After the return of the Dutch in 1945 and during the ensuing war for Indonesian independence, Daeng remained politically neutral, epitomizing the "pindah cai, pindah tampian" ideal. His angklung group performed at the initial signing ceremony for the Linggajati Agreement (an ultimately unsuccessful attempt by Indonesian republicans and the Dutch to agree on a semi-independent Indonesian federation) in November 1946; the group subsequently traveled to Jakarta to perform for President Sukarno and Prime Minister Sutan Syahrir (Rosyadi 2012, 38). They also, however, performed at the declaration of independence of the short-lived Negara Pasundan, a semi-independent West Javanese polity that, in the face of the Javanese-centric republicans led by Sukarno, promoted Sundanese autonomy by engaging in an uncomfortable alliance with the Dutch, who were eager to promote an Indonesian federation with ties to the Netherlands (see Frakking 2017, 33–34). This event was the premiere performance of Daeng's now classic arrangement of Strauss's "An der schönen blauen Donau" ("The Blue Danube Waltz"; Sumarsono and Pirous 2007, 136; Sjamsuddin and Winitasasmita 1986, 32), which remains a staple of the diatonic angklung repertory. Daeng's group also performed for the concert that celebrated the closing of the Renville Agreement—another ultimately unsuccessful truce between the Dutch and Sukarno's republican forces in 1947 (Rosyadi 2012, 38).

"Hallo-Hallo Bandung"

Walter Mignolo and Catherine Walsh (2018) consider the 1955 KAA, as well as comparable events (e.g., the 1961 Conference of the Non-Aligned Countries), as key events in the development of "legacies of decoloniza- tion" (2018, 4). They conceive colonialism as constitutive of modernity and discuss the "colonial matrix of power" that sustains both colonialism and modernity. In their view, the process of decolonization "undoes, disobeys, and delinks from this matrix" (2018, 4). Sukarno's deliberate exclusion of major world powers in the conference—according to Naoku Shimazu, "not a single 'white' or 'Western' state was present" (2011, 5)—thus qualifies as an act of decolonialization. His warnings to delegates to recognize those powers' ongoing economic and intellectual control as forms of coloni- alism qualify as well; according to Khaled Al-Kassimi, "from a decolonial delinking perspective, the Bandung Conference of 1955 remains a defining decolonial gesture" (2018, 11).

It was Daeng's disciples in Bandung who played for the 1955 KAA; Daeng himself was in Australia. The Colombo Plan, an international con- sortium founded in 1950 with a mission to promote cooperation among newly emerging Asia-Pacific countries, had sent Daeng as one of seven- teen Indonesian teachers to study English language and music education for nine months in Australia (Sumarsono and Pirous 2007, 149–150). In any case, it is fruitful to analyze Daeng's diatonic angklung groups with

42 *When in Bandung ...*

current theories of decolonial decoupling. Angklung music decouples Western-sounding music, replete with lyrical melodies, common-practice harmonies, and even multi-voice polyphony, from its colonial antecedents by using instruments constructed entirely of local materials and relying on local approaches to performance that emphasize interlocking parts and simple, distributed roles for everybody involved, with no soloists.[8]

A look at one of Daeng's arrangements will demonstrate how his approach to angklung was a perfect fit for the KAA, with its emphasis on decolonization, as well as Sukarno's promotion of the local Indonesian values of gotong royong and democratic consensus. "Hallo-Hallo Bandung" is a well-known song written by the prolific Indonesian composer, Ismail Marzuki (1914–1958). While I am not certain that it was among the pieces performed during the KAA's opening angklung concert, the song's history and significance suggest that it is probable.

Marzuki originally composed the song during the colonial period, as a nostalgic tribute to Bandung, where he had lived and worked before moving to Jakarta. After World War II, however, the song acquired new significance. In 1946, the British forces who had been dismantling the Japanese colonial administration on Java ordered all the Indonesian troops loyal to the recently declared Republic of Indonesian to leave the southern part of Bandung; instead, on March 24, the republicans evacuated everybody, including civilians, and burned south Bandung to the ground as a gesture of defiance and protest. The event came to be known as "Bandung Lautan Api (BLA)," ("Bandung Sea of Fire"), and eventually became an important symbol of the revolution and Indonesian independence. Marzuki, who had returned to Bandung to escape the unrest in Jakarta, was inspired to revise the Indonesian-language lyrics of "Hallo-Hallo Bandung" to cite the BLA as an inspiration for republican soldiers. The song subsequently became known throughout Indonesia as a song of the revolution (Setiadijaya 1996).

Daeng Soetigna's arrangement of "Hallo-Hallo Bandung" circulates widely among performers of diatonic angklung; I don't know when he first transcribed the song for angklung, but the version in Figure 2.3a is widespread (I have transnoted it into staff notation in Figure 2.3b).[9,10]

Daeng's arrangement calls for at least 22 individuals (i.e., an ensemble of the size that performed at the KAA), each playing a single angklung. The "Daftar Angklung" (list of angklung) at the bottom of the score in Figure 2.3a specifies the name/number of each angklung required for the piece in its first row; the second row provides each angklung's corresponding note in the arrangement, set in G major, in cipher notation (1=do, 2=re, etc.). I should note that this arrangement assumes the expanded range (beyond the original 1 to 30 of Daeng's original sets) which Daeng created in the late 1950s (Winitasasmita and Budiaman 1978, 24).[11] The lower octave is "numbered" with pitch names (G, A, B, c, cis [c#], etc., culminating with f#3 as pitch 0; Sumarsono and Pirous 2007, 201–202). A forward slash through a cipher indicates the diatonic note is raised a semitone; a backward slash indicates that the note is lowered a semitone. The range

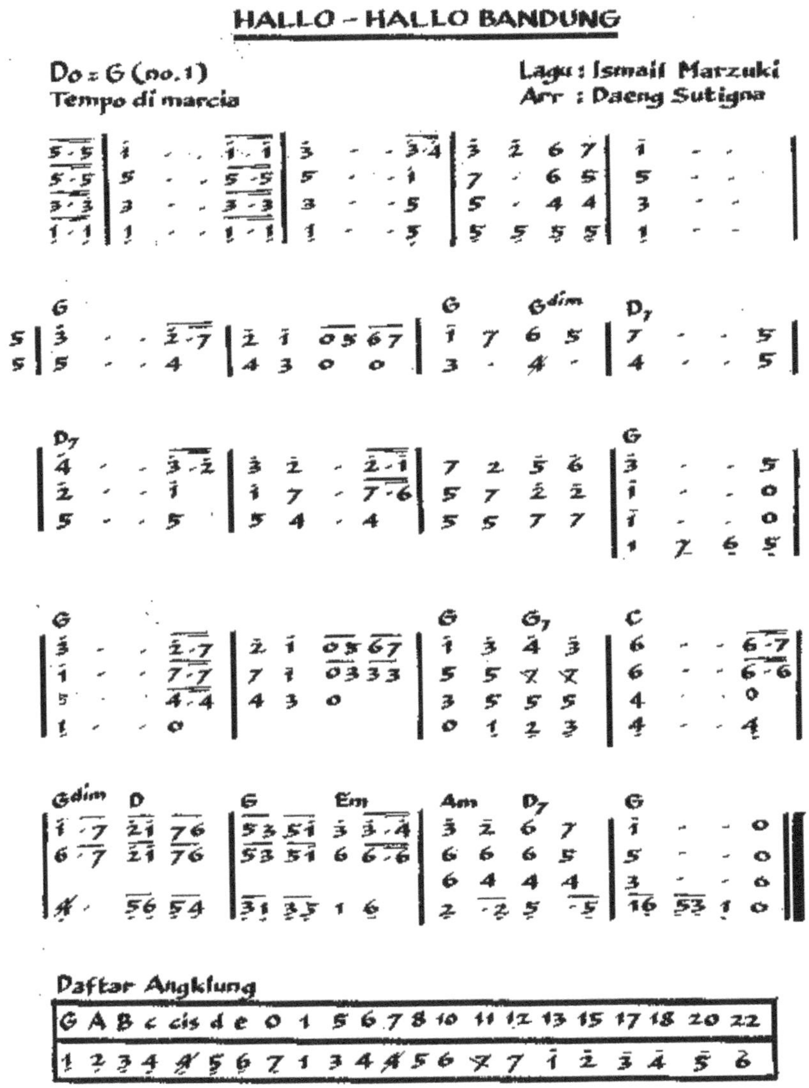

HALLO - HALLO BANDUNG

Figure 2.3a "Hallo-Hallo Bandung" (Ismail Marzuki) arranged by Daeng Soetigna.

of the ensemble is just under three octaves. Dots below the cipher indicate the low octave; no dot indicates the middle octave; a dot above indicates the high octave.

Indonesian scholars characterize "Hallo-Hallo Bandung" as a *lagu mars* ("march piece"). The song's duple rhythm (suitable "to accompany young soldiers ... marching in line, following the rhythm"; Permata 2021,

44 *When in Bandung ...*

Figure 2.3b Transnotation of Daeng's arrangement of "Hallo-Hallo Bandung."

31)[12] is characteristic. Such rousing pieces are not limited to the military; schools, corporations, and political parties often have their own symbolic lagu mars (Karyawanto 2018, 8). Such marches are artefacts of colonialism, even though they have been thoroughly assimilated by Indonesians over the centuries.

The partitur (as Indonesians call the type of score notation in Figure 2.3a) reveals mostly chorale-like textures of two, three, or four voices, with voice leading that adheres to most of the conventions of common-practice harmony that are designed to keep each voice distinct even though their timbres are similar. The arrangement begins with an

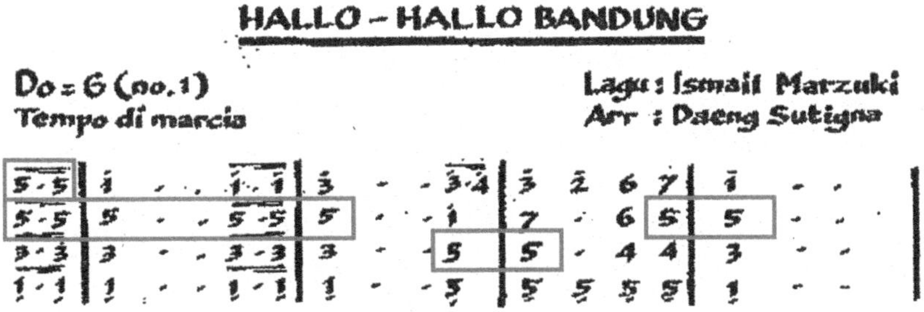

HALLO – HALLO BANDUNG

Do = G (no. 1)
Tempo di marcia

Lagu : Ismail Marzuki
Arr : Daeng Sutigna

Figure 2.4 First line of "Hallo-Hallo Bandung"; the note "5" is highlighted in to demonstrate that it is part of three distinct "voices" in the texture, even though it is played by a single individual.

introduction featuring a full four-voice texture. The first phrase of the song proper (at m. 5) has a two-voice texture. Each of the subsequent phrases adds a bit of complexity—a third voice in the second phrase (mm. 9–12), a bass line in the third phrase (mm. 12–16), and more polyphonic complexity in the final phrase (mm. 17–20).

All these musical features conform to Western—that is, colonial—models. But keeping in mind that a single player is responsible for a single pitch, it becomes clear that many individuals must contribute their single note to two, even three of the different voices. The player of the pitch notated as "5," for example, in the first system, plays (at different times) in the top voice, the second voice, and the third voice (see Figure 2.4). A listener accustomed to hearing chorales will not be aware that each "voice" in the texture is actually the result of cooperation between several individuals, or that each individual contributes to several different "voices." In other words: although the piece is abstractly conceived as the combination of several independent voices, the practical playing is conceived around the iteration of individual pitches.

Thus, the march form, the chorale texture, and the common-practice harmonic voice leading are "decolonized"—undone, disobeyed, and delinked, using Mignolo and Walsh's formulation (2018, 4)—by creating them using local materials (i.e., the bamboo instruments), producing local soundmarks (i.e., the distinctive timbre of bamboo rustling) and promoting local values (i.e., "gotong royong," the spirit of cooperation) through local performance practices (i.e., interlocking). Audiences see a musical representation of Old-Order-style "democratic consensus" in the musicians' agreement to play their single note at the correct—and only the correct—moment(s).

Angklung at the 1964 New York World's Fair

In his opening speech at the KAA in 1955, Sukarno warned of "other colonialisms," referring to American-style capitalism and

46   *When in Bandung ...*

Soviet-style socialism/communism, and initially sought to steer clear of both superpowers. Sukarno tried to assert this position symbolically at the 1964 World's Fair in New York by lobbying to place Indonesia's pavilion at the Fair halfway between the USA and USSR pavilions (Cotter and Young 1964, 26; Ross 2016, 64). The USSR eventually withdrew from the Fair, however, rendering moot any obvious symbolism attached to the Indonesian pavilion's location.

Daeng Soetigna was tapped to coordinate the Sundanese sections of the performing arts delegation for the Indonesian Pavilion in 1964 (Sumarsono and Pirous 2007, 175–176; Haas 1964, 5; Amilia 2001, 36), which featured diatonic angklung, along with music and dance in four different regional styles (Sundanese,[13] Javanese, Balinese, and Sumatran). The performance was, according to a June 7, 1965, *Newsday* article, "one of the Fair's most popular [attractions] during the 1964 season" (Caro 1965, 5). According to Imran, Malik, et al., the grand finale of the performance, held in the pavilion's restaurant, featured the entire multi-ethnic delegation playing diatonic angklung to accompany the singing of Sundanese diva Tati Saleh (2011, 72, 91). The troupe continued on to France and the Netherlands when the World's Fair season ended in October of 1964,[14] spending a total of about seven months abroad (Sumarsono and Pirous 2007, 299; Rosyadi 2012, 38; Haas 1964, 5; Amilia 2001, 45).[15]

The New York World Fair's angklung diplomacy neatly sums Sukarno's vision of Indonesian governance and the nascent country's international image. The entire delegation played in the angklung ensemble, but none of the angklung musicians were angklung specialists, thus enacting a version of a collective ideal for Indonesian society. Their repertory represented Indonesia, through Indonesian songs, as well as performing Indonesia's adaptability to the modern world, through its renditions of songs local to the places they visit (e.g., their concert for the Queen of the Netherlands included "an angklung rendition" of "Daar bij die molen" [Lindsay 2012, 203]). And, as previously discussed, the playing style, timbre, and texture of the music covered everything they played with an unmistakable Indonesian bamboo sensibility.

As early as 1960, and despite his earlier insistence on avoiding the world's superpowers, Sukarno became receptive to aid from the Soviets, explored alliances with the PRC, and became increasingly hostile to the United States. The growing rancor between Indonesia and the USA came to a symbolic head when Sukarno withdrew Indonesia from the New York World's Fair before the 1965 season started.[16] A troupe had already begun to rehearse for the 1965 season when the cancellation was announced; some of those performers were redeployed for cultural missions to North Korea, the Peoples' Republic of China, and Japan—destinations expressly designed, it would seem, to rub salt into the deepening wounds of US-Indonesian political differences (see Imran, Malik et al. 2011, 88). The 1965 group did not include Daeng Soetigna, however (Imran, Malik et al. 2011, 91–99).[17]

As the 1960s progressed, Sukarno's political stability relied on a careful balance between the military, the Indonesian communist party, and Islamists. In 1965, under pressures on a variety of fronts, this delicate balance collapsed. In the aftermath of the "Gerakan 30 September" (the September 30th Movement, with the acronym "G30S"), the military took charge of the country, and communists and the Indonesian communist party (Partai Komunis Indonesia, with the acronym PKI) were brutally suppressed, resulting in the extrajudicial murders of millions of Indonesians. It is still not clear exactly who was responsible for the attempted coup and its bloody aftermath—according to various theories, it might have been disgruntled Indonesian military leaders, or the PKI, or even the American CIA—but once the dust settled, Indonesia was ruled by a new president, General Soeharto, whose policies were much more favorable to global (American-style) capitalism.

According to David Bourchier, both Sukarno and Soeharto saw Indonesia's strength in an "essentially communalistic and cooperative" approach vs the West's "individualistic, hedonistic and materialistic" sensibilities (i.e., "liberal"). Sukarno's *Orde Lama* ("Old Order") and Soeharto's *Orde Baru* ("New Order"), which replaced it, both promoted "indigenist" approaches. Soeharto and the military, however, subscribed to a different conceptualization of Indonesian collectivism. Sukarno's "populist indigenism," emblematized by gotong royong, gave way to "conservative indigenism," exemplified by *kekeluargaan* ("family-ism") under Soeharto, which promoted a benevolent patriarchal system in which all participants understand their designated place within a preordained hierarchy rather than simple, egalitarian "mutual cooperation" (Bourchier 1998, 204). A cynical, if accurate, evaluation of Soeharto's subsequent thirty-five-year reign in Indonesia would lean—perhaps too literally— toward the "kekeluargaan" approach, as Soeharto's relatives and cronies came to dominate the Indonesian economy for decades (and continue to wield significant influence into the present).

Saung Angklung Udjo

It was in this changing political climate that one of Daeng's earliest disciples, Udjo Ngalagena (1929–2001), and his wife, Uum Sumiati, founded Saung Angklung Udjo (SAU) around 1966.[18] A *saung* is a field shed, meant for storing crops; for Udjo and his wife, this rustic image epitomized the character of the place they envisioned with multiple goals: as a performance space, as a laboratory for education, and as a tourist attraction to employ residents of their Padasuka neighborhood (in eastern Bandung) that hearkens back to old-fashioned rural Sundanese values. According to a recent SAU brochure, Daeng Soetigna, from whom Udjo learned diatonic angklung, requested Udjo to continue the work of introducing angklung to the entire world.[19]

48 *When in Bandung …*

SAU grew steadily over the decades, became a staple of the Bandung tourism industry, and remains an important site in the angklung scene. When Udjo died in 2001, his family continued to run, even expand, SAU. At least six of Udjo's children— Sam, Nan, Daeng [Oktaviandi], Yayan [Muliana], Hety, and Taufik [Hidayat]—some of whom add "Udjo" to their professional names—play active roles in the business.[20] Furthermore, Sam, Daeng, and Yayan continue Udjo's practice of exploring new ways to build, tune, and play angklung.

SAU's afternoon presentation—billed on the website as "Bamboo Performance, Everday 15.30–17.00"—is a well-rehearsed, snappily paced variety show. In 2013, the program brochure listed *wayang golek* (Sundanese rod puppet theatre), *helaran* (a choreographed representation of village ritual music with angklung tuned to *salendro*), choreographed *klasik* dances (*topeng* [masked dance] and "Tari Merak"), *calung* (portable bamboo xylophones), *arumba* (stationary bamboo xylophones), *angklung mini* (small, simple angklung ensemble), *angklung Pa Daeng* (hand-carried diatonic angklung in Daeng Soetigna's original style), a participatory angklung workshop ("bermain angklung bersama," i.e., "playing angklung together," a.k.a. "angklung interaktif," i.e., "interactive angklung"), angklung orchestra (large bamboo-dominated ensemble), *angklung jaipong* (angklung orchestra accompanying *jaipongan* dance), culminating in free-for-all dancing by the audience. The actual 90-minute performance that I recorded on May 13, 2013, included most, but not all, of the items listed above.[21,22] In 2019, a ticket cost rp 70,000, about US$5.00.[23] The program's narration is primarily in English, and a large contingent of the audience for the show that afternoon appeared to be European (mostly Dutch) tourists.[24]

SAU's entrepreneurial, capitalistic spirit is clear from the ongoing success of this daily tourist show but is even more in evidence in the large gift store that patrons visit after the show, where they can choose from a mind-boggling array of souvenirs, including musical instruments, mostly made from bamboo, and look at various bamboo-related exhibits.

The success of SAU is tethered, at least in some part, to Udjo's astute deployment of Soeharto's seemingly contradictory synthesis of the kekeluargaan and global capitalist principles within the particular circumstances of SAU's hyper-local setting and Sundanese values, and angklung's innate capacity to follow the adage, "pindah cai, pindah tampian." Udjo's path to success reads like an Indonesian Horatio Alger story. Udjo himself came from a modest background, where he learned music in a variety of contexts, including angklung and calung (bamboo xylophone music). His parents were able to send him to a Dutch-language school (HIS) for upwardly mobile Indies natives, as well as to various teacher training institutes (Poetry 2011, iv–22). He and his wife managed their finances carefully in order to both take care of daily necessities and to fulfill their dreams: to provide educations for their ten children and to

When in Bandung ... 49

establish a *padepokan* ("retreat") angklung, now known as SAU (Poetry 2011, iv–23).

SAU has long been characterized by its close relationship to the immediate neighborhood surrounding its 1.2 hectare site (about 3 acres), at Jalan Padasuka 118, in eastern Bandung (the map in Figure 3.1, in Chapter 3, shows the approximate location of SAU). One angklung expert explained to me that as a CV (limited partnership),[25] SAU's first goal is to turn a profit, of course, but that SAU also is committed to contributing to its local community (pc, anon., April 19, 2013). Currently, as it has for decades, SAU recruits new students, ages 4 to 6, mostly from the Padasuka neighborhood.

According to Milyartini, in SAU's earliest days, Udjo recruited neighbor children to augment his own sizeable brood of ten sons and daughters for an angklung ensemble that performed in the front yard to welcome small groups of tourists (2012, n.p.). Nowadays, the best students are invited to continue their training and to take part in the afternoon show that happens every day. A couple of sources told me that this audition and winnowing process is very selective, and most (up to 85%) of the children are rejected for further training (pc, anon., April 26, 2013). Still, those selected are given free tuition to advance their studies in music, as well as "Host/MC" training (Poetry 2011, iv–39). There are as many as 500 active students at any time, primarily (but not exclusively) young people from the neighborhood (Sadikin 2009, 35), and Poetry estimates that 90% of SAU's workforce comes from Padasuka (2011, iv–38).

At the very beginning of his forays into the world of angklung, Udjo developed sets of bamboo instruments tuned to Sundanese scales (*salendro*, *sorog/madenda*, and *pelog degung*). Unlike the tuners of village ceremonial angklung, which generally featured ad hoc (if salendro-like) tunings, Udjo based his angklung tunings on gamelan instruments and the writings of Sundanese and Javanese music theorists, so that his groups could perform arrangements of traditional Sundanese gamelan music in the same way that diatonic angklung could render Western music. These sets are called *angklung modern Sunda* or *angklung pentatonik*, to contrast them with the *angklung diatonik* or *angklung padaeng* (in the tradition of Daeng Soetigna). Udjo's son Sam continues to refine pentatonic tunings for angklung (Milyartini 2012; Musthofa 2018, 549).

According to Rida Fadilah Husni Majid, new SAU students first learn pentatonic angklung, and then progress to diatonic angklung styles (2013, 2)—an "evolutionary" approach reflected and expanded in the progression of SAU's afternoon stage show. Indeed, the afternoon show, in effect, presents an teleological account of angklung, chronicling its origins in agricultural ritual music, its initial transformation to a diatonic/chromatic ensemble (angklung padaeng, in which the junior students each play a single diatonic angklung), followed by angklung's diplomatic turn, represented by *angklung interaktif* (for which each member of the audience is given a

Figure 2.5 The afternoon show at SAU.
Source: photo: Henry Spiller.

single diatonic angklung and everybody learns how to play several simple songs together),[26] culminating in *angklung orkestra*, which features several post-Soeharto innovations that enable a single individual to present virtuosic, soloistic performances (see Figure 2.5).

Thus, observers witness angklung's advancement from an egalitarian instrument echoing rural values of gotong royong into an instrument of individual virtuosity, along the lines of Western classical music and global popular music—in effect, performing the modernist, capitalist values of individualism decried by both Sukarno and Soeharto, but surreptitiously embraced by the New Order regime: "Despite Soeharto's embrace of capitalism and his increasingly market-oriented policies, he rarely if ever spoke of individualism, liberalism, or even capitalism in a positive light" (Bourchier and Hadiz 2014, 22).

Taken as a whole, then, SAU echoes many of the characteristics of Soeharto's New Order. The New Order professed, as the historian Muhamad Ali puts it, "distance from socialism and capitalism in ideological terms," but the regime "actually adopted a modified capitalist system" (2004, 6). Similarly, SAU business model is capitalist, even as it promotes the indigenous values. Soeharto's strategy for lending "cultural authenticity" to his regime's "modernizing and developmentalist" programs by embracing the indigenist values of gotong royong and kekeluargaan (Bourchier 2020, 598) are reproduced on a much smaller scale in the activities of SAU. Gary Dean points out that, "Indonesia, despite paper-thin modernist veneers, is ... still very much characterised by collectivist values and by systems of patronage" (1999), and SAU's ongoing patronage of the local neighborhood is a small-scale case in point. While hardly on a scale comparable to the corruption, collusion, and nepotism of Soeharto,[27] for whom the practice of kekeluargaan included packing the boards of a vast network of charitable foundations (*yayasan*) with his own relatives and cronies, who profited handsomely by leveraging the foundations' charitable activities,[28] the members of Udjo's family profit financially from SAU's community-based humanitarian work.

It is not my intention to suggest that the Udjo family, or SAU, is at all implicated in the corruption that has characterized New Order interventions in humanitarian, charitable work. I will vouch personally for the sincerity of all the family members with whom I've interacted in their commitments to preserving, developing, and celebrating the Indonesian performing arts, and in improving the lives of those who live in the Padasuka neighborhood. Indeed, they have renewed Daeng's and Udjo's pledge to promote cross-cultural understanding by empowering people from all over the world to make music together with angklung. Such grand altruistic visions have a way, however, of colliding with more nitty-gritty politics (see Chapter 5).

Parallel Developments in Diatonic Angklung

Udjo credited Daeng for his inspiration and relied on Daeng's imprimatur to legitimate SAU's various activities. But Daeng had other protégés, too, who endeavored to attach alternative meanings (also legitimated through the power of Daeng's endorsement) to angklung. Daeng moved to Bandung in 1949, where he started angklung groups at various schools (along with his younger brother, Oteng Sutisna).[29] With school groups proliferating, Daeng started an organization to standardize instrumentation, arrangements, and teaching methods, and to provide teacher training: Badan Koordinasi Musik Angklung (Coordinating Body for Angklung Music, with the acronym BKMA; S. 2007, 295). BKMA was responsible for the first *massal* (mass) angklung performance, with one thousand students from thirty different groups, at the 5th Pekan Olahraga Nasional (National Sports Competition, with the acronym PON) in 1961 in Bandung.

Among those participating in this mass performance was Obby A.R. Wiramihardja (b. 1944), who started learning angklung as a boy, and remained deeply involved in angklung throughout his career.[30] After graduating from Akademi Industri Pariwisata (Academy of the Tourism Industry), he landed a job as a civil servant in the Departemen Pendidikan dan Kebudayaan (Department of Education and Culture, abbreviated Depdikbud);[31] his final role there, before retiring, was as Head of the Diatonic Music Section.[32] He was a prime mover in mobilizing large angklung groups to perform for the 25th and 30th anniversaries of the KAA (in 1980 and 1985, respectively), and led several angklung missions abroad (Sumarsono and Pirous 2007, 313).

Handiman Diratmasasmita played angklung in school and started making angklung under the guidance of the school's industrial arts ("shop") teacher. He himself became a music teacher at a school run by

52 *When in Bandung ...*

Daeng's brother Oteng (Sukma 2013, 33–34), and he participated in the 1961 PON mass angklung performance with Oteng and Daeng. Handiman told me that the songs they performed included Daeng's arrangements of "Satu Nusa," "Satu Bangsa," "Meninjau Alam," and "Hallo Bandung," as well as songs about the PON (pc, May 7, 2013).

At first, Handiman made angklung for his own use, but others began to buy his instruments. He learned much about making angklung directly from Daeng and is proud to report that he continues to use the same nineteenth-century methods as Daeng's teacher, Djaja, passed along to him through Daeng. After Daeng's death, Daeng's widow gave Handiman all of Daeng's angklung-making supplies (Sukma 2013, 34). With the help of a few carpenters, he continues to produce angklung at his compact workshop on Jl. Surapati in central Bandung because, he told me, Daeng and his widow asked him to, and (like Udjo and Obby) he feels a responsibility to keep Daeng's legacy alive (pc, May 5, 2013). Several angklung teachers and scholars confided in me that Handiman's products are significantly better than others, because other makers tend to cut corners in their process (see Chapter 1 for more information about Handiman's angklung making process.)

Daeng was not the only individual promoting diatonic angklung in the early 1960s. But when the minister of Education and Culture, Prijono (a member of the left-leaning "nationalist communist" party, Murba [Lindsay 2012, 206]), dubbed another angklung teacher, Kasur, as "the father of angklung," members of BKMA protested.[33] According to Sanu'i Edia S., BKMA members convinced the leadership of the Pengurus Guru Republik Indonesia (Teachers Association of the Republic of Indonesia, with the acronym PGRI) to secure a presidential medal for cultural service (Satyalancana Kebudayaan) for Daeng at their regional conference in 1964.[34] At time time, the PGRI also invented the term angklung padaeng, proclaiming that diatonic/chromatic angklung music thereafter would be so called, in Daeng's honor (Sanui Edia S., 2007, 296).

This designation did not go over well with Lembaga Kebudayaan Rakyat (institute for people's culture, with the acronym LEKRA), a left-leaning arts organization that promoted social reform in the arts (S., 2007, 296). LEKRA artists promoted angklung as a collective activity; Ho Chi Minh, for example, on a visit to Bandung in 1959, was treated to an angklung performance along with dance, newly choreographed by a LEKRA member, called "Tari Tani" (Ross 2016, 61). Unlike most choreographed Sundanese dance, which depicted heroic characters from epic stories, "Tari Tani" depicted peasants planting and harvesting rice. LEKRA members no doubt appreciated the new subject matter, but likely objected to glorifying a single choroegrapher's name for a collective form.

LEKRA was dissolved, along with the Partai Komunis Indonesia (The Indonesian Communist Party, with the acronym PKI), after the September 30th Movement. The Indonesian Ministry of Education and Culture (under a new, pro-Soeharto minister) promulgated an official decree in

1968 (No. 082/1968) recognizing diatonic angklung as a valuable educational resource because of its potential for "character building, such as working together, collaboration, discipline, precision, dexterity, responsibility, etc." (Hynson 2016).[35]

It's worth noting that the decree focuses on angklung music's capacity for character building, not on any musical potential it might have: "although angklung is not yet a refined musical instrument, it can be counted on as an educational tool," the decree reads.[36] Daeng himself typically downplayed angklung's capabilities as a vehicle for presentational music making. As we have seen, he was committed to the idea that the primary goal of angklung performance was not the entertainment of audiences, but rather the experience of performance—as an embodiment of gotong royong, and as just plain fun (Sjamsuddin and Winitasasmita 1986, 69)—as well as its possibilities for promoting diplomacy and music education. His insistence on including an audience-participation session in angklung performances confirms this orientation. In sum, Daeng's legacy lies in a particular approach to angklung—an approach that is codified, some of his followers might insist, in his specific repertory choices and arrangements, but which dovetailed seamlessly with the values of the Old Order and conveniently, if sometimes uncomfortably, with New Order standards.

Daeng's other primary disciples, Mohd. Hidayat Winitasasmita, Sanu'i Edia S.,[37] Agam Ngadimin, and Edi Permadi, all promoted this angklung legacy through education, diplomacy, and (along with Udjo) tourism, in the final decades of the twentieth century. Like Udjo, Obby, and Handiman, for the most part, all these protégés advocated close adherence to Daeng's precedents in terms of angklung pedagogy, repertory, and performance practice, as promulgated via the BKMA. One innovation this old guard did endorse, however, was the assignment of more than one angklung to each player. A performer still couldn't play more than one angklung at a time, maintaining Daeng's "one person, one note" approach, but equipping each angklung player with as many as four angklung opened up additional options for both expanded range and more complex chromatic harmony. Mohd. Hidayat Winitasasmita, for example, formulated some standardized distributions, which ensured that at least two performers had access to each of the twenty-eight main pitches (i.e., angklung tuned to pitches between f#3–a#5), and there was one performer for each bass note (g2–f3). Each player was assigned pitches from different octaves which were not harmonically compatible or likely to be played sequentially, and thus not likely to be called for at the same moment. So, for example, player 1 controls the g2, f#3, and f4; player 2 has access to g#2, g3, and g#4; and so on.

Overall, Daeng's successors managed to navigate the shifts in political philosophy between Sukarno's Old Order and Soeharto's New Order Indonesia, by continuing to emphasize angklung's inherent collectivity—a value advocated by both administrations—while avoiding overt affiliations with either communism or capitalism. In other words: "pindah cai, pindah tampian."

Angklung Paduan

Subsequent generations of angklung enthusiasts, however, pursued angklung performance as a presentational art. Students at Institut Teknologi Bandung (the Bandung Institute of Technology, with the acronym ITB, one of Indonesia's leading technical universities since colonial times), for example, took their extracurricular angklung activities to new heights. Inspired by the culture of collegiate choirs,[38] as early as 1972 they promoted excellence in performance, new arrangements, and intra/intermural competition among collegiate angklung groups. Currently known as Keluarga Paduan Angklung ITB (angklung choir family, with the acronym KPA-ITB), they borrowed from the collegiate choir scene both the term *paduan* (which suggests a harmonious, unified blend; the term *paduan suara* suggests a blend of voices, i.e., a choir) and many of a choir's performance practices, including lining up in tiered ranks and following a conductor.[39] Instead of simply repeating the canon of Daeng Soetigna's angklung arrangements of marches, waltzes, patriotic songs, and *lagu monumental* (light classics) such as "the Blue Danube," "Spanish Eyes," and "Besame Mucho," KPA-ITB tried new arrangements of new songs, striving for a broad range of music that would appeal to their young audiences.

In 1980, Obby enlisted the ITB group to help gather one thousand angklung players for the twenty-fifth anniversary of the KAA. To recruit even more players, angklung enthusiasts started extracurricular groups in Bandung schools. One such group, at Sekolah Menengah Atas Negeri 3 (government-funded high school #3 [grades 10–12], with the acronym SMAN 3), proved to be especially robust. The group's founders, Sony M. Ichsan and Djoko Nugroho, started arranging contemporary pop hits, such as The Boomtown Rats' 1979 "I Don't Like Mondays," to make the music more appealing to the high school kids (Budi Supardiman, pc, August 7, 2013). Over the decades, SMAN 3 alumni have returned to the school to coach new generations of angklung players, resulting in a group that was robust both creatively and technically. Among these alumni was Budi Supardiman, who (charmingly self-deprecatorily) described himself to me as *raja budak* ("king of the children") for his 18-year involvement with SMAN 3's angklung group (pc, August 7, 2013).

According to Budi, the old guard—Daeng's disciples—were not enthusiastic about this new approach and strove to establish and maintain an orthodoxy. But SMAN 3 won a competition in 1983 with an arrangement of "Rumah yang Manis" (a prize-winning pop song composed, in the same year, by Elsa F. Sigar, the very young daughter of pop singer Ully Sigar Rusady). Their arrangement reportedly even received a thumbs up from Daeng himself. In 1989, Dr. Sudjoko Danoesoebroto, speaking at a National Angklung Seminar at ITB, pointed out that Daeng had used popular music, such as light classics and Latin hits, to popularize angklung

When in Bandung ... 55

in the 1950s, so mobilizing current hits was indeed within scope of the *pakem* (conventional standards) of diatonic angklung music.[40]

This gradual assertion of individuality, virtuosity, and personal expression among angklung enthusiasts paralleled growing dissatisfaction, especially among youth, with Soeharto's authoritarian approach to governance and increasingly tight restrictions on democracy and freedom of expression, as well as a swing towards neoliberalism, which became a global socio-economic force beginning in the 1980s (see Ortner 2016, among others). In 1998, protests became too loud to ignore, and Soeharto stepped down as president, laying the foundation for the period known as *reformasi* (reform), characterized by fairer democratic elections, freer speech, increased regional authority, renewed interest in local cultures, and a more open and liberal approach to diversity of political opinions, the economy, and the arts.

Several years after the fall of Soeharto, in 2002, Obby established a Jakarta-based organization, Masyarakat Musik Angklung (Angklung Music Community, with the acronym MMA), which he claimed was the continuation of the BKMA. In some ways, MMA doubled down on the more conservative approach to angklung playing. Obby's 2011 book, *Panduan Bermain Angklung* (A Guide for Playing Angklung), published by MMA, promulgates Daeng's approach to teaching, playing, and repertory as an orthodoxy. Obby's book made some concessions to contemporary angklung practice, such as the (by then common) assignment of multiple angklung to a single performer, but did not acknowledge the new advancements in repertory promoted by ITB and SMAN 3; rather, Obby made Daeng's arrangements of the classics the centerpiece of the book.

Although Udjo's innovations with pentatonic angklung expanded the potential repertory of angklung ensembles to include Sundanese music, they did not alter Daeng's "one person, one note" collective approach. While this approach makes an excellent metaphor for gotong royong, it is not conducive to the kind of self-aware, self-expressive (even self-indulgent) approach to creative activities that conforms to Western-influenced neoliberal capitalism.

In recent years, Yayan Udjo, among others, has been experimenting with ways to transform angklung into a more soloistic pursuit. By mounting a set of twenty (or more) angklung upside-down in a frame, positioning the part of each angklung that is shaken at waist height, a single individual can quickly shake one angklung after another, alternating hands, to produce a melodic line without relying on interlocking with other performers. Such angklung chimes are called *angklung toél* (toél means to touch or nudge; see Figure 2.6); in essence, angklung toél transforms angklung playing from a performative expression of collectivity into a solo art. According to Musthofa, angklung toél dates from 2008 (2018, 551). Yayan has worked on several other prototypes, as well, including versions with carillon-like keyboards. Of course, it was only a matter of time before

56 *When in Bandung ...*

Figure 2.6 Chromatic angklung toel.
Source: photo: Henry Spiller.

engineers experimented with automated angklung chimes (called *angklung robot*; see Spiller 2018). Taufik Udjo also has experimented with angklung chimes of various sorts, although he focuses more on performances than on innovations (see Chapter 5).

Dinda Satya Upaja Budi (2013) reports earlier experiments with keyboard-controlled angklung chimes in the 1980s. And a Dutch (or Dutch-Indonesian) musician who was Daeng's neighbor, a Mr. Diks, created a keyboard angklung called the *diksophone* in the 1970s (2007, xxx–xxxi). When Daeng showed the contraption to the French-trained Indonesian composer, Slamet A. Sjukur (1935–2015), in 1976, Sjukur observed that "the instrument removes bamboo from its collective nature"; Daeng was taken aback by the comment, but responded in full agreement, "even good intentions can turn out wrong, eh?" (Sjukur 2007, 270).[41]

When I asked Yayan the same question about the gotong royong aspect of angklung toél, he acknowledged that his innovations move away from that fundamental Indonesian/Sundanese value. But he sees no problems with encouraging students to develop a sense of individuality, too. Besides, he continued, students in one-person-one-angklung ensembles are basically "robots"—responsible only for playing the right note at the right time, without any understanding of why a particular note at a particular moment makes sense musically. Angklung toél provides students the opportunity to learn music in a more holistic way (pc, Yayan Udjo, May 13, 2013). Budi Supardiman expressed similar thoughts on a different occasion: cooperative angklung music requires many people to play, but such soloist innovations provide an opportunity to practice alone. It's not a substitute or a replacement for conventional group angklung music-making, but rather an "addition" to such activities. It also introduces variety, so players don't get bored. And soloist versions strengthen angklung's position (as Yayan also argued) as a tool for music education (pc, Budi Supardiman, August 7, 2013).

According to Handiman (pc, May 5, 2013), the popularity of angklung in Bandung schools ebbs and flows, at least in part because of the patronage of government officials. The 1960s and 1970s were especially good, he told me, because General Dr. H. C. Mashudi (1919–2005), a long-time fan of angklung music, was the governor of the Province of West Java 1960–1970 (notably spanning the Sukarno and Soeharto administrations). He sponsored angklung performances, often from school groups, for official events.

The national Indonesian government became interested in promoting angklung in the 2010s for a variety of reasons, not least of which was its ongoing prickly relationship with Malaysia, which allegedly tried to nominate several Indonesian art forms—including *batik*, wayang, gamelan, and angklung (Clark 2013, 398)—as Malaysia's own entries on UNESCO's List of the Intangible Cultural Heritage of Humanity (ICHH). Obby and MMA participated in nominating angklung to the ICHH, and "Indonesian angklung" was added to the UNESCO list in 2010 (see Chapter 5 for further discussion).

To fulfill their UNESCO commitment to "safeguard" angklung, government officials mandated the development of an academic program focusing on bamboo music at the government-sponsored arts academy in Bandung (ISBI), then known as Sekolah Tinggi Seni Indonesia (College-level School of Indonesian Arts, with the acronym STSI).[42] Although a number of universities in Bandung sponsor diatonic angklung performance groups, including UPI, ITB, Universitas Padjadjaran, and others, the ISBI Program Studi (Prodi) Angklung dan Musik Bambu focuses instead on research into bamboo musical instruments of all sorts, for which the government provides funding.

I attended a seminar an angklung seminar at STSI on July 25, 2013, which was among the first products of this new program, and featured presentations from the program's faculty, including Deni Hermawan, Abun Somawijaya, Dinda Satya Upaja Budi, and Iyon Supiono. Their inquiries focused on two questions: (1) how to exploit angklung as a vehicle for *industri kreatif* (creative industry, i.e., income-generating artistic activities) and (2) how to exploit angklung as a vehicle for forming an Indonesian national character.[43] Students in the program explore angklung performance, especially presentational versions of agricultural ceremonial angklung and new music for angklung along with a variety of other bamboo instruments.

Angklung Web Institute (AWI)

Reformasi also has opened up space for grassroots angklung organizations. One such group is called "Angklung Web Institute," whose acronym, AWI, is the Sundanese word for bamboo. It was founded and is run by Budi Supardiman, a successful telecommunications engineer who has been a fanatic for diatonic angklung ensembles since his primary school days. Budi, who has been actively involved in most of the organizations already mentioned—SAU, SMAN-3, ITB's Paduan Angklung, and MMA—thinks that young people sometimes get lost in these institutions' focused approaches. He aims to revitalize diatonic angklung music using the internet and social media to spread interest in and information about diatonic angklung, and to provide opportunities for casual or intensive engagement with angklung to individuals who are no longer affiliated with a school program.

When I met him in 2013, Budi ran AWI from a shopping mall (at that time, the Balubar Town Center in Bandung, and later [in 2018] in the Braga City Walk) where passers-by could hear the music, see the instruments in their storage stall, and perhaps develop an interest in angklung. His website includes educational materials and Budi's arrangements of tunes from Western classical, popular, and folk repertories.

Conclusion

I am not the first person to point out angklung's flexibility in representing changes in political and economic systems in the archipelago. Obby Wiramihardja writes, for example, "Thus, angklung symbolizes the ebb and flow of Indonesian history. When the people of Indonesia are under the feet of invaders, angklung becomes the musical instrument of beggars. With the achievement of independence, angklung once again becomes a musical instrument we can be proud of" (Wiramihardja 2007).[44] Daeng Soetigna's version, excerpted here from a speech he gave in English, is more elaborate:

> Long ago when our culture was free from external influences, ... bamboo instruments played an important role in the musical life of our people. ... When Western type musical instruments, looking beautiful and shiny, started pouring in from Europe at a later time, gradually the interest in our native bamboo instruments decreased. Most of them were soon forgotten, and some of them even disappeared altogether ... people's interest in [angklung] started waning and it almost sank into oblivion. When I was an adult, the fate of the angklung reached its acme of misery. It was very saddening because it ... reappeared as an instrument of beggers [sic], wandering from door to door in trying to extract alms from the charitable. After having occupied the honourable position of a musical instrument that symbolised the greatness

of the nation, the angklung had become the symbol of poverty and distress ... Thus ended the history of the angklung as a dignified musical instrument. In 1938, however, 1 became interested again in the angklung. ... I was compelled to try to make them myself, and thanks to the instructions of an old man, by the name of BAPAK JAYA, ... I managed to make a set of angklungs the notes of which I adapted to the Western scale. ... Gradually other advantages of this simple instrument emerged, advantages in the realm of education. ... That was the beginning of a new page in the history of the angklung ... [which] has now become popular throughout the Indonesian archipelago. Its fame has in addition spread abroad; to Singapore, Malaysia, Thailand, the Philipines [sic], Australia, New Zealand and other countries.

(Sjamsuddin and Winitasasmita 1986, 67–73)

Daeng's account imagines a precolonial past, replete with glorious angklung traditions, that degenerate into abject, impoverished angklung survivals in the music of beggars under colonialism, then finally culminates with angklung's elevation to a universal art form, a gift from a newly independent Indonesia to the entire democratic world.

The side-by-side practice of both collective and soloistic approaches to angklung represents both the seemingly incompatible left-leaning collective *and* neoliberal capitalist individualistic approaches. The ongoing divergence between angklung padaeng (Daeng-style angklung) and angklung paduan (choir-style angklung) is another way in which angklung performance practices simultaneously represents both approaches. Indeed, it is probably angklung's ability to be both—simultaneously—that assures its ongoing popularity, as Indonesians continue—as they have since independence—to navigate their own path between the modern world's economic/political systems. Pindah cai, pindah tampian.

Notes

1 The 1926 remodel was spearheaded by the prominent architect, Charles Prosper Wolff Schoemaker. Currently the building houses a museum dedicated to the Konperensi Asia-Afrika.

2 One of Daeng's disciples, Handiman Diratmasasmita, credits another individual, Prof. Dr. Mochtar Kusumaatmadja, SH, LLM, for developing the notion of angklung as a tool of soft diplomacy. Kusumaatmadja (b. 1929) was Minister of Justice from 1974 to 1978 and Minister of Foreign Affairs from 1978 to 1988, and later was a professor at Universitas Padjadjaran in Bandung (Sumarsono and Pirous 2007, 312). Handiman goes on to provide a list of diplomatic efforts in which Handiman himself was involved, including providing angklung to Indonesian embassies in foreign countries; a trip to Iran in 1970 to teach angklung to the Shah's family in the Niavaran Palace; the mass angklung performances at the 25th and 30th anniversaries of the KAA; and a mission to the Solomon Islands to teach angklung making and performance, led by Udjo Ngalagena, in 1985 (Diratmasasmita 2005).

60   *When in Bandung ...*

3 The Arsip Nasional Republik Indonesia (Indonesian National Archive) released short documentary about the KAA with archival photographs and footage, including very briefs glimpses of the angklung ensemble and "Tari Kukupu" (7:10–7:37); see www.youtube.com/watch?v=-3dG7wB9WcM or www.youtube.com/watch?v=zMDkoFLrIwU.

4 Roberts and Faulcher write that "Angklung music was a prominent representative of Indonesian cultural heritage during the Bandung Conference, with President Soekarno and Vice-President Hatta holding a reception that included angklung orchestras," citing Jack 1955, 6 (Roberts and Faulcher 2016, 228fn27).

5 Mashudi (1919–2005) was the Head of Staff of Military Officers in West Java in 1955, became the governor of West Java (1960–1970), and spent several decades in the regional and national leadership of the Gerakan Pramuka Nasional (National Scouting Movement; Sumarsono and Pirous 2007, 314); in those later capacities he was a supporter of diatonic angklung activities (Handiman Diratmasasmita, pc, May 7, 2013).

6 In a speech, delivered in English to foreign delegates to a music conference in Jakarta in 1968, Daeng reported that Djaja died only a week after they had together succeeded in making the first set of diatonic angklung (Sjamsuddin and Winitasasmita 1986, 70).

7 Using shared notation in this fashion is still the norm for contemporary diatonic angklung rehearsals, although the poster sometimes is replaced with a computer image projected onto the wall or a screen (Amelinda 2016).

8 Accounts of angklung ensembles frequently compare this interlocking approach to European handbell choirs (e.g., Perris 1971; Hynson 2016), but there is no obvious historical link between the two traditions. Handbell choirs likely originated in England in the seventeenth century, as a method for practicing tower bell change ringing (Wilson and Coleman 2001; Price and Shull 2001).

9 A version with different calligraphy, but essentially the same notes, appears in Obby Wiramihardja's introduction to angklung music, strengthening the case that this is in fact Daeng's arrangement (2011).

10 A rendition by the Angklung Hamburg Orchestra is available at www.youtube.com/watch?v=ZDA8j7MgAK8

11 Winitasasmita and Budiaman state that this range extension happened around 1958, while Sumarsono and Pirous say it was in 1960 (2007, 175). In either case, this exact arrangement must have not been available for the 1955 KAA.

12 "digunakan mengiringi para pemuda pejuang ... dalam bentuk barisan dengan gerak langkah tegap mengikuti irama"

13 According to Irawati Durban-Ardjo, the Sundanese dancers performed "Tari Sri Gati" (Imran, Malik et al. 2011, 72). According to the participant Tati Saleh, the Sundanese contingent included, besides Daeng Soetigna and herself, four dancers (Indrawati [Lukman], Irawati [Durban-Ardjo], Tuti, and one of Daeng's daughters, Utut [Gartini]), and two musicians (Atik and Iim; Amilia 2001, 37). Soemarsono and Pirous report that among the troupe was another of Daeng's children, Iwan Suwargana, who played gamelan in the pavilion and married Loesye [sic] Walelangi and settled in the Netherlands (2007, 186).

14 A *Newsday* article reports farewell parties at several pavilions, including the Indonesian Pavilion, "late into the night" on October 19, 1964 (Byerly 1964, 4).

15 Aam Amilia's biography of Tati Saleh also lists some of the non-Sundanese participants in the Indonesia delegation to the Fair. The group's director was the well known choreographer Bagong Kussiardjo; from Central Java, Sardono

When in Bandung ... 61

W. Kusumah, Stejowarini, Mas Said, Tjokrowasito (a.k.a. K.P.H. Notoprojo, a.k.a. Pak Cokro); from Bali, Gusti Ayu Raka, Bandem, and Wenta; from Sumatra, the Orkes Bukit Barisan under the direction of Yuni Amir (Amilia 2001, 37).

16 Although a *New York Times* article on January 24, 1965, suggests that Sukarno was still planning to send a delegation of performing artists, on March 12, 1965, Sukarno ordered the pavilion to withdraw because of "the open support given by the United States to the neocolonialist project of Malaysia," according to another *New York Times* article with that date.

17 The 1965 troupe was headed by Prof. Dr. Prijono, and Sanu'i Edia S., a student and colleague of Daeng's and an angklung enthusiast, was the director of the musicians (Imran, Malik et al. 2011, 91–92).

18 Some sources say 1967 or 1968. Rita Milyartini states, based on interviews with Udjo, that Udjo was manufacturing angklung as early as 1962, and that the first performance for foreign tourists (six French visitors) was in 1968 (Milyartini 2012, 176; see also Musthoa 2018, 549).

19 Daeng's biographers note that while Daeng was hospitalized toward the end of his life, he "tugas-tugas pendokumentasian depercayakan kepada muridnya yang lain, Udjo (dikenal dengan sebutan Mang Udjo Ngalagena, pendiri Saung Angklung 'Padasuka'"; Sumarsono and Pirous 2007, 193), i.e., "he entrusted the task of documentation to another student, Udjo (known by the name Mang Udjo Ngalagena, founder of the Saung Angklung 'Padasuka'").

20 I personally have never met Sam Udjo (Udjo's second child), although other researchers who have spent more time than I have at SAU speak of his important role there (e.g., Hynson 2016; Milyartini 2012), or Nan or Hety. I met Daeng [Oktaviandi] Udjo (Udjo's eighth son) when he brought a large angklung group to the San Francisco Bay Area in 2012 to perform at the San Francisco Indonesian Consulate's annual Indonesian Independence Day celebration in Union Square. Daeng Udjo and his entourage subsequently donated sets of diatonic angklung to UC Davis (where I am on the faculty). Yayan [Muliana] Udjo (Udjo's sixth child) generously spoke to me when I visited SAU on May 13, 2013. It was he who led the angklung interaktif portion of the afternoon show that day. I'll say more about Taufik [Hidayat] in Chapter 5.

21 Soedarsono's description of SAU's "Bamboo Afternoon," published in 2002, is almost exactly the same (Soedarsono 2002, 350–352).

22 The SAU website's two-and-a-half-minute introductory video presents a representative sample of most of these performances (www.angklung-udjo.co.id)

23 Indeed, SAU has become one of the Bandung area's major tourist attractions. For example, CBS Television's "The Amazing Race" visited Bandung for their 2013 season. The producers selected the area's most famous iconic local attractions as sites for their contestants to complete improbable tasks—ram fights, the bird market, and SAU, where the contestants were tasked with putting an octave's worth of diatonic angklung in the "correct" (i.e., ascending scale) order. (Season 23, Episode 9, "Part Like The Red Sea" (aired November 24, 2013).

24 Abdurochman Dwiyono reports annual attendance statistics at SAU between 2001–2011 rose from 20,246 (31% domestic, 69% foreign) in 2011 to 178,778 in 2011 (85% domestic, 15% foreign; Dwiyono 2012, 4). It is likely that these numbers reflect an increase in local school and local participation in other SAU programs, not a change in the afternoon show. Musthofa provides 2017 figures

62 *When in Bandung ...*

of 205,324 domestic visitors and 26,240 foreign visitors (that would be 87% domestic, 13% foreign; 2018, 549). The performance space for the show seats 400 (Poetry 2011, iv–49).

25 In Indonesian business law, CV stands for (the Dutch) "Commanditaire Vennootschap," i.e., a limited partnership, as opposed to a Firm (Fa) or a corporation (PT).

26 See Hynson 2016 for a detailed description of the angklung interaktif portion of the show at SAU.

27 In Indonesian, *korupsi, kolusi, nepotisme*—a phrase so frequently heard toward the end of the Soeharto era that its acronym—KKN—was enough to evoke it.

28 Even Retnowati Abdulgani-Knapp's sympathetic, "authorized" biography of Soeharto allowed that the activities of these foundations "certainly stretched the concept of gotong royong just a bit too far" (2007, 234).

29 Oteng Sutisna (b. 1910) eventually taught music education at IKIP, Bandung, studied in the US, and was visiting professor of Indonesian Studies at Washington University of St. Louis in 1969–70, when he gave a set of angklung to Arnold Perris, which was part of the inspiration for Perris's 1971 article, "The Rebirth of the Javanese Angklung" (Perris 1971; see also Sumarsono and Pirous 2007, 312).

30 The source that places Obby in this performance actually claims it was for the 6th PON, which was scheduled for 1965 in Jakarta (Rosidi 2003, 297) but never took place because the September 30th Movement (G30S) threw the nation into chaos.

31 currently (since 2011) known as Kementerian Pendidikan dan Kebudayaan (Ministry of Education and Culture, abbreviated Kemdikbud).

32 Kepala Seksi Musik Diatonis Direktorat Kesenian Ditjen Kebudayaan

33 Prijono sponsored Kasur for an extended visit to Singapore and Malaysia, where he taught angklung making and playing, and laid the groundwork for angklung scenes there that are still thriving. See Zubillaga-Pow 2014, 125.

34 They also so honored R.M.A. Koesoemadinata and Koko Koswara.

35 *Keputusan Menteri Pendidikan Dan Kebudayaan Republik Indonesia No. 082/ 1968 Tentang Penetapan Angklung Sebagai Alat Pendidikan Music*, which Hynson translates as "Decision of the Republic of Indonesia Ministry of Education and Culture number 082/1968 About the Application of Angklung as a Music Education Tool" (Hynson 2016).

36 Hynson's translation of the original "walaupun angklung belum merupakan alat musik yang cukup sempurna tetapi dapat dipertanggungjawabkan sebagai alat pelajaran pendidikan" (Hynson 2016).

37 Sanu'i Edia S. (b. 1933) was a young student of Daeng's in 1968 when he conducted three pieces performed by Daeng's group from Bandung, "Guriang," for foreign delegates to a music conference in Jakarta. The pieces were "a march by J. Gilbert," "JALI JALI," and "a Sulawesi folksong ATI RAJA" (Sjamsuddin and Winitasasmita 1986, 73). He was involved in a number of angklung missions abroad, and was the Kepala Bagian Kebudayaan (Head of the Culture Section) for the Province of West Java 1992–1999 (Sumarsono and Pirous 2007, 314).

38 According to their website, the Paduan Suara Mahasiswa (PSM)-ITB (student choir) was founded in 1962 and is the oldest student choir in Indonesia (https://psm-itb.com/profil/).

39 See http://angklung-web-institute.com/content/view/93/74/lang_en/.

40 "LAGU BARAT DENGAN ANGKLUNG?" Budi Supardiman, web document, http://angklung-web-institute.com/content/view/92/74/lang_en/

41 "instrumen itu mencabut bambu dari kodratnya yang tumbuh berkelompok." ... "niat baikpun ternyata bisa keliru, ya" (Sjukur 2007, 270).

42 Now called Institut Seni Budaya Indonesia (Institute of Indonesian Art and Culture, with the acronym ISBI).

43 Another STSI researcher, Asep Nugraha, conducted research that provides evidence that angklung was not common in Malaysian territories until it was introduced there (in the 1960s) by Indonesian visitors (2015, 8).

44 "Demikian, angklung seolah-olah melambangkan pasang surutnya sejarah bangsa Indonesia. Ketika bangsa Indonesia berada dalam telapak kaki penjajah, angklung hanya menjadi alat musik pengemis. Dengan dicapainya kemerdekaan, kembali angklung menjadi alat musik yang dapat dibanggakan" (Wiramihardja 2007).

3 Bamboo Wisdom

leuleus jeujeur liat tali
"flexible bamboo fishing rod, tough line"
("wisdom is like fishing: it requires both the flexibility of a
bamboo fishing rod and the constancy of unbreakable fishing line")

The Cikapundung river is among Bandung's most significant geographical features. It bisects the city as it flows from the high, mountainous areas at the northern end, through the city center, all the way past the southern city limits (see Figure 3.1). During colonial times, Dutch settlers built grand houses on generous plots of land on the Cikapundung's banks north of the city center, where the higher elevation provided relief from the tropical heat. After the Dutch were expelled from Java in 1949, however, Sundanese migrants moving from rural areas into Bandung often squatted on the large plots of land along the river once owned by the Dutch and built houses and *kampung* (neighborhood warrens) without permits, resulting in what Gustaaf Reerink characterizes as "informal slums" (Reerink 2015, 202–207). Bandung emerged as Indonesia's third largest city at the end of the twentieth century, and the population approached three million people. In the absence of appropriate infrastructure to support the burgeoning population, the Cikapundung became little more than an open sewer.

In the twenty-first century, the city's emerging middle class initiated a grassroots environmental movement in Bandung. A World Bank report in 2012 categorized all seven rivers in West Java, including the Cikapundung, as "heavily polluted." The good news: there were no fewer than 42 grassroots community groups doing their own small parts to clean things up in their neighborhoods (World Bank 2012; see also Lubis Nugroho 2012). Interest in cleaning up the Cikapundung also spread to the poorer modern-day kampung residents, who, after all, lived right on the banks of the river. Residents of the Dago neighborhood, which surrounds the northern end of the Cikapundung, met at Taman Budaya, the regional government-sponsored cultural center located on the grounds of the historic Dago Thee Huis, to discuss possible responses to environmental problems.

One such project was collecting and repurposing litter. A multi-generational group of a dozen or so from the neighborhood fashioned

DOI: 10.4324/9781003302797-4

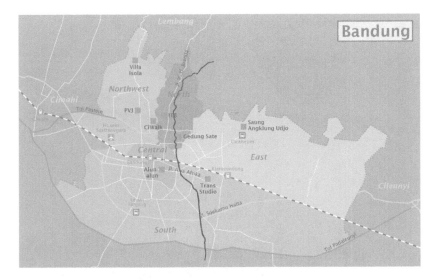

Figure 3.1 Bandung and the Cikapundung River.
Source: Wikicommons, "Bandung Wikivoyage districts map," created by ErwinFCG (licensed under the Creative Commons Attribution-Share Alike 4.0 International license), modified by the author to include the approximate path of the Cikapundung river.

all sorts of trinkets from trash, including simple musical instruments which they played for their own amusement. As time went on, this group switched from trash to bamboo as their material of choice (for reasons I will discuss shortly), assumed the name Galengan Sora Awi (abbreviated GSA), and solidified a unique style, repertory, and audience. By 2012, when I first met them, they had stable personnel, a set of specific instruments, and a well-developed repertory that drew from a variety of Sundanese song genres.

In their brochure, GSA unpacks their name: "Via a narrow path (*galengan*) we strive to realize and express our philosophy through the medium of bamboo (*sora awi*)."[1] *Galengan* is the Sundanese term for the very narrow berm that separates *sawah* (wet rice fields), and which provides a dry, if narrow, path for farmers to navigate among their fields without getting stuck in the mire. *Sora awi* is literally the voice of bamboo.

For GSA, the path to renewing and reviving their connections to human groups and to the landscapes that nurtured them, even in contemporary Bandung, is paved with bamboo.

In 2013, when I returned to Bandung to investigate modern expressions of bamboo music, I rented an apartment within earshot of Taman Budaya specifically to connect with GSA. And, sure enough, I heard GSA rehearsing at Taman Budaya on my first evening there. I wandered over to reintroduce myself. The members of GSA informed me that they would be

Figure 3.2 Galengan Sora Awi performs at the Cikapundung Hiking Orienteering Games (CIHOG), March 30, 2013.
Source: photo: Henry Spiller.

performing the following day for the Cikapundung Hiking Orienteering Games (CIHOG), at Babak Siliwangi park, near the busy Simpang market district at Dago's southern end (see Figure 3.2).

Bamboo Retentions

GSA's use of idiosyncratic, homemade bamboo musical instruments is the linchpin of the group's profoundly local sensibility. Bernard Stiegler's notions of primary, secondary, and tertiary retention, outlined in his 1998 *Technics and Time*, provide an appropriate theoretical framework for understanding the significance of bamboo in GSA's work.[2] Individuals, upon encountering an object from a past they don't themselves remember, must activate their own primary retentions (their own immediate memories), and secondary retentions (episodic memories and impressions from their past) to make sense of the object. GSA's bamboo instruments are, I argue, sites of "tertiary retention." According to Stiegler, tertiary retention is the process by which human-made objects transmit memories of their makers' experiences to new users of the object without any direct interventions or contacts between the makers and the new users. As Frédéric Pouillaude puts it, new users must incorporate the object's "material condensation of practices and theories of sound" (those "categorial and perceptual distinctions around which a given musical practice is organized" that are preserved in the instrument's form [2017]) into their own constructions of identity, time, and place. Joshua Tucker mobilizes Stiegler's theory to make a startling claim: that musical instruments, via tertiary retentions, can "transmit knowledge across boundaries of space and mortality, ensuring that individuals are shaped by experiences they have not lived personally" (Tucker 2016).

GSA's move to bamboo began when one of the participants—Akim Tarkim, who is a blacksmith, metalworker, and woodworker by trade—noticed an anachronistic bamboo instrument called *celempung* in one of the display cases that line Taman Budaya's lobby (see Figure 3.3). In West Java, celempung refers to a tube zither constructed from a bamboo log by incising two or three strings from the bamboo's skin and raising

Figure 3.3 GSA rehearsing in the lobby area of Taman Budaya, Bandung. Akim Tarkim is visible in the corner, wearing a cap. His son, Ujang, plays *baragbag* (bamboo drums). At left, Gopar plays one of Akim's modern *celempung*. Gopar hits the celempung's strings with a stick with his left hand to produce pitched sounds. Note that one of the strings has a weight attached to it, which lowers its pitch considerably. With his right hand, he strikes the end of the instrument to produce unpitched percussive sounds. The original celempung that inspired Akim is visible in the display case above Gopar's head.

Source: photo: Henry Spiller.

68   *Bamboo Wisdom*

them on bridges. The strings are often weighted with wooden or bamboo appendages that alter the pitch and timbre of the strings considerably.[3]

This celempung somehow resonated with the GSA participants' aspirations for their music-making activities. Bamboo, like rubbish, was plentiful in the Dago area. The instrument bore the stamp of Sundanese workmanship, referenced a sense of connection with the past, and evoked a sense of local identity—a textbook example of a "tertiary retention." Akim and his compatriots were energized by their ongoing experiences—primary retentions, in Stiegler's formulation—of creating musical instruments and playing music together. Like most Sundanese, they had internalized the oft-reinforced narrative that bamboo is a key constituent of Sundanese identity—a secondary retention. As GSA's brochure later summarized, bamboo "expresses [Sundanese] values, reflects a way of life, and gave birth to Sundanese culture" and serves as "a symbol of togetherness and local knowledge—an ancient plant whose services have contributed to shape Sundanese art and culture."[4] The celempung in the display case, which some unidentified Sundanese ancestor long ago hand-crafted from bamboo, concisely materialized the kinds of connections GSA yearned for between the physical environment of their neighborhood, the active and intimate social aspects of playing music, and an age-old, if unchronicled, history of local creativity. Akim became obsessed with the notion of out-fitting his comrades with all-bamboo musical instruments.

Celempung

At its most basic, a celempung in West Java is a bamboo log from which two or three "strings" have been incised from the bamboo's skin and raised on bridges. A wooden or bamboo weight on one of the strings alters its pitch and timbre. There are similar tube zithers all over island Southeast Asia; Artur Simon calls them a Neolithic Malay invention (Simon 2010, 25).

Jaap Kunst and his co-author, Raden Tumenggung Arya Wiranatakoesoema, lavish attention on celempung in their article, "Een en Ander Over Soendaneesche Muziek," where they describe an ensemble known as *celempungan* in considerable detail (Kunst and Wiranatakoeseoma 1921). Kunst distills this lengthy discussion into a concise description in *Music in Java*:

> The *chelempung*-orchestra is fortunate in being widely-spread. The name is derived from the idiochord bamboo instruments, which are found in it in two different functions, i.e., as kendang and as ketuk. The other instruments in this combination—another essential element of which seems to be a female voice—are: rebab, suling, goong awi, and—not always, however—a kachapi.
>
> (Kunst 1973, 382)

Kunst's *"chelempung-*orchestra" involved one or two inventive musicians who could reproduce several interlocking ostinatos, one on each string, to provide a complete-sounding Sundanese accompaniment. The weighted string produced a gong-like sound, suitable for the ends of phrases. (Modern performers can even wave their hands over the instrument's air-hole to modulate the volume of the sound, creating a tremolo that simulates the characteristic undulating timbre of a gong.) Celempung players also could supplement these ostinatos with intricate patterns inspired by Sundanese *kendang* (double-headed barrel drum) playing by hitting the bamboo in various places with a hand or a stick.

After Indonesian independence (1945), the ensemble called celempungan was still widespread—but in a modernized version, in which bamboo idiochords were replaced with other instruments: *siter* or *kacapi* (plucked zithers with steel strings), kendang (a set of barrel drums), and *goong* (a large hanging gong). It's worth noting that Theodore Grame has suggested that a Sundanese preference for such straight zithers may be an artifact of the difficulty of bending or shaping bamboo (Grame 1962, 9).

Samin, who led the Radio Parahyangan's outstanding celempungan group in 1999,[5] explained his understanding of the ensemble's history to me. He told me that the ensemble is named after the celempung, an instrument that had two strings played by striking them with a stick; the player also hit the body of the instrument with the hands. According to Samin, the celempung was made of wood. He was referring to an intermediate version of the celempung that luthiers developed in the 1920s to "modernize" the idiochord bamboo instrument (pc, Samin, February 9, 1999). It was this version, constructed from wood, with steel strings, that traveled to Japan in 1976 with a Sundanese delegation for an "Asian Traditional Performing Arts" seminar and was documented in detail by Fumio Koizumi (Koizumi et al. 1977). It is interesting to note that Samin's and Koizumi's histories both erase the original bamboo version of the instrument.

Akim made his first celempung around 2008 (pc, May 28, 2013) and perfected his approach to making celempung by harnessing his skills as a craftsman, examining existing celempung, experimenting with such variables as the width and thickness of the strings, and engaging overall in a lot of trial and error. His celempung are larger than historical models (pc, Udung, June 18, 2013), and he covers the open end of the bamboo tube—the part that players hit to create drum-like sounds—with rubber to make playing less painful. He also puts a small hole in the closed end of the tube to allow the drum-like sounds to emerge. Akim has likely long been aware of the instruments of another celempung maker—Abah Olot (see Chapter 4)—but it appears that each has developed innovations on his own. Figure 3.4 shows Akim playing one of his celempung, along with annotations for the instrument's various parts (described in more detail in the following section).

70 Bamboo Wisdom

stick   strings   bridges   weighted string   rattan wrapping   rubber covering   left hand

Figure 3.4 Akim playing one of his celempung with the various parts labelled.
Source: photo: Henry Spiller.

Making Celempung

To make a celempung, Akim begins with a raw green culm of the bamboo variety he calls *awi bitung* in Sundanese (*bambu betung* in Indonesian; *Dendrocalamus asper*) about 76 cm long and 12 cm in diameter (see Figure 3.5a). The culm comprises one complete internode, that is, a section of hollow bamboo stem bounded on either end with a solid node, which is about 56 cm long, along with incomplete internodes, about 12 cm long, at either end. Awi bitung no longer grows locally, so Akim purchases the raw materials from a lumber dealer (Admin Inilahkoran 2014). He begins with green bamboo because the fibers are still pliable, making it easier to fashion the strings.

The strings are created by separating a thin strip of the bamboo's "skin" along the length of the complete internode. First, Akim nails in a couple of metal strips into the nodes to mark the ends of the strings, and to keep the strings from separating from the bamboo beyond the nodes. He incises grooves in the bamboo to begin to create the strings. He carefully deepens the grooves, using various chisels (and a screwdriver used as a chisel) to separate the string from the tube. Once he's got the chisels in deep enough, he lifts the new string up with two chisels from either side to separate the "skin" string from the rest of the bamboo (see Figure 3.5b). Once the separation is established, it's relatively quick to insert a chisel all the way in and run the chisel up and down to separate the string completely from the bamboo. He uses a hammer to insert short dowels at either end of each

Figure 3.5 Akim makes a celempung. a. bamboo culm; b. separating strings; c. adding the bridges; d. adding the weight.
Source: photos: Henry Spiller.

string as bridges, which keep the strings elevated above the body of the bamboo (see Figure 3.5c).

To add weight to one of the strings, he creates a hole, about 3 cm in diameter, at the midpoint of one of the strings and about 2 cm away. He attaches a pre-fashioned wooden or bamboo weight on the string so that it is suspended over the hole. If the weight vibrates against the bamboo, he removes material from the bamboo to allow the weight to vibrate freely (see Figure 3.5d). A variation of this standard model involves suspending the weight between two strings (in which case the hole is between the two strings as well).

At this point, he sets the celempung aside to dry, usually by hanging it in the workshop. The drying process can be hastened with a fire, but takes weeks or months in any case. Once dry, he completes the celempung by wrapping locally sourced rattan around the bamboo at the nodes, which cover the metal strips and further ensure that the strings don't separate further from the log, and by testing and adjusting the tuning of the strings by moving the bridges. He creates holes (about 3 cm in diameter) in each of the nodes to allow the air to be released. He then glues a foam rubber cover, about 1 cm thick, over the end of the celempung that is meant to be hit with the hand; once the glue is dry, he trims the rubber with a hacksaw blade, and punches another hole in the middle of the rubber cover.

Akim also builds an instrument he calls *celempung renteng*, which consists of several celempung, carefully tuned and arranged in ascending

Figure 3.6 Akim's celempung renteng.
Source: photo: Henry Spiller.

pitch order—a sort of celempung chime or xylophone, which has gained popularity as a novelty instrument for pop and jazz musicians (see Figure 3.6). In Sundanese, the word renteng means arranged in a row (Eringa 1984, 631; Heins 1977, 72–73). Each of the component celempung that make up the celempung renteng has two strings, which Akim says must be precisely in tune with each other, and with the weight, for the sound and pitch to be clear. He tunes the strings by moving the bridges and tunes the weights by adding or removing material from the bottom of the weight.

GSA's Novel Instruments

Akim maintains a thriving business making celempung and celempung renteng for other musicians, but celempung per se is not part of GSA's typical instrumentation. Akim modified the celempung's basic form to create new instruments that would suit the group's music-making goals. He put together a set of celempung-like instruments to imitate the timekeeping instruments in other ensembles, such as the three *ketuk* in the *ketuk tilu* ensemble, or the gong chimes in gamelan ensembles (*ketuk, kenong, kempul, kebluk*, etc.; see Spiller 2004). Such instruments typically measure time in a manner the ethnomusicologist Jaap Kunst has described as *colotomic*: each instrument marks the division of a time period into smaller units, with the higher-pitched instruments subdividing the units delineated by lower-pitched instruments. The result is a cycle, in which hierarchical time units are audibly marked with specific instrumental timbres (see Spiller 2004). Such rhythmic cycles are the most typical form given to the ostinatos that are one of the two fundamental layers of Sundanese traditional music. In gamelan music, the longest colotomic cycles are marked by the stroke of a *goong* (large bronze or iron gong with a central boss), which provides a low-pitched, oscillating sound that marks a satisfying end to a musical phrase.

Goong awi—Akim devoted considerable effort to reproducing a large gong's emblematic timbre. He started with a piece of large-diameter awi bitung bamboo and affixed to the instrument's strings a large weight to generate a very low frequency pitch. Making this pitch audible would ordinarily require a huge resonator to reinforce and amplify the sound—too large to be practical. Instead, Akim outfitted the *goong awi*, as he calls it—literally, "bamboo gong"—with a built-in microphone, which, when connected to a sound system, amplifies the sound through loudspeakers (see Figure 3.7). The best metal gongs, when struck, produce a sound that undulates, both in pitch and amplitude, producing what musicians call an *ombak* ("wave"), the aesthetics of which are quite sophisticated (see Giles

Figure 3.7 Goong awi.
Source: photo: Henry Spiller.

1974). Akim mounted the goong awi on a frame that provides adjustable suspension (by laying the bamboo tube on taut strings) to maximize the instrument's vibrations. He told me he takes pride in his goong awi's ombak, which are produced by making the idiochord strings as thin as possible (pc, August 12, 2013). Amplified, the goong awi makes a convincing substitute for a goong. Without amplification, however, the instrument is virtually mute, as became all too obvious on several occasions when power outages made the goong disappear completely during rehearsals and performances.

Baragbag (kendang awi)—The drumming produced on kendang—a set of wooden two-headed barrel drums that include one large drum (called *indung*) and two or more small drums called *kulanter*—is also emblematic of modern Sundanese music. Each of the drum heads has a different pitch (although drummers are only moderately concerned with the exact pitch of each stroke), and there are several different ways to strike the drums; drummers thus have a wide range of timbres from which to draw. Each kendang body (*kuluwung*) is carved from a single piece of dense, hard wood, usually *kelapa* (coconut), *kawung* (sugar palm), *muncang* (candlenut), or *nangka* (jackfruit) wood. The outside may be conical or barrel-shaped; regardless of the outside shape, the inside is hollowed out so that there is a shallow depression on each end (beneath the heads), which opens into a wider cavity in the middle of the drum (see Figure 3.8). Each of the shallow

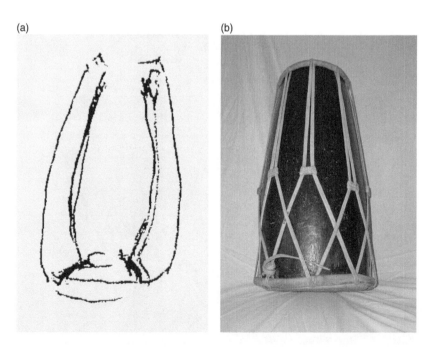

Figure 3.8 a. Otong Rasta's cross-section sketch of the hollow inside a kendang (pc, June 12, 1981); b. kendang.

Source: photo: Henry Spiller.

depressions is covered by a head (*wangkis*) made of thick animal skin that is wrapped around a rattan ring slightly larger than the end of the drum.[6] The two ring/head assemblies are placed over the ends of the drums and laced to one another over the drum with a single long leather thong (*rarawat*) in a criss-cross pattern. Each of the resulting pairs of criss-crosses is joined by a small braided rattan ring, called *ali-ali*, *gelang*, or *wengku*, that enables the player to tighten or loosen the tension of the drum heads (pc, Otong Rasta, June 12, 1981; Kubarsah 1996, 72–77).

Kendang are associated not with bamboo culture, but rather with later incursions to the archipelago by South Asian cultures and religions. Reproducing the sounds of kendang with bamboo, therefore, presented its own set of challenges. The acoustical profile of kendang sounds relies not only on the weight and density of the wooden shell, but on the unique inside shape as well. These qualities are impossible to reproduce with bamboo.

Akim started with large hollow bamboo culms, which he covered with inner-tube rubber. His son, Ujang (a.k.a. Handi Purnaman), a talented self-taught musician, figured out how to play kendang-like patterns, even if the timbre and arrangement was a little bit different. Akim called his invention *baragbag*, which Ujang speculates is an onomatopoeic representation of the drums' slightly flabby (compared to kendang) timbre. Akim eventually replaced the rubber with goat skins to improve the sound (see Figure 3.9).

Gambang awi—According to Akim, the GSA musicians got tired of playing only unpitched percussion instruments, so Akim put together a couple of xylophones fashioned from bamboo slats. The name *gambang*,

Figure 3.9 Ujang (a.k.a. Handi Purnaman) plays Akim's baragbag (a.k.a. kendang awi).

Source: photo: Henry Spiller.

Figure 3.10 Gambang awi.
Source: photo: Henry Spiller.

which refers to traditional wooden xylophones in gamelan ensembles, seemed appropriate. Akim's first *gambang awi* provided one octave's worth of diatonic pitches. Akim focused on diatonic tunings because Ujang, who was helping the other musicians figure out what to play, had experience primarily with diatonic music. Akim later added more pitches—in the form of a second rank of bamboo slats (see Figure 3.10). Akim correctly points out that many Sundanese pentatonic tunings are easily approximated with twelve-tone tempered chromatic tuning ones, as pop Sunda musicians have demonstrated for decades by performing songs in Sundanese pentatonic modes with guitar and keyboard accompaniment. The ordering resembles a chromatic keyboard, but the pitches are not quite the same. Rather, the pitch vocabulary allows the musicians to choose pitches that sound "right" to them when playing tunes in a variety of diatonic modes and Sundanese pentatonic modes, including *salendro*, which is not even approximately reproducible with tempered chromatic tuning (pc, Akim and Ujang, May 28, 2013; see also Zanten 2014, 335).

Other instruments—Most of GSA's remaining musical forces do not represent radical departures from traditional instruments: *karinding, tarompet, suling*, and a singer.

Karinding is a bamboo or palm-wood guimbarde (or mouth harp) that has a long history in West Java as an instrument for personal entertainment.

Karinding has recently experienced a revival in Bandung, thanks in a large part to the efforts of a group of death metal musicians who, under the name Karinding Attack, began promoting karinding and other bamboo instruments among Sundanese teen-agers for playing metal-style music (see Chapter 4). Teddy Kusmayadi is GSA's karinding player; he also makes karinding out of both bamboo and palm wood.

Tarompet is a quadruple reed aerophone (see Figure 3.11). It is one of West Java's most versatile melodic instruments. Because it is loud, it is especially useful for outdoor music, including some forms of gamelan, some ceremonial angklung ensembles, and for the drumming music that accompanies demonstrations of the Sundanese martial arts known as *penca silat*. Akim is GSA's tarompet player, and he also makes tarompet from all local, natural materials for his own use and for sale to other musicians. He makes the body of the instrument from *jati* (teak) or *keruing* (*Dipterocarpus confertus*). The complex reed (*empet*) consists of dry coconut leaves attached to the hollow quill of a Manila duck feather (Admin Inilahkoran 2015). A crescent-moon shaped mouthpiece, made of coconut shell, helps the performer maintain the requisite circular breathing.

The tarompet typically the only non-bamboo instrument in GSA's instrumentarium; Asep Bobeng told me that it is not feasible to make tarompet from bamboo. Akim also makes a Sundanese single-reed aerophone, called *taleot*, which is conventionally made from bamboo. Its soft sound, however, is not appropriate for many of GSA's arrangements (pc, March 30, 2013).

Suling (bamboo ring flute; see Chapter 1) is another go-to instrument in West Java for playing melodies. Unlike tarompet, which is usually viewed as rather rustic, it is associated with aristocratic musical genres, *tembang Sunda* and *gamelan degung*. A solo singer—especially a female singer—is characteristic of many Sundanese styles and genres, ranging from the aristocratic tembang Sunda to all sorts of traditional and modern gamelan music, as well as *pop Sunda*, *dangdut*, and other modern creations.

CIHOG

With these resources, GSA has the means to present a wide variety of Sundanese music. In order to examine how they manage to imitate various ensembles to present their varied repertory, I return now to their 2013 performance at the Cikapundung Hiking Orienteering Games (CIHOG). At the same moment that GSA started to play on the stage, I encountered Agus I. P. Wiryapraja in the crowd; he introduced himself as the founder of GSA.[7] As they performed, he explained that GSA's opening piece was a "Nusantara Medley," composed of songs from around the Indonesian archipelago. I observed that most of the musicians played ostinatos on unpitched percussion instruments. The actual tunes—cast in a variety of modal systems, in keeping with the astonishing diversity of musical traditions in Indonesia—were rendered primarily by two Sundanese

Figure 3.11 Tarompet (l) and suling (r) flanked by two gambang awi.
Source: photo: Henry Spiller.

instruments with the capability to produce many different pitches, namely tarompet and suling (see Figure 3.11).

The two bamboo xylophones (gambang awi) contributed chords that suggested appropriate harmonizations, as in "Beungong Jumpa" (Magnolia flower), which was included in the medley to represent Indonesian's western-most province, Aceh in North Sumatra. It is a recent song, in the melodic minor mode (with no sixth degree, but both natural and flat seventh degrees), composed by Ibrahim Abduh. GSA also includes the Javanese "Suara Suling" (also known as "Gambang Suling") in the medley, composed by the famous composer and puppet master for *wayang* (Javanese and Sundanese puppet theatre), Nartosabdho. It is cast primarily in Javanese *pathet lima*, a five-note hemitonic pentatonic tuning system with one additional substitute pitch (see Becker 1980, 95). The medley concludes with a song from Indonesia's easternmost province, Papua (western New Guinea).

As discussed in Chapter 1, Sundanese music of all types is characterized by a musical texture with two contrasting musical layers: (1) ostinato patterns with regular rhythms, often rendered by several musicians playing interlocking parts, and (2) florid melodies, often with considerable rhythmic freedom. This texture itself has roots in bamboo technology, in that it combines the two main types of sounds that bamboo can make—percussive sounds produced by hitting bamboo, which are easily organized into rhythmically regular ostinatos, and whistling sounds made by blowing into bamboo tubes, which lend themselves to flexibility in both pitch and rhythm. In its layering of free melody and ostinatos, GSA's bamboo instruments indexed the Sundanese landscape and gave a distinctly local flavor even to this medley of non-Sundanese tunes.

Next, GSA's singer, Lia, took the microphone and addressed the crowd in the local language, Sundanese. She announced that they would perform "Kembang Gadung ("yam flower"), which is a song from the lower-class men's social dance tradition called *ketuk tilu*. In ketuk tilu events, the song "Kembang Gadung" accompanied the first appearance of the *ronggeng* (professional female singer-dancers; see Spiller 2010); in ketuk tilu events, the song played as the ronggeng lined up to present themselves to the male audience.

The standard ketuk tilu ensemble includes only a hanging gong, a three-pot gong chime, a set of drums, a singer, and a two-string bowed chordo-phone called *rebab* (see Spiller 2010). The traditional lyrics ask that the performance be blessed by heaven.[8] GSA's version, however, uses a newer version of the lyrics, made popular by pop Sunda stars such as Teh Euis, which rather self-consciously looks back to the ronggeng tradition as a source of uniquely Sundanese wisdom. Teh Euis's version features dynamic synthesizer licks mixed with Sundanese flute playing and drumming.[9] In GSA's version, various bamboo idiophones stand in for the three ketuk; the tarompet takes the rebab's role; and the baragbag drums imitate ketuk tilu drumming patterns.

Akim's heavily amplified bamboo idiochord goong awi replaced the gong. When I commented on how surprisingly convincing this gong sub-stitute sounded, Agus remarked that the instruments were all made of bamboo; some were ancient, but some (like the bamboo gong substitute) were newly invented.

Lia stood up and performed simple dance gestures as she sang, recalling the traditional ronggeng of the ketuk tilu tradition, and audience members, mostly but not exclusively male, took the cue to begin to dance in front of the stage, as they would at any event geared toward men's dancing.

GSA's next song, "Botol Kecap" ("bottle of sweet soy sauce"), may have roots in another men's dance tradition from Ciamis (Herdiani 2017, 467), but GSA is copying more recent incarnations of the song, especially pop Sunda versions typically performed with keyboards, guitars, and drum machines. It is cast essentially in the Sundanese pentatonic melodic mode known to some as *mataraman* or *pelog degung*, which combines both small intervals (approximately a minor second) and large intervals (a major third; i.e., from low to high, b c d f# g). "Botol Kecap" also occasionally includes extra notes (e and a) to approximate a diatonic scale. It also lends itself to conventional tonic-dominant harmonization. GSA's accompani-ment featured their two bamboo xylophones, whose hybrid diatonic/penta-tonic tunings imitated the keyboard instruments and guitars associated with Sundanese pop accompaniments. Sensing that people in the audience wanted to move, they also added drumming that was conducive to dancing.

Lia remained standing to sing "Akang Haji ("brother Haji") (a.k.a. "Sorban Palid"—"fallen turban"), another well-known pop song, to which

80   *Bamboo Wisdom*

GSA added a bit of a reggae groove. The group's current manager, Asep Bobeng, with whom I was standing at that point, took credit for the reggae gesture, explaining that he thinks audiences take notice when well-known songs have a novel twist. According to Indra Ridwan, "Sorban Palid" was recorded as early as the 1930s by a singer named Nji Mené, with accompaniment from European instruments, and was broadcast all over Java (Ridwan 2014, 10). Wim van Zanten has analyzed a variety of recordings of "Sorban Palid"; some feature gamelan accompaniments, others use Sundanese zithers, while yet others include keyboards and synthesizers (Zanten 2014). The song mentions that the titular turban—a symbol of the protagonist's pilgrimage to Mecca and a source of vainglorious pride—falls into the Cikapundung, and Lia gestured toward the river as she sang about it.

Next came "Bangbung Hideung," a song associated with Sundanese *wayang golek* rod puppet theatre. The text starts with a description of the eponymous *bangbung hideung* (black beetle), but the poem develops into a complex metaphorical description of unrequited love. GSA's version of "Bangbung Hideung" is inspired by a commercial arrangement from 2009, recorded by pop diva Rika Rafika, which presents "Bangbung Hideung" as a medley with another wayang song, "Banodari" (Ridwan 2014, 191–197). Rafika's version opens with an electronic house music ostinato, along with male voices chanting the title words.[10] GSA's version takes Rafika's wayang references a step further: in their rendition, they imitate the style of a wayang *kakawen*—an unmetered mood song, accompanied with a xylophone ostinato, which is how the song would be presented in a wayang performance. GSA also adds the low-pitched buzzing twang of a karinding (bamboo guimbarde)—which actually imitates the sounds of a beetle. Mimicking the Rafika arrangement, GSA transitions to "Banodari" with an accelerando and, once the faster tempo has stabilized, features the very loud, dynamic drumming associated with *jaipongan*, a music and dance craze first popularized in the 1980s, which has become an icon of modern Sundanese culture.

GSA ended their set with "Kembang Tanjung" ("Spanish cherry tree flower") a well-known *jaipongan* song; it features the loud, dynamic drumming associated with that genre, which was first popularized in the 1980s and has become an icon of modern Sundanese culture. The area in front of the stage was filled with eager audience members who were inspired to dance.

GSA's Approach

This CIHOG performance epitomizes many of GSA's unique characteristics. First of all, they maintain an eclectic repertory of Sundanese (and, more broadly, Indonesian) songs from a variety of genres, including (but not limited to) those I just described, namely, regional folk songs, ketuk tilu, pop Sunda, wayang golek, and jaipongan. Although each genre is normally accompanied by a specialized set of instruments—the ketuk tilu ensemble, different *gamelan* ensembles, and pop Sunda guitar/keyboard bands—GSA's homemade bamboo instruments did a credible job of accompanying them all, both in terms of Sundanese music's basic instrumental textures that combine fixed-pitch ostinatos with florid melodies, and in accessing all the required tonal systems—traditional Sundanese pentatonic tunings as well as Western diatonic modes.

A second fundamental GSA characteristic is the group's careful management of their set lists to conform to the specific needs of the audience for which they are playing. Although their repertory includes other types of songs as well—children's songs, Sundanese and other regional folk songs, *dangdut* (Indian-influenced popular music), so-call *klasik* ("classical") gamelan tunes, and music for *penca silat* (Sundanese martial arts), for example—they mobilize only those items that conform to the needs of particular events. As I learned later, they even learn new songs and develop new arrangements for specific occasions. For CIHOG, GSA knew the crowd would expect an event in which compelling drum rhythms and a female singer would inspire them to dance (see Spiller 2010), so they chose their repertory accordingly. Finally, GSA's performances almost always involve events associated with environmentalism, such as these Orienteering Games, but also the Dago neighborhood's monthly "Car Free Day"; other occasions on which they perform are corporate team-building exercises sponsored by Bandung businesses, such as telecommunications giant Telkomsel, who sends groups of employees to the area around the Cikapundung River to plant trees. The fact that GSA's instruments are made of bamboo stimulates all participants' primary, secondary, and tertiary retentions to create a powerful association both with the area's natural environment and with Bandung's nascent environmental movement.

GSA maintains a repertory of about thirty songs or so. The musicians all have different musical backgrounds and skill levels, but they are committed to making collaborative arrangements. They typically pick songs they already know and find out—by trial and error—how to play the songs on their instruments. The manager, Asep Bobeng, often evaluates the group's collaborative arrangements and makes suggestions about tempo, instrumentation, and rhythmic feels. He also makes suggestions about repertory, especially in conjunction with particular events. For example, when preparing for a series of primary school performances, Bobeng asked the group to put together a medley of Sundanese children's songs. A collaboration with a couple of Zumba fitness instructors inspired a collection of up-tempo tunes. Bobeng also masterminded the "Nusantara medley," which opened GSA's CIHOG performance, in order to lend the group a more national, rather than exclusively regional, identity and widen their appeal. For a theatrical performance of Sundanese playwright Arthur S. Nalan's

82   *Bamboo Wisdom*

play, "Kawin Ucing" ("cat wedding"), Bobeng went through the script and suggested incidental music selections; among other wedding-themed tunes, GSA adapted the "classical" *gamelan degung* piece, "Pajajaran," because *degung* music is associated with weddings in West Java.

Performing as Amateurs

As somebody who has spent countless hours studying and playing music with Sundanese musicians in traditional *latihan* (lesson-rehearsal) settings, I found GSA's rehearsal process to be unusual in several respects. Participants in Sundanese latihan typically recognize, at least covertly, a hierarchy of which people have the knowledge and competence to take the musical lead. GSA's process was much more egalitarian. Latihan typically have a social side as well, with the attendance of non-participants, much conversation, and tea and snacks. Although GSA rehearsals were convivial events, there was rarely the kind of social interactions—eating, drinking, gossiping—that characterize latihan. On the other hand, the members of GSA, despite their diversity in age and social circumstances, are an exceptionally close-knit social unit.

The way in which GSA solidifies their arrangements through a slow, iterative, egalitarian process reinforces these characteristics. Nobody takes the lead in setting the arrangements. Rather, they begin with a generalized idea of a song, or a medley, and simply start to play it to see what emerges. Over time, through many iterations, they settle on a tonal center, accompaniment patterns, eventually crystalizing set (yet flexible) arrangements. The singer, Lia, for example, rarely specifies starting pitches, or even modal requirements; instead, she sings what she hears, and the other musicians figure out how to complement her singing.

GSA regards the Cikapundung river as a center for their activities. The group has received permission to maintain a *saung* (rustic bamboo-and-rattan structure) on the banks of the Cikapundung, on property managed by a government water treatment facility. This shack, which the members call Cika Cika ("fireflies"), is a site for "back to nature" team-building events for corporations, sponsored by an organization called Barayakota (featuring singalongs conducted by GSA members), as well as for GSA's own private celebrations. I attended several such events in 2013, but the most elaborate was to celebrate the full moon in June—an activity for which the Sundanese have an enviably poetic verb: *ngabungbang* ("to enjoy the moonlight"). While there was still light, GSA members and their guests made simple music together. After dusk, participants shared an elaborate traditional feast on the upper level of the saung, then retired to the bank of the river to enjoy the moonlight.

GSA's status as a group of amateurs—in the sense that they are lovers of art who are not necessarily trained to produce it—helps to make sense of their gravitation toward bamboo musical instruments. The relative

Bamboo Wisdom 83

simplicity with which bamboo is transformed into musical instruments, and the ease with which such instruments can be coaxed into producing meaningful musical sounds, valorizes local knowledge, unwritten folkways, and neighborhood sociality.

GSA's bottom-up approach to reconnecting to a Sundanese identity is rooted firmly in their specific locale. Sundanese music comprises a panoply of ensembles, genres, and styles, which have long been in dialogue with one another and with music from the outside. GSA forges connections between the environment, the past, and the present by performing an eclectic repertory of Sundanese styles and genres—which ordinarily would require several special-purpose ensembles—on their home-made bamboo instruments for events that are associated closely with the physical environment of Bandung. In effect, bamboo's inherent flexibility—as memorialized in the adage *leuleus jeujeur liat tali* (flexible bamboo fishing rod, tough line)— provides a medium for the members of GSA to recontextualize several different repertories of Sundanese music (the "tough line" that connects modern-day Bandung residents to their cultural roots).

Returning to Stiegler: In his theorizing about the meaning and agency of objects, Stiegler has also argued that twenty-first-century digital technology has democratized the capability to create objects, such as films and recordings, that once were the exclusive purview of specialists (2014, 26). For GSA, however, it is not new media, but rather the revival of a very old technology—bamboo—that enables them to produce the musical instruments and genres once limited to specialists. Their musical activities fit well with the post-modern "do-it-yourself" (DIY) principles that drive alternative music scenes all over the world and are also associated with environmental and social reform movements.

According to their brochure, GSA's mission is to "provide a platform to unite local creative potential and to make bamboo a medium for artistic expression."[11] Their name—Galengan Sora Awi—gestures toward the precariousness of this mission in modern, urban Bandung. The members of GSA have homed in on bamboo—as a material, as a soundmark, as a cultural symbol, and as an integral part of the landscape—as the path to navigate the narrow space between Sundanese traditional rural culture/values and the city of Bandung's increasingly urban, modern way of life. The path takes advantage of the primary, secondary, and tertiary retentions that connect bamboo to both Sundanese culture and the landscape of West Java.

Sundanese audiences share GSA's secondary retentions about bamboo's significance in their culture and draw similar conclusions about the tertiary retentions conjured by the band's bamboo musical instruments. The group's careful attention to pleasing their audiences, by catering to their expectations for familiar songs, danceable rhythms, and event-specific repertory—attending, in other words, to their audiences' primary retentions—magnifies these effects.

Notes

1 "Melalui sebuah Jalan Kecil [galengan] Kami coba menyampaikan Ide, gagasan serta potensi berkesenian dan kemudian diekspresikan, disuarakan melaui media bambu [sora awi]."
2 I first encountered Stiegler's ideas in the work of Joshua Tucker (2016).
3 It would be fascinating to explore how the term celempung came to be associated with the elegant zithers in Central Javanese gamelan, but it is beyond the scope of this chapter.
4 "Merupakan satu sumber daya alam yang mengungkapkan nilai-nilai, memberikan pandangan hidup, melahirkan budaya dan membentuk ragam kesenian serta alat-alat musik bambu. ... Bambu merupakan simbol kebersamaan dan kearifan lokal sekaligus sebagai tanaman purba yang telah banyak memberikan jasa sehingga telah ikut mengukir wajah seni budaya Sunda."
5 Both Radio Parahyangan and its celempungan group are now defunct.
6 Traditionally, the heads are made from cow or water buffalo skin; but goat skin produces the brighter, higher-pitched sound that is preferred for most contemporary applications.
7 I was sorry to learn, as I was writing this book, that Pa Agus died in January 2019.
8 See www.youtube.com/watch?v=Xca0ISBfElE
9 See www.youtube.com/watch?v=pLh48WpM5oI
10 www.youtube.com/watch?v=6kMYXRuk2s0
11 "... membentuk sebuah wadah untuk menyatukan potensi–potensi lokal kreatif kembali dan menjadikan bambu sebagai media ekspresi berkesenian."

4   Roots Values

kudu kawas awi jeung gawirna
("We should be like bamboo on its cliff")

Bandung is a relatively young city, founded in the first decade of the nine-teenth century. Its location was determined in a large part by the Dutch colonial government, which compelled the local *bupati* (hereditary aristo-cratic ruler), Wiranatakusumah II, to move his capital to lie on the new *Grote Postweg*—the great post road, built during the governorship of Henrik Willem Daendels (1808–1811). The *Postweg* was a modern trans-portation breakthrough that revolutionized cross-country travel on Java, although its revolutionary significance was later supplanted by the island's first railroad, built in 1867.[1]

Despite this eminently modern and pragmatic history, Bandung has a profound local identity, steeped in Sundanese history, folklore, and spir-ituality that long predates its putative founding. The bupati followed trad-itional Sundanese philosophy in picking the precise site for the new city's center, choosing a spot with an auspicious confluence of an even number of rivers (Sumardjo 2011, xvii), near a holy spring just west of one of the rivers, the Cikapundung (see Chapter 3), which guaranteed the protection of the goddess Nyi Kentring Manuk. He built his new palace facing the dormant volcano whose distinctive shape garnered it the name Tangkuban Perahu—"overturned boat"—to capitalize on the mountain's mystical associations (Amor Patria 2014, 130).

Sundanese legend holds that Tangkuban Perahu is the tangible remains of an Oedipal drama from the region's mythical past. Queen Dayang Sumbi, the tale relates, discovered that Sangkuriang, the great hero she was about to marry, was in fact the son she lost many years before. To avert the incestuous marriage, she demanded of Sangkuriang an impossible task—creating a lake and building a pleasure boat with which to sail on it in a single night. When she discovered that Sangkuriang was well on his way to completing the feat, she arranged for some cocks to crow, tricking Sangkuriang into thinking dawn had arrived before he finished his task. In anger and frustration, he threw the boat into the lake, where it overturned and became part of the Bandung area's unique landscape (see Figure 4.1).

DOI: 10.4324/9781003302797-5

Figure 4.1 Tangkuban Perahu, viewed from northern Bandung.
Source: photo: Henry Spiller.

By the early twentieth century, the Dutch made Bandung their colonial capital, and filled the city with spectacular Art Deco civic and residential architecture—much of it designed by the noted architect, Charles Prosper Wolff Schoemaker (e.g., Gedung Merdeka; see Chapter 2, Figure 2.2).

More recently, modern skyscrapers, hotels, and toll roads—and even plans for light rail systems—have all brought Bandung into the twenty-first century. No matter how modern Bandung becomes, however, the potent Sundanese spirituality that determined its original location continues to simmer just under the surface. A financial institution now occupies the site of the original holy spring, but the bank employees carefully maintain and honor the fount, which they were happy to show me after I convinced them that my intentions were good (see Figure 4.2). Some people believe the waters have supernatural powers.[2]

These deep roots are reflected in the proverb, "kudu kawas awi jeung gawirna," which invites Sundanese people to observe how bamboo (*awi*) thrives by insinuating its root systems into the cliffs (*gawir*) on which it grows, and how those root systems in turn help maintain the cliffs' stability in the face of erosion. The exhortation to "be like bamboo on its cliff" promises stability and success for current Bandung residents in return for maintaining the traditions and local wisdom of their Sundanese forebears, even in thoroughly modern Bandung.

Figure 4.2 The author at the Bandung holy spring, now in the basement of a bank.

Karinding

Following the fall of President Soeharto's New Order government in 1998, many Bandung residents sought ways to reinvigorate Bandung's Sundanese essence along the lines of the proverb. The (re)turn to bamboo by Bandung residents in the twenty-first century is not just proverbial, however, it is quite literal: the centerpiece of a youth movement in West Java that promotes the value of local Sundanese wisdom in grappling with the complexities of global modernity is a small and quite simple bamboo musical instrument called *karinding*. According to Kimung (a.k.a. Iman Rahman Angga Kusuma, as quoted in Pramudya 2019), a historian, teacher, author, and death metal musician who has been influential in kindling interest in karinding among Sundanese fans of underground music in the first two decades of the century, this movement embraces other symbols of autochthonous Sundanese culture as well. It is not unusual to encounter young people sporting *iket* (traditional men's tied cloth headcoverings), *pangsi* (traditional trousers), or *kujang* (a characteristically Sundanese weapon; see Chapter 1). And some study and practice *aksara Sunda kuno* (a uniquely Sundanese system for writing used between the fourteenth and eighteenth centuries, derived from Old Kawi.[3] Kimung, along with others, adopted/adapted the cultural theory term "glocalization" (*glokalisasi* in Indonesian) as early as 2007 to describe the underground community's efforts to "think globally and act locally" (e.g., Abdilah 2007). Studying and playing karinding provides a means to focus on Sundanese history and language, and to adapt the values of indigenous Sundanese religious/devotional practices called *Sunda wiwitan* for the needs of the twenty-first century (Dayana 2017, 353). Karinding may be thought of as—quite literally—the bamboo that proverbially both clings to and stabilizes the precarious cliff of Bandung's modernity.

Karinding is the Sundanese version of an instrument of the sort generically called (in English) jew's harp, mouth harp, jaw('s) harp, trump, or guimbarde. Following the lead of Hornbostel and Sachs (1961), I use the French-derived "guimbarde" as a generic English term over the more common but problematic "jew's harp."[4] Guimbardes usually have a flexible tongue (or elastic plaque) that is fixed to a frame at one end so that it can vibrate when excited. Guimbarde players typically hold the instrument in front of the mouth, which is slightly open, so that the air compressions caused by the lamella resonate in the mouth cavity. By varying the shape of the mouth cavity, the player can emphasize different overtones and formants and change the timbre of the resultant sound. Different breathing patterns and various manipulations of the larynx and surrounding muscles provide possibilities for further timbre changes, and even for pitch modifications (see Figure 4.3).

Figure 4.3 Teddy Kusmayadi plays *karinding*.
Source: photo: Henry Spiller.

Acoustical analyses of such instruments have shown that the lamella itself is not actually the source of the vibrations that the mouth cavity amplifies and modulates; rather, the vibrations result from the lamella's opening and closing the space between the two arms that surround the lamella, setting up a periodic air turbulence in the mouth cavity. For this reason, the overtone series that reaches the mouth cavity is harmonic, rather than the non-harmonic overtones that the idiophonic lamella itself produces (Ledang 1972, 102; Adkins 1974, 670). And thus guimbardes from all over the world, which are made out of many different materials, including wood, metal, bamboo, and bone, sound very similar (Ledang 1972, 95). John Wright suggests that such instruments have a wide, although not universal, distribution throughout the Eurasian landmass (2001).

Indonesian versions of guimbardes are made from bamboo, palm wood, or metal, and come in a variety of shapes and sizes, with different techniques for setting the lamella in motion and for amplifying the resulting vibrations. Instrument names in Indonesia include *tong, uding, ruding sulu* (Kalimantan), *berimbak* (Maluku), *tebe* (Savu), *nggunggi* (Sumba), *knobe besi, knobe oh* (West Timor), *genggong* (Bali and Sulawesi), *karombi, oli, ore-ore mbondu, alingen* (Sulawesi) (Yampolsky et al. 2001). In Central Java, guimbardes are called *rinding* (Kunst 1973, 360).

A Sundanese karinding (see Figure 4.4) is typically fashioned from a relatively flat piece of bamboo (typically tamiang) or dried palm branch (*Arenga pinnata*) about 20 cm long and 1 or 2 cm wide. Its third dimension

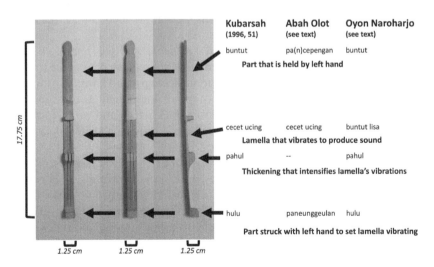

Figure 4.4 Parts of a Karinding, according to Kubarsah (1996, 51), Abah Olot (various sources, see text) and Oyon Naroharjo (various sources, see text).

Source: photos: Henry Spiller; karinding made by Abah Olot, 2013.

90   *Roots Values*

is mostly quite thin (1 mm); however, there are usually two or three parts that are relatively thick (1 cm). One thick part typically separates the handle from the part that contains the lamella and its frame. Another thick part is in the middle of the lamella, to give it more stability, as well as more weight and thus a lower vibrating frequency. The part that is struck (*paneunggeulan*) is also thick to withstand the constant beating.

According to several sources, who mostly rely on the lore of Abah Olot (a karinding maker who will be introduced in more detail later in this chapter), there are three main components. First, a handle, called *pa(n)cepengan* ("that which is held"), which the player grasps firmly with the left hand. Sometimes the handle is carved into a decorative shape, such as a kujang or a *gunungan* (a kind of wayang puppet; Arinda 2016). Second, a thin tongue or lamella, incised out of the bamboo, that remains attached at one end but otherwise free to vibrate within the frame from which it was cut, that is called *cecet ucing* ("cat's tail"). Third, the *paneunggeulan* ("that which is beaten"), to which the *cecet ucing* is attached, and which the player strikes, usually with the right-hand index finger at its first joint, to set the lamella into vibration (Kimung 2013; Kimung 2016; Suwandi 2013, 25–26; Art Etsa Logam 2013; Arinda 2016).

Oyon Naroharjo, who represents a tradition of karinding playing in Tasikmalaya, uses different names for the three parts already described: *buntut* ("tail," i.e., pa(n)cepengan or handle); *buntut lisa* ("tail's wooden pin," i.e., cecet ucing or lamella); *hulu* ("head," i.e., paneunggeulan, or the part that the player strikes to make sound). He also identifies a fourth part, *pahul* ("spoke")—a thickening of the karinding material at the end of the lamella that intensifies its vibrations (Indrawati 2006, 34–35; see also Kubarsah 1996, 51).

Another type of karinding, called *karinding toél* (or *towel*), is not struck but rather plucked or strummed, and is a relative newcomer to the Sundanese scene, pioneered by the ethnomusicologist and karinding innovator Asep Nata (see Chapter 5). This type of instrument is regarded as both easier to make (because it has fewer thick parts) and easier to play. Guimbardes in some other parts of Indonesia provide a string to set the lamella vibrating, but not in West Java.

According to Kunst, in the "Tasik district the jew's harp is called karinding only when cut from arènwood [i.e., palm or kawung]; when made from bamboo it is there called *karèng*" (Kunst 1973, 360). Coolsma's 1884 definition of karinding—"a kind of whistle made from a branch of the kawung palm"[5]— doesn't mention bamboo as an option (Coolsma 1884, 152). In current usage, however, both bamboo and palm instruments are called karinding. Karinding maker Teddy Kusmayadi told me that bamboo is much easier to work with than palm wood (pc, June 24, 2013); some sources suggest that palm wood karinding are louder than the bamboo version (e.g., Arinda 2016).

In the past, a separate bamboo tube, closed with a node at one end, held horizontally with the karinding's handle inserted partway (as described

Figure 4.5 Ki Amenk and Wisnu play karinding with Karinding Attack; note the bamboo microphone stands for the karinding.
Source: photo: Henry Spiller.

by Jaap Kunst 1973, 360 [also Kunst and Wiranatakoesoema 1921, 248]), was an integral part of karinding performance practice—it served to amplify the mouth-resonated karinding sounds. The tube sometimes served double-duty as a carrying case for the karinding as well. Contemporary performances usually omit the tube, however; if amplification is desired, karinding players use a microphone and PA system. In a nod toward the past, however, the microphone stands are often made from bamboo (see Figure 4.5).

The etymology of the term karinding is not clear. There are several dubious theories circulating among contemporary Sundanese karinding aficionados. The first, promoted by Abah Olot, suggests that it is formed of two words: *kakak* (elder brother) and *rinding*, which Abah Olot believes meant "art" or "music" in the past; thus, he claims, karinding is something that precedes music (Riyadi 2011, 19; Yonatan 2010, 2; Art Etsa Logam 2013). Another theory, popularized in a contemporary poem (by Nazaruddin Azhar) based on karinding legends from Tasikmalaya, is that the instrument was named after a loud insect called *kakarindingan* (Yonatan 2010, 2; Kimung 2013); another source provides the detail that

92   *Roots Values*

the instrument's shape resembled the insect's tail (Indrawati 2006, 25–26).[6] A story collected by Cace Hendrik in Ciramagirang relates a legend that a buffalo herder named Kari invented the instrument to help him pass the time while herding buffalo ("ngangon munding" in Sundanese); an abbreviation of the phrase "KARI nganong muNDING" produces the word karinding (Hendrik A. P. 2009; quoted in Kimung 2013). It is quite possible, of course, that the syllables "rinding" are simply an onomatopoeic representation of the instrument's sound, and similar sounding words name guimbardes from other parts of Indonesia (and from the Philippines, e.g., *kubing, subing, aruding* (Trimillos 1983, 45; Simon 1985, 120–121; Maceda 1998, 215). The prefix "ka" in Sundanese is a marker for a noun.

Karinding is mentioned in passing in an untitled Sundanese manuscript, about a spiritual seeker named Sri Ajnyana (Noorduyn and Teeuw 2006), which appears to have been written around the sixteenth century.[7] In a description of the bedroom of the beautiful goddess Puah Aci Kuning, who is testing Sri Ajnyana's commitment to moral behavior by tempting him to engage in forbidden sexual pleasure, two musical instruments appear near the bed: a *kacapi* (zither) and a *kari(n)ding* (Noorduyn and Teeuw 2006, 234 [lines 831–832]). There is no description in the poem of these instruments' sounds or the manner in which they would have been played. It seems possible, however, that the karinding's persistent association with courtship (see below) might explain its presence in the bedroom. According Noorduyn and Teeuw, uniquely Sundanese words and ideas appear frequently in such texts and serve to place the stories into their audience's local world, in contrast to both the Javanese and the Indian elements that permeate the narratives. They also cite as local an earlier passage that compares the buzzing of bees and wasps (named with specifically Sundanese names and attending to a riot of particularly Sundanese flowers) to a concert of music from various instruments, both bamboo and bronze (Noorduyn and Teeuw 2006, 230 [lines 626–643]).

A handful of Western documents from the nineteenth and early twentieth centuries represents outsider views of karinding in a variety of settings. Jonathan Rigg's 1862 Sundanese-English dictionary includes a definition that suggests he mistook the bamboo resonating tube to be the karinding itself:

> a musical instrument made of a tube of bambu about one foot long and one inch in bore, at the end of which is held a small instrument with a tongue to it. This instrument is struck by the finger and blown upon, when a sound like a jew's harp is produced.

> (Rigg 1862, 203)

Likewise, Edward H. Knight, who wrote descriptions of the Javanese instruments at the 1878 Paris Exposition in *Lippincott's Monthly Magazine*, described bamboo "jewsharps" as "about a foot long, and with a string to fasten to the ear"; he, too, apparently mistook the bamboo resonator for

Roots Values 93

the guimbarde itself. I speculate that the "string to fasten to the ear" might have been a mechanism for keeping the bamboo tube in the right position without having to hold it (Knight 1878, 416).

When translating the Bible into Sundanese in 1891, Sierk Coolsma used the Sundanese terms "*soeling*" and "karinding" for the Hebrew *ḥălil* in *Jeremiah 48:36* (usually translated in English as "pipe" or "flute"), suggesting that the translator thought these instruments would be most evocative for his Sundanese congregants (Coolsma 1891, 859).[8]

Benjamin Ives Gilman recorded a karinding player at the 1893 World's Columbian Exposition in Chicago, Illinois; it is among the earliest extant recordings of music from Java. All accounts indicate that Sundanese residents of the Exposition's Java Village played karinding for their own entertainment, as well as for the vicarious pleasure of American visitors who overheard them. Gilman's notes remark only that he recorded "a performance on this curious instrument" (Lee 1984, 17). He makes no mention of any auxiliary resonating tube.

In collaboration with the Regent of Bandung, R.T.A. Wiranatakoesoema, Kunst brought a pair of karinding players to demonstrate their art to the gathered Dutch experts for the First Congress of the Java Institute (June 17–20, 1921; "P." 1921, 329). Kunst and Wiranatakoesoema included more information about these performances in their article, "Een en Ander Over Soendaneesche Muziek" (Kunst and Wiranatakoesoema 1921, 248–249), including a list of eleven pieces and notes about various contexts for karinding performance (read on for more on these topics).

Karinding in Sundanese History

Over the centuries, the Sundanese karinding has proven to be a versatile instrument (Kunst and Wiranatakoesoema 1921, 248; Kimung 2016). For example, its simplicity and portability made—and make—karinding ideal for entertaining oneself during idle moments while caring for crops or animals (Suwandi 2013, 12; 26). In the past, some sources report, lonely workers in the fields traded karinding dialogues over large distances (Art Etsa Logam 2013). As mentioned above, the Sundanese residents of the Java Village at the 1893 World's Columbian Exposition in Chicago played karinding for their own amusement. According to Kunst and Wiranatakoesoema, writing in 1921, women played karinding morning and evening to entertain themselves and their children (1921, 249). In modern-day Cisolok (a village which self-consciously revives and maintains traditional Sundanese values), karinding are playthings for the children (Kimung 2016).

Octogenarians from the region around Mount Manglayang near Ujungberung (about 12 km east of Bandung) remember that karinding and celempung provided the accompaniment for rehearsals of *penca silat* (Sundanese martial arts) in their youth (Suwandi 2013, 27; Art Etsa Logam 2013). According to Kunst and Wiranatakoesoema, karinding was also the

94   *Roots Values*

centerpiece for an endurance game, in which male participants competed to see who could play karinding the longest. The wagers typically involved tobacco or matches, although Kunst and Wiranatakoesoema also relate the tale of a father who determined which of two rivals would get to marry his karinding-loving daughter by challenging them to such a competition (1921, 249).

The preceding story is perhaps an extreme example, but the karinding has a long-standing association with courtship in West Java. An origin story from Cineam—a village near Tasikmalaya (about 140 km southeast of Bandung) that boasts a contemporary karinding scene spearheaded by Oyon Naroharjo (Suwandi 2013, 27; Indrawati 2006)—sets the karinding's invention in the mid-fourteenth century, during the time of the medieval Galuh kingdom. A young man named Kalamanda fell in love with a woman, Sekarwati, who was reputed to have summarily snubbed all of her many suitors. Through powerful meditation, Kalamanda learned that the key to Sekarwati's heart would be a musical instrument that could express his true love. So, he fashioned the first karinding, played it outside Sekarwati's window, and won her heart; they lived happily ever after (Suwandi 2013, 26–27; https://kilangbara.wordpress.com/2016/10/14/karinding-ti-citami ang/; Indrawati 2006, 25–26). In another story, karinding's power to attract women leads to a less desirable outcome. Ki Slenting, it is told, bewitched so many women with his karinding playing that the community eventually punished him for his depravity with a death sentence (Kimung 2013). Adolescent boys playing the karinding to attract the attention of girls has apparently been a common custom in many parts of West Java (Suwandi 2013, 15). But it was not only men who played the karinding to spark their romantic lives. Kunst and Wiranatakoesoema describe a ritual enabling a woman to increase her chances of finding a suitable husband; the ritual involved bathing (dressed in white) in seven different springs under the full moon, playing karinding all the while (1921, 249).

In Cimanggung, Parakan Muncang (about 40 km east of Bandung), Abah Olot (a.k.a. Endang Sugriwa) represents the fourth generation in a family line that makes and plays karinding and other bamboo instruments (Suwandi 2013, 28). He names his father, Abah Entang, and his grandfather, Abah Maja, as his mentors, and asserts that karinding has been a part of many village ceremonies there for generations, including village thanksgiving celebrations (*lembur* and *buluan*), ceremonies for eclipses (*gerhana*), and full moon ceremonies (*caang bulan, ngabungbang*; Suwandi 2013, 28; Art Etsa Logam 2013). According to Kunst and Wiranatakoesoema, villagers played the karinding during solar and lunar eclipses to drive away the supernatural agents that were causing the eclipse (1921, 249).

Tomy Suwandi also acknowledges karinding's association with eclipses but suggests that its role was primarily as a warning device (Suwandi 2013, 28–29). Kimung reports that karinding was involved in covert communication between freedom fighters during the revolution, as well as more recent separatist movements (e.g., Darum Islam/Tentara Islam Indonesia

Figure 4.6 Karinding as a fashion item.
Source: photo: Henry Spiller.

[DI/TII] and PKI; Kimung 2019). The instrument's association with the PKI and LEKRA is one reason, Kimung suggests, that instrument fell out of favor during Soeharto's New Order (Kimung 2011b).

It is worth noting that karinding was (and is) also an item of fashion. Karinding designs reflect whether the instrument is meant to be played by a man or a woman. Women's karinding are fashioned to look like—and can be used as—a hair pin, while men's karinding are shorter and can be carried in a tobacco case (Kimung 2013; Suwandi 2013, 26; Herlinawati 2009, 101). Among youthful Bandung karinding enthusiasts, it is currently fashionable to carry one's karinding inserted into one's iket (headcloth; see Figure 4.6).

Many modern Sundanese accounts of karinding history state that Sundanese farmers played karinding to drive away pests—insects and/or rodents—from their fields (e.g., Daryana 2017, 353; Art Etsa Logam 2013; Suwandi 2013, 3, 11; Hakim et al. 2012, 3; Herlinawati 2009, 100, 108). Echoing the advertising claims of a variety of modern contraptions that claim to repel pests with "ultrasonic" sounds—audible to pests but not to humans—delivered at "low decibels" (i.e., low volume or intensity) to prevent harm to humans, the Sundanese accounts cite only karinding's "low decibel" output as justification for these claims for pest control. The ethnomusicologist Asep Nata, who is an important figure in Bandung's karinding revival (see Chapter 5), confirmed to me that "karinding pest control" is an internet meme with little credibility. He told me, tongue-in-cheek, that he himself tried playing the karinding to drive away the many mice who live on the ISBI campus, with indecisive (at best) results. He did refer me to a report about an elementary-school science project, which won

96   *Roots Values*

a prize at a Singapore science fair, that claimed to demonstrate success in repelling ten white mice by playing the note "F" on a karinding,[9] but definitely did not endorse their findings.

Repertory

Karinding repertories are extremely diverse—not surprising, given the instrument's wide distribution and versatility. In the notes for his 1968 karinding recording, Ernst Heins reports that "[t]he player can produce any folksong or gamelan tune known to him"[10] (Heins 1968). In contrast, Kunst and Wiranatakoesoema, reporting on the karinding demonstration at the 1921 Java Institute Congress, name eleven very specific repertory items, along with some translations of the "piece" names.

1. Toetndang (toet = spider's abdomen; ndang = web. So: like a cobweb; melody without end)
2. Boentjis.[11]
3. Loetoeng loentjat (= jumping monkey)
4. Tonggeret (the name of the well-known, noisy insect).
5. Djipang (welcome song)
6. Djemplang (with this word of unknown derivation, suggesting a *renteng* piece)
7. Oetaeio (= winding)
8. Doger (name of an ensemble from Tasikmalaya)
9. Keupat eunang (= the swinging of a woman's arms when walking).
10. Lempaj (= elongated, slim)
11. Panodjo (= bounce)

(Kunst and Wiranatakoesoema 1921, 249)[12]

It is worth noting, however, that they also comment that because the karinding's range is limited, "the difference between the melodies is not always striking" (Kunst and Wiranatakoesoema 1921, 249).[13]

At least one of Kunst and Wiranatakoesoema's names overlaps with the four standardized *pirigan* ("accompaniment patterns") taught by Abah Olot as the canon of modern karinding playing, namely "tonggeret" (see below). Many of the other titles in Kunst and Wiranatakoesoema's list make more sense when interpreted as accompaniment patterns (more specifically, as ostinatos suitable for particular contexts) rather than piece names as well. "Toetndang" in particular suggests to me an onomatopoeic rendering of a karinding ostinato.

Abah Olot and his students, including Kimung, promulgate a repertory limited to four pirigan: *tonggeret*, which imitates an insect that makes a sound at dusk; *tutunggalan*, for signaling (e.g., eclipses), which is also called *gogondangan*;[14] *iring-iringan*, which is a "kind of march" that lends solemnity to a wedding ceremony (for example); and *rereogan*, a substitute for *dog-dog* drumming, which is appropriate for comedy performances (once known as *reog*) or for ceremonial purposes (Suwandi 2013, 28–29).[15]

These ostinatos provide a foundation for considerable creativity by members of the karinding community. After listening to the Gilman recording of karinding from 1893, Kimung observed (writing in a facebook post invitation to a "Konser Kelas Karinding" on October 18, 2013), that the patterns are very free, that there are no pirigan (the four "accompaniment patterns" the Bandung karinding community knows today). And perhaps, he continues, this recording can answer the question on the minds of today's karinding musicians, who are constantly looking for how karinding was played before the current surge in popularity: apparently much more freely than how it is played today.[16]

Another stream of karinding tradition rests in the hands of Oyon Naroharjo, from Tasikmalaya. According to Indrawati, who wrote a thesis based on her interviews with Oyon, Oyon traces his lineage to a 1930s karinding player named Mbah Kaman, who passed his lore to a friend named Murniah, who then taught it to future generations, including Oyon, who started learning in 1954 (Indrawati 2006, 27). Although he learned karinding as a solo instrument, to be played to pass the time while resting, Oyon developed a group style with five to eight karinding players. In 1966, he formed a group called Lingkung Seni Sekar Komara Sunda, which developed a system for teaching karinding (Indrawati 2006, 28). Oyon left West Java in 1968, but after his return in 1992, he revived his group, which performed on occasion in Bandung; he also opened a *warung* (food stall), where he and members of his group performed on karinding to drum up interest in the instrument (Indrawati 2006, 32).[17]

Karinding's Decline

Although karinding survived in some out-of-the-way pockets (e.g., Abah Olot's community, and Oyon's group in Tasikmalaya),[18] by the second half of the twentieth century, the playing of karinding was rare. I've already mentioned the recording released in 1968 by Ernst Heins, that included a brief karinding except; in a review of the recording, the Sundanese scholar Iwan Natapradja notes that karinding "is almost never heard anymore" (Natapradja 1972, 315). The ethnomusicologist Endo Suanda, who spent his childhood in the 1950s in a small village near Majalengka in West Java, told me that he himself never saw a karinding in the village, nor did his father ever recall ever seeing one (pc, June 3, 2013). Noted musician Burhan Sukarma likewise indicates that he was unaware of karinding growing up in Karawang in the 1950s (pc, August 29, 2020).

I have already reported a theory that karinding's association with the PKI and LEKRA is one reason for the instrument's fall from grace during Soeharto's New Order regime (Kimung 2011b). But the more conventional explanation is that karinding—a quiet instrument most suitable for

98 *Roots Values*

personal amusement or courtship—simply became irrelevant in the loud, busy, modern world.

Nevertheless, karinding continued to be played, in both obscure and not-so-obscure contexts. The pop and avant-garde musician/composer Hari Roesli (1951–2004) at times included karinding in his performances in the 1970s and 1980s (Art Etsa Logam 2013; Kimung 2013; pc, Adam Tyson, December 19, 2019). The pop singer Chrisye opens his 1999 hit version "Semusim"[19] with a taste of karinding (see Kimung 2013; Kimung 2019). Popular singer-songwriter Doel Sumbang also employed karinding into his recordings (Kimung 2019). Karinding references were not limited to the worlds of pop music. The choreographer Irawati Durban Arjo, writing in 1989, suggests that karinding—among other musical genres not typically associated with dance—were included in the accompaniments for newly conceived dance dramas as well (Durban Ardjo 1989, 174).

In the mid-2000s, energized by the reformasi movement's affirmation of local cultures and values, Sundanese artists, scholars, and traditional cultural advocates such as Dodong Kodir, Asep Nata, Yoyo Yogasmana, and Opa Felix, experimented with karinding (Kimung 2013). Komunitas Hong, for example, founded by Mohamad Zaini Alif in 2003 to revitalize Sundanese children's games and other folklore, included karinding in its activities. But the most wide-ranging—and perhaps the most surprising— approach to karinding in the past decades is the merger of Bandung's thriving underground death metal scene with the lore and the sound of karinding.

Karinding Meets Death Metal

Bandung is a major center for Indonesia's thriving "underground" music scene (Baulch 2003 115, 156; Clinton and Wallach 2015)—a wide-reaching umbrella term that includes a variety of non-mainstream, even anti-mainstream genres. According to Jeremy Wallach, underground embraces "four basic genres: punk, hardcore, metal, and alternative" (2005, 19), with countless subgenres, including black-metal, death-metal, grindcore, hardcore, power-metal, thrash-metal, and punk (James and Walsh 2015, 28).

Metal, broadly conceived, has been part of Indonesia's musical life since at least 1975, when Deep Purple performed the first concerts by a major American or British band ever in Jakarta,[20] in a concert promoted in Java's major cities (Jakarta, Bandung, Semarang, and Surabaya).[21] An estimated 150,000 people attended the two Jakarta concerts (Crescenti 1976); clearly there was already a pent-up demand for metal music. Wallach suggests that many Indonesians do not "regard the music as particularly foreign," and estimates that there has been a well-developed "network of underground metal scenes located in towns and cities throughout the Indonesian archipelago dedicated to the grassroots production, distribution, and consumption of metal music" since the late 1980s (2005, 280).

Roots Values 99

Denizens of the Indonesian underground scene absorbed the global scene's values and political inclinations, which often clashed with the policies and tactics of Indonesia's New Order government (led by Indonesia's second president, Soeharto), which promoted what Jeremy Wallach has characterized as a "'top-down' culture of timidity, fear, and docility" (Wallach 2005, 17). With the goal of creating and solidifying a unified Indonesian identity across the country's 300-plus ethnic and language groups, the Soeharto regime enacted a variety of policies that suppressed public discussion of differences in ethnicity (*suku*), religion (*agama*), race (*ras*), and inter-group relations (*antara-golongan*), referred to with the acronym SARA (Muljadji 2016, 16). Indonesian youth, inspired toward activism through their involvement with global underground scenes, contributed to the eventual downfall of Soeharto's regime (Wallach 2005, 17; Martin-Iverson 2014, 185) and the emergence of a political culture of reformasi (reformation), beginning in 1998, that emphasized democratic reforms and local autonomy.

Deena Weinstein wryly observes that "Mapping metal, especially its active 'underground,' is a messy task at best" (2011, 41), and this maxim holds especially well in Indonesia, where thousands of bands identify themselves as one (or several) of a bewildering array of metal genres and subgenres.[22] But death metal, she asserts, "has the largest contingent of bands and the most extensive global reach" (2011, 41) in the underground scene. Jeremy Wallach speculates that while death metal is more popular in urban areas, the occult overtones of black metal are more appealing to villagers in rural areas (2005, 19).

According to James and Walsh, Bandung is "home to the largest death-metal scene in Asia" (2015, 28), and Bandung's first death metal bands released recordings in the mid-1980s (2015, 38). Clinton and Wallach examined results from "Google Trends" and determined that Indonesians did more searches on the terms "heavy metal" and "death metal" than residents of any other countries (2015, 278–279). They explain: "Indonesia's position is no surprise given the enormity of the Ujung Berung [sic] scene in Bandung, West Java, which is perhaps the largest death metal scene in the world."

Ujungberung is the name of an administrative unit in the furthest eastern part of the city of Bandung, about 10 km from the city center, where some seminal death metal bands, such as Burgerkill and Jasad, formed in the 1990s. These musicians, along with younger musicians eager to make their mark in the death metal scene and throngs of fans, comprised a loose artistic coalition, called the Ujungberung Rebels, to help produce metal festivals as well as provide advice and role models for younger musicians.

James and Walsh report (quoting the death metal musician Man, of the band Jasad) that there were as many as 128 active bands in 2011; Kimung (who, in addition to his karinding activities, was a founding member of leading death metal band Burgerkill) reported 150 bands around the same time period (Kimung 2011a, 12). James and Walsh independently verified

100 *Roots Values*

at least 61 bands on the Indonesia page of metal-archives.com (2015, 29); my own more recent check on metal-archives.com suggests that of the 186 metal bands based in Bandung, 106 included some form of "death metal" as their genre.[23]

Although the various underground subgenres share much cultural context, according to James and Walsh, the death metal scene "exists side by side with the largely separate black-metal, punk, and hardcore scenes in Bandung, each of which has its own specific discourses, dress, leaders, heroes, culture, and boundaries" (James and Walsh 2015, 31). In general, these underground scenes, according to Sean Martin-Iverson, are outward-facing, based in part on "mediated connections of exchange that form the global DIY hardcore network" (Martin-Iverson 2014, 188; see also Wallach 2005, 19), and being Sundanese is not "especially salient for DIY hardcore activities" (Martin-Iverson 2014, 188).

The Bandung death metal scene is exceptional in this regard, however, in its promotion of specifically Sundanese symbols and values. In 2006, the musicians established a sort of quasi-institutional infrastructure, called Bandung Death Metal Sindikat (BDMS). BDMS, since its inception, has advocated the inclusion of Sundanese elements—clothing, performance genres, and social values—in metal music (Kimung 2011a, 12; Daryana n.d., 4). A number of death metal musicians told me that the Brazilian metal band, Sepultura—especially their 1996 album *Roots*, which prominently features Latin rhythms and percussion instruments as well as melodic nods to Brazilian indigenous musics—served as an inspiration for their own embrace and promotion of local Sundanese materials (see also Daryana n.d., 6). Embracing Sundaneseness was likely enabled by reformasi's easing of New Order policies on local languages and cultures, which were "largely undermined during Suharto's Java-centric New Order regime" (Lippit 2016, 17).

According to Kimung, the first inclusion of Sundanese traditional performance in a death-metal show was at Death Fest II in 2007 (Kimung 2011a, 13), which featured a performances of penca silat (Sundanese martial arts accompanied by music) and *debus* (demonstrations of extraordinary physical endurance) by Gerakan Pemuda Sunda Pajajaran (GPSP, "Pajajaran Sundanese Youth Movement"). GPSP is a group dedicated to restoring traditional Sundanese practices, especially those associated with the *rakyat* (common people), to prominence in modern West Javanese life. GPSP introduced the musicians to some community elders regarded to have deep understandings of old practices. Those associated with BDMS and Ujungberung Rebels tried to learn and participate in a variety of such practices—rituals, slogans, songs, ways of dressing—and to introduce these practices to their young fans as well (Kimung 2011a, 14).

A sobering tragedy, involving the actual deaths of Bandung death metal fans, helped reinforce the Ujungberung Rebels' commitment to Sundanese values and set the stage for a fusion of death metal aesthetics

Roots Values 101

with Sundanese bamboo musical instruments. On February 9, 2008, eleven teenagers suffocated to death at a concert featuring the local metal band Beside at the Asia Afrika Cultural Center (AACC) on Jalan Braga (formerly a Dutch-era cinema called the Majestic) in Bandung. The tragic deaths were apparently the result of overcrowding, poor planning for medical and other emergencies on the part of the organizers, and excessive force from the police who tried to clear the auditorium too quickly (Diliyanto 2008).[24]

This calamity, which came to be known as *Tragedi AACC* ("AACC Tragedy") and *Sabtu Kelabu* ("Gray Saturday"), had some immediate repercussions. The underground community was demoralized on many fronts. And it became extremely difficult to obtain permits for metal shows in Bandung (Pramudya 2018), forcing bands to perform elsewhere—in nearby Cimahi, for example, or abroad. There also were long-term effects, some of them positive. The underground community united to provide better security and more detailed emergency plans for their events, and to present clear-headed opposition to restrictions placed on them by the government and the police. A decade later, relations between the city and the underground community are not necessarily smooth, but at least the underground is acknowledged by all as an important part of Bandung's creative scene (Pramudya 2018).

Bandung's underground musicians were horrified that their performance practices could lead to such senseless deaths, and determined that uncritical adoptions of global metal aesthetics, including its violent overtones, may have contributed to this very un-Sundanese tragedy. Some musicians were eager to forge new musical directions that aligned more closely with their own local Sundanese values and exigencies, even as they continued to identify with global metal movements.

It was through their connections with Sundanese community elders that two Ujungberung Rebels musicians, Ki Amenk and Man, first encountered karinding, and were intrigued by its anachronistic and sublimely local qualities. Their enthusiasm for the instrument infected many others in the community, and soon a whole cadre of karinding players emerged. One of the Sundanese elders, Mang Engkus, also introduced them to Abah Olot (a.k.a. Endang Sugriwa), who was reviving the art of making *karinding* and other bamboo implements (Kimung 2010) and maintained a workshop/studio in the small community of Cimanggung (about 20 km east of Ujungberung) in 2004 (Devi S. 2019).

Abah Olot's family had made and played karinding for at least four generations. Olot learned to make them as a boy from his father, but he turned to crafting furniture as an adult to make a living. According to a 2010 article, Olot heard somebody say that the karinding was extinct and decided that it was his responsibility to return home and ensure that his family's legacy of karinding was preserved (Kustiasih 2010).

The budding death metal karinding players performed for a soft launch party in late 2008, with the reinforcement of Abah Olot's own bamboo

102   *Roots Values*

musical group (known as Giri Kerenceng); this appearance was billed (in English) as "Karinding Attack" (Kimung 2011a, 16). The musicians invited Abah Olot to teach at Common Room, a center for alternative arts activities in Bandung, where Ujungberung Rebels musicians sometimes rehearsed and socialized (Kimung 2011a, 17). Abah Olot left a variety of bamboo instruments at Common Room, where the musicians had ample opportunity to experiment with them (pc, Kimung, August 19, 2013). Abah Olot was pleased to watch as his karinding, which young people in his own community were not particularly eager to learn, became increasingly popular in Bandung's large underground scene due to his association with Common Room.

A few core musicians played karinding in a variety of situations, including TV interviews, acoustic shows, and electronic/DJ events. To commemorate the one-year anniversary of the Tragedi AACC, these core musicians mounted a twenty-minute *papalidan* (trance ritual), in which they played karinding together with the goal of reaching a trance state to create a mood of remembrance before the other performances began to honor the victims and their families (Kimung 2011a, 19). These performances, along with intensive practice sessions at Common Room, established what Kimung calls the "embryo" of a group of musicians seriously pursuing bamboo music.[25] By the end of February, 2009, the group appeared for the first time officially under the name Karinding Attack.[26]

Karinding Attack

Death metal is characterized musically by growled, guttural vocals (or "death grunts"); aggressive drumming, featuring patterns characterized by rapid sixteenth-note patterns divided between snare drum, bass drum, high-hat, and crash cymbal (called "blast beats"); guitars with strings tuned to pitches that are lower than the standard tunings ("downtuned"); and a lyrical focus on gore (Bell 2011, 277). For the most part, Bandung death-metal musical style is consistent with these global norms, with the possible addition of vocal styles adapted from the singing and narration of *dalang* (puppet masters; Daryana n.d., 5). Furthermore, Bandung death metal bands tend to wear clothes that hark back to Sundanese roots, especially *iket* (head cloths; see Daryana n.d., 5), promoting a new (or renewed) appreciation and regard for local values and wisdom (see Abdullah 2014, 13). In contrast to most global metal fans' predilections toward radical politics, James and Walsh suggest that Bandung's death metal scenes are "only marginally less socially conservative than Indonesian society as a whole" (James and Walsh 2015, 33). Bandung groups are less likely to present critiques of organized religion, in accord with West Java's almost universal embrace of Islam, but more likely to promote resistance to oppression and political corruption (James and Walsh 2015, 30).

"Refuse/Resist"

An examination of how Karinding Attack musicians cover the death metal anthem, "Refuse/Resist," by the Brazilian band Sepultura, provides insight into their translation of death metal idioms into bamboo instruments. Although Sepultura, led by guitarist Max Cavalera, included some nods to Brazilian percussion in "Refuse/Resist" (Harris 2000, 20), the song is rather conventional. The bass and guitar are downtuned so that their lowest pitches are d1 and d2 (rather than e1 and e2), respectively. The original, released in 1993 on the Roadrunner label, features a standard metal instrumentation (two electric guitars, bass, drums), a typical death metal form with several sections, each characterized by a specific "riff" (short melodic guitar/bass motif), and lyrics that describe the devolution of the world into violent, destructive chaos, which listeners are enjoined to "refuse, resist."[27]

The song opens with six seconds of a recording of a human heartbeat,[28] then the music proceeds as summarized in Figure 4.7.

Each riff section features the guitarists and bassist performing idiomatic versions of the riff, while the drummer provides rapid-fire blast beats. Arguably the most characteristic riff in the song is the one labelled "instruA" in Figure 4.7, which assaults listeners with a syncopated repeated melodic tritone interval that evokes the sound of an emergency siren. The lyrics (in the verse and chorus)[29] are delivered with a growled "death metal" voice, mostly on the pitch Gb (sometimes D).

I have seen Karinding Attack perform their cover version of "Refuse/ Resist" on several occasions.[30] Figure 4.8 summarizes how their cover version televised on April 26, 2012, adapts each section (riff) of the piece.

Their live version at Padepokan Seni (in South Bandung) on May 31, 2013, was mostly the same, but it also featured three performers on *berimbau* (Brazilian musical bows associated with capoeira), invited from a local capoeira group, to add a little Brazilian color as well. The performance also featured an outsider metal vocalist, who was brought in to provide appropriately growled vocals because their founding vocalist, Man (of the death metal band Jasad) wasn't available (for reasons to be discussed shortly).

Karinding Attack's music demonstrates how death metal's primary characteristics are reproducible on bamboo instruments. The low-pitched, buzzy fundamentals of Sundanese karinding capture the distorted sounds of detuned electric guitar and bass strings, which are enhanced in Karinding Attack's cover by the weird droning of various types of blown gongs.[31] The taleot's strident double-reed sound stands in for an effects-laden electric guitar. The varied percussive sounds of celempung and celempung renteng (see Chapter 3) stand in for both the standard metal blast beats, as well as the local color of Brazilian (or other "ethnic") percussion. The versatile suling (along with more obscure Sundanese wind instruments) can stand in for the flights of fancy in which electric guitar players sometime indulge.

104 *Roots Values*

Timing (min:sec)	Length of Riff	Label and Riff	Reps	Comments
0:00	n/a	heartbeat	n/a	Sound of a human (fetal) heartbeat
0:06	1 m	INTRO 	4	4/4, mm = ♩~120; each measure is a call and response between bass/drums (first two beats) and other percussion (*samba bateria* instruments; second two beats)
0:15	1 m	INTRO A 	8	After 4 mm, guitar joins bass in tritone riff two octaves higher
0:31	4 mm	INTRO B 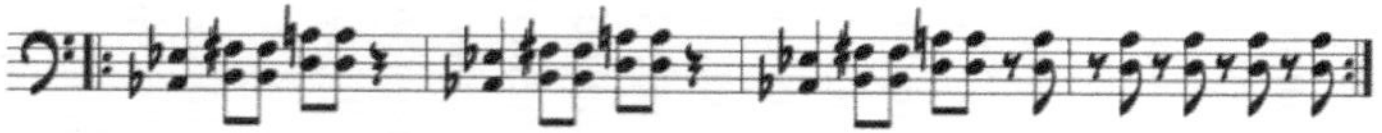	2	two-note "power chords"
0:47	1 m	VERSE 	8	Lyrics delivered in a growling style on the pitch Gb
1:04	1 m	INTRO A	4	
1:12	1 m	VERSE	8	Lyrics delivered in a growling style on the pitch Gb
1:28	7 mm	CHORUS 	1	
1:43	2 mm	SOLO A 	2	4/4 mm = ♩~160; rhythm guitar only (first repetition); bass and drums join (second repetition)
1:49	1 mm	SOLO B 	8	free solo guitar

Figure 4.7 Formal and riff analysis for "Refuse/Resist" (Sepultura).

2:01	1 m	SOLO A		4	free solo guitar continues
2:12	1 m	INSTR A		4	Back to original tempo (mm=120)
2:20	1 m	VERSE		8	Lyrics delivered in a growling style on the pitch D, then Gb
2:37	7 mm	CHORUS		1	Lyrics delivered in a growling style on the pitch Gb
2:52	1 m	INSTR A		8	Final syllable of "resist" sustained for the entire section; guitar joins bass in tritone riff two octaves higher for second 4 mm.
3:08	1 m	OUTRO 		5	Same as intro, w/ a triplet variation; fifth repetition includes only the first 5 notes

Figure 4.7 Continued

Label and Riff	Sepultura Version	Karinding Attack Version
heartbeat	Sound of a human (fetal) heartbeat	Solo suling, playing an *arang-arangan* (soaring, free-rhythm solo) in the sorog mode. It is then joined by low notes on the blown gong.
INTRO 	4/4, mm = ♩ ~120; each measure is a call and response between bass/drums (first two beats) and other percussion (*samba bateria* instruments; second two beats)	Call and response between two karinding (imitating the bass part), doubled by the blown gong, answered by the celempung renteng (imitating the bateria part).
RIFF A 	After 4 mm, guitar joins bass in tritone riff two octaves higher	The two karinding imitate the rhythm of the motif as well as the buzzy timbre of the detuned guitar and bass; they use a modified "tonggeret" pirigan technique, which involves breathing in and breathing out to create two distinct karinding pitches, which recall Sepultura's tritones. A taleot (folk double-reed shawm) joins to play the guitar part that doubles the bass at a higher pitch. The two celempung and the celempung renteng take on the drum part.
RIFF B 	two-note "power chords"	Karinding and blown gong imitate the riff's rhythm, without matching the pitch contour.

Figure 4.8 Formal and riff analysis for "Refuse/Resist" (Karinding Attack).

Roots Values 107

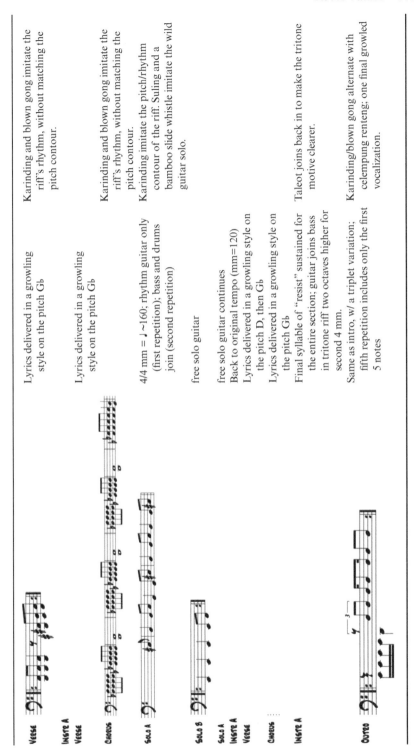

Figure 4.8 Continued

108 *Roots Values*

And while not every singer is capable of delivering death metal's ominous growl, a number of local Bandung musicians have cultivated the skill—enough so that an ensemble of simple, traditional bamboo instruments can mount compelling—if relatively quiet—renditions of death metal music.

It is important to stress that Karinding Attack is not a cover band; I discussed their version of "Refuse/Resist" as a pragmatic way to introduce their adaptations of metal aesthetics. Most of their material is original and exhibits uniquely Sundanese sensibilities in terms of both content and style. They released a CD in 2012, titled *Gerbang Kerajaan Serigala* ("Gate of the Wolf Kingdom"), which featured two tracks that were performed in their various appearances that I witnessed in 2013.

"Lapar Ma"

Formally, "Lapar Ma" ("I'm hungry, Mother") is similar to "Refuse/ Resist." It opens with four repetitions of a one-measure riff consisting of a call from the vocals ("Lapar, Ma!") with a strident eighth-note response from the other instruments (karinding, celempung, celempung renteng), followed by several repetitions of a two-measure phrase that features a two-note ostinato decorated with lead guitar-like licks performed on a suling. Each strophe of rapid-fire lyrics, in the Sundanese language, delivered in a growling death-metal voice, relate the gruesome details of a state of constant hunger, answered by a refrain of "Lapar" ("hungry"). Kimung explained that Karinding Attack prefers to use Sundanese and Indonesian lyrics in most of their songs because many of their listeners are not proficient in English (pc, Kimung, August 19, 2013).

Like many metal songs, the second section of the song involves a rhythm change; in this case, the ostinato accompaniment becomes much slower, while the singer (still growling) describes all sorts of local Sundanese delicacies, some in delicious detail, some in language verging on the repulsive. Various 2012 performances accompanied this section of the song with projected video backgrounds of food preparation ... and open-mouth mastication. A third section (with another distinct rhythmic feel, enhanced with squeaky sounds from toy bamboo instruments) ironically evokes a popular song about street food, "Colenak," composed by Nano S. (and recorded by countless Sundanese pop singers).[32]

The first section, with its urgent tempo and lyrics that complain about constant hunger, contrasts with the lugubrious second section, with lyrics that paint a phantasmagorical portrait of gluttony, to paint a realistic portrait of the emotional state of poverty-induced hunger. Overall, it is an effective social protest against the inequalities of modern food politics.

"Maaf"

But is "Lapar Ma" about radical politics, or rather about ardent resistance to oppression and political corruption, in the terms with which James

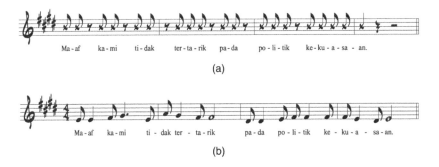

Figure 4.9 "Maaf" motifs: a. Rhythmic motif for second section of "Maaf." b. Melody for third section of "Maaf."

and Walsh characterize global death metal music (2015, 30)? Another Karinding Attack song, "Maaf" ("Excuse me" or "Sorry"), addresses the group's attitude toward politics more directly. Musically, it shares many of the formal and stylistic features of "Refuse/Resist" and "Lapar Ma."[33] It opens with a medium-speed ostinato, accompanied with blast beats on the karinding and celempung, to accompany a series of paired couplets that equivocate between the two sides to every issue: "this group, that group"; "this approach, that approach"; "this party, that party." The next section contrasts the blast beats of the first section with a rhythmic motif aligned to the speech rhythm of the song's quintessential trope: "maaf, kami tidak tertarik pada politik kekuasaan" ("sorry, we are not interested in the politics of power"; see Figure 4.9a).

Then a third section deploys the slogan, this time with a regularized duple rhythm, along with a catchy tune (which the audience can sing and/ or clap along to; see Figure 4.9b) that serves as an ostinato to accompany speech-rhythm, possibly improvised, verbal reflections on the state of modern Indonesian politics.

Kimung explained to me that Karinding Attack musicians are assertive about staying out of formal politics. He claimed that candidates for political office in Bandung sought the band's endorsement on many occasions, in response to the band's popularity and their influence over an active cohort of young people. But the group made a self-conscious effort to remain neutral. This desire to stay out of politics was the genesis of "Maaf," Kimung explained (pc, Kimung, August 19, 2013).

When I first encountered Karinding Attack in 2012, it was Man (Jasad), a popular and charismatic singer and tireless advocate for young people, who introduced me to the band. He was one of the first among the Bandung metal community to embrace karinding and was influential in making the instrument popular among Bandung youth. So, I was surprised, when I returned to Bandung in 2013, that Man was not involved in most of Karinding Attack's activities and did not participate in any of

110   *Roots Values*

their live performances. Kimung explained that Man was curtailing his involvement with Karinding Attack in 2013 precisely because he had made the decision to be involved in local electoral politics—that is, precisely the politik kekuasaan (politics of power) that Karinding Attack repudiates in the song.[34]

Karinding Attack may be uninterested in "the politics of power," but they are definitely committed to shaping the political and ethical inclinations of the next generation. Besides the social messages of their songs, they accomplish this goal through outreach to youth communities, including the ongoing *kelas karinding* ("karinding class," with the acronym KEKAR), a free karinding course for interested students, taught by members of Karinding Attack, at Common Room.[35]

The official curriculum strives to ground three traditional Sundanese values, expressed by the three words, *yakin*, *sadar*, *sabar* ("confident, conscious, patient"), in the individual and communal practice of karinding music. These philosophical lessons are mapped onto the three physical parts of the karinding (as introduced earlier in this chapter). Confidence is instilled in teaching students how to hold the instrument using the *pacepengan* ("that which is held"), which demonstrates to students their potential to succeed. Patience is invoked in learning, slowly, by trial and error, how to hit the *paneunggeulan* ("that which is beaten") to make the *cecet ucing* ("cat's tail"; tongue/lamella) vibrate to make the karinding sing. Consciousness emerges when the students realize that the sounds they create are not their own—rather, they're the karinding's—but that the student has a crucial role in controlling and shaping the sound, teaching the value of awareness of and respect for others (pc, Kimung, April 24, 2013; Kimung 2016).

The KEKAR teachers generously allowed me to participate in the class on a number of occasions in 2013. The other boys welcomed me as a fellow traveler (despite my being well beyond anything resembling "boyhood"). In my first class, I was taught first how to get the karinding's lamella to vibrate—to produce the basic sound, which my teacher called "tong." The next step involved breathing in while producing the tong sound, which raises the tong's pitch. The third sound is breathing out while striking the karinding, which creates the sensation of a falling pitch. These three sounds, I learned, are the basic components of the pirigan called tonggeret. In subsequent classes, the advanced students were paired off: one student provided the basic accompaniment pattern (i.e., pirigan tonggeret), while the other student improvised melodies by emphasizing the 3rd to 7th harmonics of their karinding.

While my fellow students were learning to improvise, however, I was singled out, in subsequent lessons, to refine my basic technique. Doing it correctly, my teacher told me, requires patience and relaxation. He suggested specific technical modifications—forming my lips and mouth into a sort of "o" shape; breathing in and then out normally, as if running;

not changing the shape of my mouth. If I was successful in practicing these modifications, he assured me, there would be a positive effect on my brain.

Thus, in my experience, the course imparted these the values of yakin, sadar, sabar ("confident, conscious, patient") indirectly—by focusing on the mundane details of karinding technique. My KEKAR teachers relentlessly insisted that I master the basics of karinding technique; but they also found ways to relate basic technique to philosophical values even to an inflexible student such as me. The lesson I learned—that playing the karinding is much more difficult than it appears on the surface—indeed contributes to instilling the more general philosophical significance of karinding (confidence, patience, and consciousness) in those who take the time to learn it.[36]

Conclusion: Approaches to Karinding

Hinhin Agung Daryana views karinding as a container of "local wisdom" that can impart Sundanese values to new generations (Daryana 2017, 353). In Indonesia's reformasi period (the first two decades of the twenty-first century), performers such as the musicians in Karinding Attack grafted those values onto global popular music. They took advantage of coincidental surface similarities, including the karinding sound's similarity to distorted, detuned guitars and the celempung's capacity to produce blastbeat-like percussion parts, to fuse Sundanese values with an already popular youth movement, as distilled in international death metal. Death metal challenges its fans to consider the dark sides of big issues—the excesses of government control, global capitalism, and the repression of marginalized peoples—through often grotesque imagery of death, mutilation, and the supernatural. Although earlier generations of Indonesian had much too much personal familiarity with such evils—cruel Dutch colonial policies, the excesses of the native aristocracy, the revolution, Sukarno's Old Order, and especially Soeharto's brutal, dictatorial New Order—Indonesia's record in such matters improved markedly during reformasi. The literal enactment of death and mutilation at the 2008 Tragedi AACC, where some young Sundanese metal fans were trampled to death at a concert, served as a wakeup call—a reminder that Sundanese tradition offered a kinder, gentler approach to life and human relationships.

Turning to bamboo as an instrument to reinforce local values was an almost overdetermined move. As I mentioned at the outset of this chapter, the revival of karinding literally *and* metaphorically honors the proverb, "kudu kawas awi jeung gawirna (we should be like bamboo on its cliff)." A Karinding Attack T-shirt captures the turn with the slogan, "Happy bamboo not heavy metal" (paired with an appropriately macabre death metal image).

My interactions with Karinding Attack musicians and their young fans had a similar vibe—rhetorically and sartorially they often expressed the

112 *Roots Values*

gruesome lyrical and musical gestures of death metal music. Nevertheless, I came away with warm memories of genuine sweetness, both to me (as an improbable interloper into their scene), and especially to one another. While the musicians of Karinding Attack look ferocious on stage (whether they are playing loud electric music in the death metal bands or karinding and celempung with Karinding Attack), they are caring, even affectionate with their young followers.

Karinding Attack provides a model for a new kind of ensemble, which typically consists of three to eight teenagers playing karinding and celempung and singing. Such groups form in schools (sometimes as an official extracurricular activity) and in neighborhoods. The members compose songs about matters that concern them, accompanying themselves with bamboo musical instruments. They often share their work on social media.

Such groups deploy the qualities—namely yakin, sadar, sabar ("confident, conscious, patient")—that the individual musicians have embodied by studying the lore of karinding and its kindred bamboo musical instruments, to meet the modern world head-on with an unapologetically Sundanese expressive vocabulary.

Notes

1 Today's Jl. Asia-Afrika, Jl. Sudirman, and Jl. A. Yani are the route of the Postweg (Roelcke and Crabb 1994, 23).
2 See http://selancar68.blogspot.com/2010/12/cerita-sumur-bandung.html
3 See https://en.wikipedia.org/wiki/Sundanese_script
4 I prefer to avoid the misleading term "harp," which rules out "jaw harp" and "jaw's harp"; and, unfortunately, the excellent word "trump" has recently acquired undesirable connotations. There is no obvious connection between the instrument and Jewish people or Jewish music; the term may have resulted from a mispronunciation of the Northumberland term *gewgaw* (Wright 2001). Hornbostel and Sachs note that such instruments' names are often misleading: they run through a list of guimbarde names in various European countries to demonstrate that the same basic instrument is mischaracterized as a drum, a harp, a fiddle, and a trumpet:

> the German *Maultrommel* is not a drum, nor the English Jew's (properly jaw's) harp a harp, nor the Swedish *mungiga* a *Geige* [fiddle], nor the Flemish *tromp* a trumpet; only the Russians are correct when they call this same instrument, a plucked lamella, by the uncommitted term *vargan* (from Greek όργανο, "instrument").
>
> (Hornbostel and Sachs 1961, 5)

Indeed, Hornbostel and Sachs cite confusion over what to call guimbardes as an exemplar of why the world needed their "objective" classification system in the first place. In an ironic twist on the origins of the term "jew's harp" as a mispronunciation, some Indonesian writers have coined and used an entirely new English-language term, "Zeus harp," which they claim is related to the Greek deity of the same name. Armand Riyadi (2011, 1) cites a 2006 publication by Ridwan Hutagalung that mentions "zeusharp" (*Features of World*

Music. Mustika: Bandung, p. 52); I have not been able to locate the Hutagalung publication to confirm, but that may be the first such reference. Other writers, especially bloggers, have adopted the term in the meantime. I speculate that "Zeus harp" is itself a mishearing/mispronunction of "jew's harp." At least one source specifies that a Zeus harp is made from iron or steel (as opposed to bamboo or palm wood; Herlinawati 2009, 101).

5 "een soort dwarsfluitje, dat gemaakt wordt van een tak van den kawoeng."

6 The Nazaruddin Ashar poem is available at https://kilangbara.wordpress.com/2016/10/14/karinding-ti-citamiang/

7 Palm leaf manuscripts in Old Sundanese only occasionally can be reliably dated. The philosophy and values in this particular poem suggest it is part of what some scholars call West Java's "mandala period," approximately the fourteenth to the sixteenth centuries, before the common adoption of Islam in West Java, in which such didactic works were frequently written in spiritual hermitages (Siswantara 2015; Paulus et al. 2018; Lyra, Indira, and Muhtadin 2019, 62).

8 In this verse, the prophet Jeremiah laments Moab's desolations with mentions of musical instruments: in Sundanese, "'Sabab kitoe hate kaoela, ngalengis koe hal Moab, saperti soeling; djeung angen kaoela ngalengis koe hal oerang Kir-Heres, saperti karinding ....'" In English, "Therefore My heart wails for Moab like flutes; My heart also wails like flutes for the men of Kir-heres" (*New American Standard Bible*). It's worth noting that Coolsma defined karinding as a "kind of whistle" in his 1883 Sundanese-English dictionary, which helps justify his usage of the term in this particular translation (Coolsma 1884, 152).

9 Asep Nata posted images of the April 19, 2011, edition of a newsletter, *Pelangi Santa Angela*, from the Santa Angela school in Bandung (www.santa-angela.sch.id), on his blog (http://karindingtowel.blogspot.com/2011/08/karinding-towel-berpengaruh-terhadap.html), which reported their science fair win.

10 Heins identifies the tune on the recording as "Tjiung Kumahkar."

11 Green beans, referenced in a common angklung song.

12 "1. Toetndang (toet = boentoet = achterlijf van een spin; ndang = web. Dus: als een spinneweb; melodie zonder eind). 2. Boentjis. 3. Loetoeng loentjat (= springende aap) 4. Tonggeret (de naam van het wel bekende, luidruchtige insect). 5. Djipang (welkomstlied) 6 Djemplang (met dit woord, van onbekende afleiding, wordt ook een der renteng-tonen anngeduid). 7. Oetaeio (= kronkelingen) 8. Doger (naam van een instrument-combinatie uit het gebied van Tasikmalaja) 9. Keupat eunang (= het slingeren der armen eener vrouw bij het loopen). 10 Lempaj (= langgerekt, slank) 11. Panodjo (= stuiter)"

13 "is echter het verschil tusschen de melodieën niet steeds even opvallend."

14 E.g., Oktavia and Kusmawardi 2013, 5.

15 There is a youtube video of Abah Olot demonstrating the four pirigan, as well as providing explanations (in Sundanese, with Indonesian subtitles) at www.youtube.com/watch?v=RMnMjZ-r2q8.

16 "Dan mungkin rekaman ini bisa menjawab para musisi karinding hari ini yang terus mencari bagaimana pola permainan karinding yang buhun itu: ternyata jauh lebih bebas dari apa yang kita mainkan hari ini" (Facebook post, October 19, 2013, www.facebook.com/111411779491/photos/a.116337494491.102467.111411779491/10151817064449492)

17 Indrawati mentions the following songs: "Nanyaan," "Angklung," "Dengkleung," "Leang-leang," "Lagu Mega Pudar / Bulan Surup," and "Jungjae." These are, for the most part, familiar folk or children's songs. Her

114   *Roots Values*

notation for these songs appears to represent the vocal melodies, and the fact that she includes lyrics for some of the songs suggests she is notation vocal melodies, not karinding accompaniment patterns.

18 According to Abah Olot, karinding remained popular in the 1960s to 1970s in some communities, and "almost every house had karinding (Hampir setiap rumah mempunyai karinding)," but public interest diminished in the 1980s, when "modern musical instruments began to dominate (karena alat musik modern mulai mendominasi)" (Oktavia and Kusmawardi 2013, 4).

19 www.youtube.com/watch?v=1Ydinw9gpnM, the karinding is most audible during the track's first ten seconds. The song also features the venerable Waldjinah, one of Indonesia's most popular singers.

20 According to Deep Purple bassist, Glenn Hughes, in an interview recorded in 2010 ("Deep Purple Mark IV Indonesian Tour—Highlights from Jakarta 1975," www.youtube.com/watch?v=KwYP8U3kpss, at 0:46)

21 A poster for the concerts posted at https://thericecookershop.com/deep-purple-live-jakarta-1975/ provides dates and prices, and lists locations in each city where tickets could be purchased.

22 On November 1, 2019, there were 1,769 entries for bands from Indonesia on *Encyclopaedia Metallum*, a crowd-sourced database of heavy metal bands at the website metal-archives.com. The site maintains strict guidelines about what qualifies (and doesn't qualify) as "heavy metal."

23 I consulted metal-archives.com on November 1, 2019. Unlike James and Walsh, I did not consider bands from nearby cities such as Soreang and Cimahi. I do not know if my higher count indicates that there are more bands now, or simply more bands with the time, ambition, and access to the internet required to maintain listings on the site.

24 Three concert promoters were eventually convicted of negligent homicide; two were sentenced to ten months in prison, one to three years (anon. 2008).

25 At first, the community included Mang Engkus, Mang Utun, Ki Amenk, Man Jasad, Kimung, Okid, Wisnu, Hendra, Iman Zimbot, Gustaff, Ranti Gustavo, Kimo, Ari, Kiki, Diki, and others (Hakim 2012, 4).

26 Karinding Attack personnel were Mang Engkus, Mang Utun, Ki Amenk, Man Jasad, Kimung, Okid, Wisnu, Hendra, Iman Zimbot (Hakim 2012, 4). Only one member, Imam Zimbot (sometimes spelled Jimbot [official name is Iman Rochman]) has a background in traditional Sundanese music; he comes from a musical family, and studied traditional music at Universitas Padjadjaran (Lippit 2016, 77).

27 The official video, available at www.youtube.com/watch?v=6ODNxy3YOPU, features images of military actions in city streets, met with violent resistance.

28 Sepultura lore identifies the heartbeat as that of Max Cavalera's (then) unborn son.

29 available at https://genius.com/Sepultura-refuse-resist-lyrics,

30 Karinding Attack's appearance on TV One Indonesia (April 26, 2012) included a performance of "Refuse/Resist," available on YouTube: www.youtube.com/watch?v=pk6CslefTl0.

31 The performers assert that these dijeridu-like instruments have Sundanese precedents.

32 A 2016 recording of "Lapar Ma," featuring Man as the lead singer, is available at www.youtube.com/watch?v=1_hG0DhljGY. An earlier version (also

with Man) is available at www.youtube.com/watch?v=bxgNl_2XPZ8 (starting at 3:16). Videos from a 2012 concert (www.youtube.com/watch?v=moW3KT0c ct0 and www.youtube.com/watch?v=RpU9XvOWoWA) feature evocative videos in the background of food preparation ... and chewing. A version of Nano S.'s "Colenak," performed by Een Rataningsih, is available at www.yout ube.com/watch?v=oz-M88lOhKA.

33 www.youtube.com/watch?v=QWwnPEH3DZE (Mar 17, 2012). www.youtube. com/watch?v=2yj-YSzkB3k (Apr 23, 2011).

34 Man did participate in a Karinding Attack rehearsal that was visited by the local press during my fieldwork, validating Kimung's claim that there was no "falling out." Man has participated in some of Karinding Attack's performances in recent years as well.

35 Art Etsa Logam 2013 suggests that the course is also available in other venues, including schools, as well.

36 For more information on the kelas karinding at Common Room, see Daryana 2017 (358); Art Etsa Logam 2013; Oktavia and Kusmawardi 2013.

5 Entanglements

Tamiang meulit ka bitis
"entangled in one's own *tamiang* bamboo"
("hoist with his own petard")

Tamiang meulit ka bitis is a Sundanese proverb that means literally "*tamiang* (a variety of bamboo) twists around the leg." It is understood figuratively as "entangled in one's own tamiang," in the sense of Shakespeare's "hoist with his own petard," that is, "affected negatively (and ironically) by one's own attack."[1] More generally, it gestures toward the poetic justice that often is inherent in such backfires.

The proverb coincidentally echoes the title of the archaeologist Ian Hodder's 2012 book, *Entangled,* in which he aims to "look at the relationships between humans and things from the point of view of things" (2012, 10). "Entanglement as a term aims to allow a materialism but embedded within the social, the historical, the contingent" (Hodder 2012, 96).

Musical Entanglement

Consider the proverbial tamiang (*Schizostachyum blumei*), which is a bamboo variety with thin walls, narrow diameter (ranging from 10–20 cm), and long internodes (30–60 cm) that have little variation in diameter. These qualities would seem to make tamiang ideal as a raw material for applications such as suling (bamboo flutes) and fishing poles (Fern n.d.).

Taking Hodder up on his suggestion to start from the point of view of things could reverse this approach and regard tamiang's physical properties as generative rather than reactive. Hodder identifies "affordance, abstraction and resonance as different dimensions of entanglement" (2012, 137). Tamiang's physical qualities are an example of *affordance*; these qualities of tamiang afford certain kinds of outcomes and set up potentials for particular results (Hodder 2012, 49). It is not so much that tamiang is ideally suited for suling, but rather that suling is a technology that makes productive use of tamiang's innate qualities. In other words, perhaps the first Sundanese musicians did not begin by looking for the ideal material with

DOI: 10.4324/9781003302797-6

which to make some preconceived flute, but instead built their musical systems—sounds, textures, and instruments—from the affordances of the materials that were readily available.

These initial affordances inevitably had a systemic effect on Sundanese musical sensibilities—a process Hodder calls *abstraction* (2012, 120). Chapter 1 touched upon the traces of bamboo technology on Sundanese music that are evident in the timbres and textures of modern Sundanese music. These soundmarks, I argued, are abstractions in that they extend these affordances of bamboo into more generalized principles of musical style; in this case, a Sundanese predilection for musical textures that combine fixed-pitch/regular-rhythm accompaniments with lyrical, free-rhythm melodies. This chapter begins with my speculations about bamboo's possible role in the development of another fundamental identifying feature of Sundanese music: the characteristic pentatonic tuning systems, *salendro* and *pelog degung*.[2] I draw upon insights from the early twentieth-century physicist Charles Wead and the Philippine ethnomusicologist José Maceda to argue that these tuning systems ultimately derive from symmetrical patterns of fingerholes in the Sundanese suling.

The most common form of suling is the six-hole *suling panjang* (long suling), made of tamiang bamboo. Wead, writing around the turn of the twentieth century, noted that Sundanese suling fingerholes in particular have a distinct pattern with two groups of three equidistant holes (Wead 1902).

Indeed, present-day Sundanese instrument makers rely on symmetrical measurements to place the holes in a suling and other wind instruments (see Figure 5.1a). I interviewed the Sundanese instrument maker, Mang Akim, about his *taleot* (single-reed bamboo shawm; see Chapter 3). He told me that he measures the circumference of the bamboo with a string, and uses that measurement as the distance between the holes (pc, August 21, 2013). Endang Toto, a suling maker, measures the length of the bamboo tube and places the first fingerhole at the halfway mark. The next two holes are 1/20 of the length away from the previous hole. The large gap between the two groups of three holes is 1/10 of the total length (Suwarna 1999, 31).[3] When I observed Toto make suling in 2018, he used a tape measure to determine the distances between holes, based on the overall measurement of the stock (see Figure 5.1b).

The ethnomusicologist José Maceda theorizes that because the fingerholes for bamboo flutes in many parts of Southeast Asia (including the Sundanese suling panjang) were drilled according to equal measurements made of the bamboo tubes (see Figure 5.2), it follows that the specific pitches of tuning systems are epiphenomena of the physical placement of holes in symmetrical visual patterns, and that they are not derived from acoustical relationships (Maceda 1990). This notion diverges radically from the principles of deriving scales and tunings from string length ratios and acoustic harmonics (and their presumed relationship to cosmic order), which have been the basis for Western (via the ancient Greeks) and Chinese music theory for millennia.

118 *Entanglements*

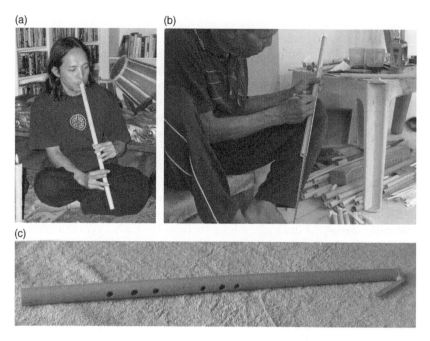

Figure 5.1 Suling. a. Ismet Ruchimat plays suling panjang. b. Mang Toto measures the halfway point to drill the first hole in a suling he's making. c. arrangement of holes on a suling panjang into two groups of three equidistant holes.
Source: photos: Henry Spiller.

The nineteenth-century physicist Hermann von Helmholtz, for example, discounted equidistance as a viable principle for the construction of scales (although it likely did not even occur to him to consider *visual* equidistance). "It might perhaps have seemed most simple to make all such degrees of pitch of equal amount, that is, equally well distinguishable by our sensations" (Helmhotz 1963, 363). He goes on to point out that even though the West uses equal divisions for rhythm, and even though the modern chromatic scale has equal divisions, "… there seems at no time or place to have been a system of music in which melodies constantly moved in equal degrees of pitch, but smaller and larger intervals have always been mixed in the musical scales in a way that must appear entirely arbitrary and irregular until the relationship of compound tones is taken into consideration" (Helmholtz 1863, 363). (By "compound tones" Helmholtz means the composite sound of a musical tone's fundamental and all of its overtones or partials; Helmholtz 1863, 22.)

The genesis of ethnomusicology itself lies in efforts to discern such patterns of overtones in all musical scales. Erich M. von Hornbostel and Jaap Kunst, for example, collaborated on an elaborate "cycle of blown

Entanglements 119

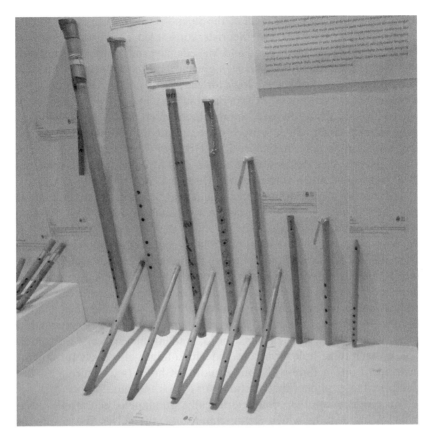

Figure 5.2 A display of bamboo flutes from all over the Indonesian archipelago, most with equidistant fingerholes, on display at the Sri Baduga Museum, Bandung.
Source: photo: Henry Spiller.

fifths" theory to explain the existence of scales throughout the world that did not appear to conform readily to Pythagorean principles of scale generation from string harmonics. Hornbostel and Kunst came up with an alternate system of harmonics/overtones generated, they claimed, by overblowing tubes stopped at one end, which included twenty-two possible pitches. They believed this ur-scale to have originated in ancient China, and that it subsequently spread throughout Asia. Javanese and Sundanese salendro and pelog tone systems were among Hornbostel's and Kunst's examplars in promoting such theories (see Kunst 1948; Kunst 1973, 24–44).

The salendro (spelled *sléndro* in Javanese) tuning is particularly problematic because the precise measurements of its intervals vary considerably in practice. The nineteenth-century phonetician Alexander J. Ellis concluded that "the equal division of the Octave into five pentatones of 240 cents [is] the probably unrecognised ideal of the Salendro tuner" (Ellis 1885, 511).[4]

For the most part, these theorists considered equidistance only as reckoned by the ear. Both Wead and Maceda have independently suggested that it is *visual* symmetry—privileging what the eye sees rather than what the ear hears— that provides a logic for generating pitch systems and scales for Southeast Asian music in general (and Java in particular). Evidently, what Maceda calls a "divisive" approach, in which the octave is divided to determine specific pitches, is much more prevalent in Southeast Asia than the "cyclic" approach, characteristic of Greek or Chinese notions of scales, which derives scale degrees using a cycle of a repeated interval, such as a fifth, transposed into a single octave (Maceda 1990).

Indeed, the two groups of three equidistant holes on the six-hole suling panjang can account for the basic pitch vocabularies of at least two fundamental Sundanese scales. The salendro scale is usually described as an octave divided into five approximately equidistant intervals. Using Alexander Ellis's "cents" metric, which theoretically divides a single octave into 1200 equal intervals (a single one of which is too fine a distinction for human ears to distinguish), each salendro interval is 240 cents (by way of comparison, a tempered major second is 200 cents, while a tempered minor third is 300 cents, so a salendro interval lies just about halfway between two piano keys). When playing in salendro, a suling player keeps the middle hole of each three-hole group covered with a finger, effectively turning the instrument into a flute with four equidistant holes (see Figure 5.3). The audible effect is pitches that are (more or less) equidistant.

To produce another characteristically Sundanese pentatonic scale, called pelog degung, which is non-equidistant, the player first covers the top hole of each group (resulting in a small interval, approximately 80–100 cents), then the remaining two holes at once (resulting in a large interval, approximately 340–360 cents). A third, medium interval (approximately 240 cents—the original salendro interval) completes an octave (see Figure 5.4). This salendro interval lies between the note produced by covering all the holes and overblowing the suling and the note produced by leaving all the holes open.

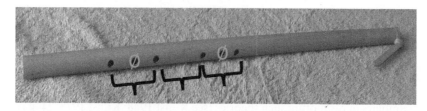

Figure 5.3 Keeping the middle holes of each of a suling's three-hole groups closed to simulate four equidistant holes for salendro.

Source: photo: Henry Spiller.

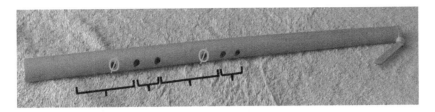

Figure 5.4 Covering suling holes to create pelog degung's small and large intervals.
Source: photo: Henry Spiller.

The musicologist Manfred Bukofzer (who convincingly debunked the theory of blown fifths [Bukofzer 1937]), treats the six-hole suling as evidence that salendro and pelog are related, although he doesn't discuss the equal hole spacing as a factor (n.b. the words "goeloe" [gulu] and "limo" [lima] in Bukofzer's writing refer to Javanese pitch names):

> Fortunately, we know of an instrument of the Gamelan which, in spite of its fixed pitch, is used in both Pelog and Salendro. This is the bamboo recorder, the Soeling, with six finger holes. When the player changes from Pelog to Salendro, he keeps his fingers permanently on the second and fifth finger holes which, open, would give the tones goeloe and limo. In former times, these holes were plugged with wax.
> (Bukofzer 1939, 247)

Although salendro, according to some, tends in theory toward equidistant, 240-cent intervals, there is in practice much latitude in the actual sizes of salendro intervals that are still considered to be "in tune." The same is true for various pelog tunings as well. This variability has long puzzled ethnomusicologists. However, if one considers that the primary determinant of pitches was not how they sounded, but rather how they looked—that the origins of these tunings is visual symmetry, not acoustical coherence—then the tolerance for pitch variability begins to make more sense. José Maceda suggests that such approaches to tuning flutes have a long history in the Philippines and likely other parts of Southeast Asia, and likely predate the development of bronze instruments (Maceda 1979, 165–168; Maceda 1990, 192).

Returning now to Hodder's notions of affordance and abstraction: West Java's two primary contrasting pentatonic pitch systems (salendro and pelog degung) can be interpreted as abstractions of the affordances of bamboo. The persistence of these tunings, even in Sundanese musics that do not use bamboo, exemplify Hodder's third level of entanglement: *resonance*, the "process by which at a non-discursive level coherence occurs across domains in historically specific contexts" (2012, 126). Hodder chooses a musical example—nineteenth-century European romanticism— to

122 *Entanglements*

illustrate the concept. He details the strands of technology (e.g., iron fabrication and precision manufacturing for the piano), politics (e.g., nationalism and "folk" music and ideas of "freedom"), psychology (new attention to the role of emotions), and other "entangled" domains that are prerequisites for any coherent understanding of romanticism in European music (2012, 126–132).

Like nineteenth-century European romantic music, Sundanese traditional musics are entangled across a variety of domains. Sundanese gamelan is rooted in bronze technology, which itself is entangled in a complex web of social and political strands. I would like, however, to suggest that, in order to cohere within pre-existing musical aesthetics, gamelan music perpetuates bamboo-derived tunings and their variability, even though gamelan technology doesn't lend itself to the visual symmetries from which the tunings might derive. Similarly, more recent innovations, such as pop Sunda, gain coherence when bamboo-derived tunings are invoked. Although pop Sunda utilizes global instruments (guitars and keyboards) that are designed to produce European-derived tempered diatonic scales and functional harmony, pop Sunda is characterized by pentatonic scales that are resonant of salendro and pelog degung.

According to Hodder:

> … all things that humans produce …resonate through our bodily interaction with them in the world. They come to 'feel right' in particular contexts. Or else we reject them because they cannot be made to cohere, either through abstraction or bodily resonance. Conscious abstraction and bodily coherence work with affordances to produce a particular way of being entangled, in which humans have bodies of a particular kind and things have forms of particular kinds.
>
> (2012, 132)

Returning to the proverb, "entangled in one's own tamiang": when filtered through Hodder's approach to thinking about things, it lends the air of local wisdom to a Sundanese musical essence that is indeed profoundly "entangled" in the bamboo technology that enabled it.

Matters of Care

Scholars in a variety of fields have, like Hodder, pondered the nature and meaning of "things," including musical instruments, and how they are at once both products *and* producers of human culture. And, again like Hodder, they generally theorize things as "assemblages," building on Deleuze and Guattari's notion of how real-life, agentive systems are complex, involving heterogeneous, flexible components (2004 [1980]; e.g., Latour 2005, Bennet 2010, Stiegler 1998). Some authors further theorize assemblage subcategories of various sorts: "sociotechnical assemblages" (Puig de la Bellacasa 2011), "sociomaterial assemblages," (Clarke and Star

2008, 142), "technoscientific assemblages" (Paxling 2020), even "more-than-human, other-than-human, inhuman, and human-as-humus" assemblages (Haraway 2015). Some musicologists, such as Joshua Tucker and Eliot Bates, have applied these ideas to musical instruments (Tucker 2016; Bates 2012), which I will characterize as "musico-technical assemblages." In general, although all these authors use different vocabulary and metaphors, they all echo Hodder's notion that "things" are produced through complex interactions of the affordances of raw materials, supplemented by abstractions and resonances. They typically also assign some sort of "agency" to things, acknowledging and theorizing their existence independent of human interactions.

According to Maria Puig de la Bellacasa, considerable *care* is required to maintain both technologies *and* the world. Echoing Joan Tronto and Berenice Fisher (Fisher and Tronto 1990, 40; Tronto 1993, 103), Puig de la Bellacasa defines care as "everything that we do to maintain, continue and repair our world" (Puig de la Bellacasa 2011, 3). Puig de la Bellacasa inspires me to consider the different kinds of care that the individuals in this book's various case studies give to the bamboo musico-technical assemblages with which they are allied, and to suggest that they provide care in order to ensure that the assemblages continue to exercise their own particular kind of agency. In short: the humans care, and the assemblages care back. By caring for bamboo musico-technical assemblages—by nurturing them, giving them new life and new contexts—the assemblages (in turn) bestow their coherence onto Sundanese modernity.

In what ways do people actually care about bamboo—what do they have to gain from developing caring relationships with different bamboo assemblages, and what do those assemblages do for their human partners? And how is that care delivered? Each of the three case studies in the preceding chapters considered very different bamboo-based assemblages; each has demonstrated different facets of care, and each represents very different goals and outcomes. All three, in the broadest sense, attempt to reconcile tradition (with bamboo musico-technical assemblages as metonyms of that "tradition") with modernity.

I introduced each chapter of this book with proverbial epigraphs. In this conclusion, I interpret—maybe overinterpret—the various Sundanese proverbs to epitomize the care relationships between people and bamboo—or more specifically, bamboo assemblages, including musical instruments. Care relationships are not always altruistic: Puig de la Casa points out that "neoliberal governance has made of caring for *the self* a pervasive order of individualized biopolitical morality" (2011, 9). And, as Martin, Myers, and Viseu have noted, "care is a selective mode of attention: it circumscribes and cherishes some things, lives, or phenomena as its objects. In the process, it excludes others" (Martin et al., 2015: 627). Revisiting the book's case studies, and putting them into dialog with other approaches to caring for bamboo, for angklung, and for karinding, provides an opportunity to examine what is gained—and what is lost—in each care relationship.

124 *Entanglements*

Who Cares About Bamboo?

Pindah Cai, Pindah Tampian—Diatonic Angklung

This old saw implies that a basic structure, with a simple, universal function—a bamboo bathhouse—may be the same physically in different communities, but that each community maintains unique protocols about its use. I argued in Chapter 2 that, like the tampian bathhouse, diatonic angklung ensembles were adapted to represent different interpretations of the enduring Indonesian value of *gotong royong* (mutual cooperation) by colonial, nationalist, non-aligned, communist, and neoliberal forces.

In this case, different parties have come to care about the specific form and sound of a particular musico-technical assemblage—angklung—as well as abstractions and resonances of that assemblage as visible symbols of gotong royong. It should not come as a surprise to anybody, however, that abstractions such as gotong royong—and associated assemblages (angklung)—can be redeployed to promote rather different resonances.

Chapter 2 detailed some ideological battles in which diatonic angklung has served as an avatar for more fraught political clashes, namely communism vs capitalism and Indonesian identity vs Malaysian identity. In this chapter, I dig a little deeper into the implications of including angklung on UNESCO's "Representative List of Intangible Cultural Heritage."

The United Nations Education and Cultural Organization (UNESCO) adopted the Convention for the Safeguarding of the Intangible Cultural Heritage (CSICH) in 2003, which broadly defines "intangible cultural heritage" (ICH) as "practices, representations, expressions, knowledge, skills— as well as the instruments, objects, artefacts and cultural spaces associated therewith—that communities, groups and, in some cases, individuals recognize as part of their cultural heritage" (UNESCO 2020, 5).

The real-world advantages that such a designation provides are debatable. Different localities value UNESCO's imprimatur differently: "in some places a UNESCO designation is seen as a financial boon, in some places it is a point of pride and identity, in some places it is a burden, and elsewhere it is merely an adornment or, for that matter, not even on the radar screen" (Foster 2015, 152). In other words, the "brand" (as Foster calls it) or imprimatur (my word) that UNESCO recognition lends can be highly valued, even if it not necessarily understood. Indeed, regional and local affiliates— often with their own parochial interests—have considerable influence in proposing ICHs for official recognition by UNESCO (see Seeger 2015). In some locales, the whole point of UNESCO's program "has appeared to shift away from this focus [on conserving and preserving natural and cultural heritage] towards one motivated by politics and economics" (Adie 2017, 51).

As a result, as Bendix et al. suggest, "a great deal of UNESCO's agenda is 'lost in translation' or invariably transformed, as heritage conventions enter the level of state governments, … endowing actors at state, regional

Entanglements 125

and local levels with varied levels of power over selective aspects of culture that prior to UNESCO initiatives had rarely seen attention or control on the part of the state" (Bendix et al., 2013, 14).

All these details help contextualize the "public outcry in Indonesia after Malaysia allegedly nominated for inclusion on UNESCO's Representative List of Intangible Cultural Heritage several supposedly Indonesian cultural forms, including batik, wayang, gamelan and angklung" (Clark 2013, 398). Clark also reports, however, that Malaysia never actually applied to UNESCO for batik or angklung, and that "UNESCO has no record of any unsuccessful nominations by Malaysia" (Clark 2013, 407; see also Chong 2012, 31).

Knowing of my research project about bamboo music, a couple who are well-connected in Indonesian government circles, especially when it comes to Indonesian cultural missions to foreign countries, invited me to join them to attend an extravaganza called "Grand Symphony Angklung" in Jakarta. (I will identify them here as Mas and Bu, respectively.) Mas drove us, from Bandung, via the toll road—a three-and-a-half-hour ride through abysmal traffic and blinding, torrential rain—to Theatre XXI, a posh performing arts venue in Jakarta's prestigious central district. I was feeling very special as we picked up our "VIP" invitations … at least until I saw the doors marked "VVIP," and even "VVVIP." No matter, even we lowly VIPs were treated to a sumptuous buffet, which Bu and I enjoyed while Mas parked the car.

Bu introduced me to Taufik Udjo, one of Mang Udjo's sons (see Chapter 2), one of the show's musical directors. As I perused the program, I realized that this event involved the highest echelons of Indonesian society. The event was cosponsored by the "Lembaga Kerjasama Ekonomi Sosial dan Budaya Indonesia-China (LIC— Institute for Indonesia-China Economic and Social Cultural Cooperation) and the "Komunitas Pecinta Angklung" ("Community of Angklung Lovers"). The program emphasized UNESCO's "Inscription of Indonesia [sic] Angklung on the Representative List of the Intangible Cultural Heritage of Humanity" in 2010. The opening message from Prof. Dr. H. Sukamdani Sahid Gitosardjono (of LIC) drew parallels between Indonesia's and China's efforts to preserve traditional culture and celebrated the many goodwill delegations of angklung players to China. Dr. A.M. Hendropriyono (also of LIC), in his message, stressed that character-building is just as important as economic development, and reiterated the theme (by now familiar to readers of this book), that angklung is an excellent way to impart truly Indonesian values.

According to the program, this "Grand Symphony Angklung" was meant to "Present the art of angklung and its appreciation, including traditional, modern, and digital expressions. Play songs from all corners of the world: National Pop Songs, Regional Songs, Western Songs, and Chinese Songs."[5]

Artists on the program included Dwiki Dharmawan, a well-known producer, jazz musician, and film director (along with his orchestra); Nazar

126 *Entanglements*

Wildan, a virtuoso performer on "keyboard" angklung instruments (along the lines of those I described in Chapter 2 as Yayan Udjo's experiments); Dira Sugandhi and Dewi Githa, Indonesian pop singers; Mark Okoth Obama Ndesanjo, an author and pop pianist, based in China, who happens to be the half-brother of former US president Barack Obama; and a couple of wunderkind virtuosi—one Chinese (on the *yanggun* hammered dulcimer) and one Indonesian (on angklung toél).

The program also featured a group called "Touch of Seven," consisting of the wives of prominent Indonesian generals/politicians playing angklung toél.[6] Bu told me that none of the wives have ever played angklung before, but that Taufik Udjo had rehearsed them two times per week in the three months before the concert. Touch of Seven, dressed in matching outfits, played all their music from memory, and gave an impressively competent performance.

The audience (at least a thousand, by my estimate) was greeted with an impressive setting—an orchestra and lots of angklung-based instruments, as well as several large screens. The production featured slick video presentations, along with the live musical performances, featuring performers dressed in a curious combination of formal Indonesian and Western clothing styles: matching *kabaya* (blouses) for women; tuxedos and black bow ties (for men); an *ikat* (patterned woven fabric) vest for the conductor.

In a nod to "traditional" bamboo music, the first live music (after some video introductions) featured hints of rituals: marching angklung, proceeding from the back of the auditorium to the stage, along with related performances (*rengkong* and *lesung*). They were quickly eclipsed, however, by diatonic angklung groups on stage, including the Touch of Seven.

The first major solo act was Mark Okoth Obama Ndesanjo, who greeted the crowd in English. Indonesians in 2013 were quite enamored with US president (2009–2017) Barack Obama, who spent time in Indonesia as a boy while his mother, Ann Dunham, conducted anthropological field research there, and so they welcomed Obama Ndesanjo, who bears a striking physical (and vocal) resemblance to his half-brother, with considerable enthusiasm. He told the crowd he loves Indonesian food and quoted Indonesia's motto—"Bhinneka tunggal ika." "It's true," he says; "there's unity in diversity." Obama Ndesanjo sat at the grand piano and began to play "Es Lilin," an iconic Sundanese song. He was soon joined by suling and kendang, as well as tasteful angklung stylings from Touch of Seven and even a spate of characteristically Sundanese *senggak* (men's interlocking vocal interjections). Obama Ndesanjo's main contributions to the musical texture were dramatic piano glissandos. Eventually a singer (Dewi Gita) joined in as well. The whole number took about ten minutes.

A PowerPoint slide show next told the audience that the Dutch banned angklung in the nineteenth century, relegating it to beggars. The next slide related the story of Daeng Soetigna's diatonic/chromatic angklung innovations (unfortunately a typo pinpoints the date as 1983 instead of

1938), and of Mang Udjo's subsequent angklung innovations, including "angklung tradigi" (i.e., "tradition and digital"). With the stage still in darkness, we heard Dwiki Dharmawan playing a quasi-Debussy phrase on the piano, which was answered by a very bluesy lick on angklung toél. When the lights came up, we saw that a young boy, dressed in a tuxedo, was playing the angklung toél. He was clearly a prodigy, and the audience gave him warm applause. Dwiki interviewed the boy; he was thirteen years old and had been playing angklung toél for five years.

The announcer clarified that although angklung is originally from "tanah Sunda" (the Sundanese homeland), in fact it belongs to all of Indonesia, that it's a tool of gotong royong and of diplomacy, and that is why UNESCO named it intangible cultural heritage. But, the announcer continued, UNESCO will withdraw the designation if Indonesians didn't "maintain angklung" ("perpertahankan keberadaan angklung"); she admonished everybody in the audience to "protect, maintain, promote, and preserve" it ("melindungi, memelihara, mempromosikan dan melestarikan").

Indeed, the UNESCO convention requires "periodic reporting" every six years, although it is not clear what the consequence of a negative report would be (Adie 2017). The Indonesian Ambassador to UNESCO told the news magazine *Kompas* that "within four years if Indonesia could not preserve and develop it, the recognition of the cultural heritage of the object could be revoked" (Pradoko 2013, 33; see also Nugraha 2015, 4).

PowerPoint slides informed us that angklung is becoming globally popular, while the raw materials required to make angklung are increasingly difficult to find. We then watched a video of the women of Touch of Seven doing their part to stave off this ecological disaster by planting bamboo, clad in matching T-shirts.

Meanwhile, on stage, Obama Ndesanjo started to play John Lennon's "Imagine" on the piano, joined by Touch of Seven and others. A singer joined in, changing some of the lyrics ("nothing to kill or die for" becomes "nothing to kill or hunger") but leaving Lennon's atheist paean "and no religion too" unaltered—surprising me in this theist environment.

Next came a teenage Chinese virtuoso, who played tunes that the Chinese audience members recognized on the *yanggun* (hammered dulcimer), accompanied by Touch of Seven and other angklung musicians. The grand finale featured Obama Ndesanjo, various angklung musicians, orchestra and choir, and both the generals Sudrajat and Hendropriyono (on guitar and arumba [a bamboo xylophone], respectively), in a rousing rendition of ABBA's "Chiquitita."

Sudrajat and Hendropriyono invited others (including Hendropriyono's wife, Tati, who is a member of Touch of Seven) on stage to acknowledge their contributions to the event, and they provided some closing thoughts. Hendropriyono asked rhetorically, "why are we here? We are concerned about the situation of angklung. I like the sound—do you? You agree! But it's rarely heard now. Our kids prefer modern music. Angklung is the

128   *Entanglements*

heritage of Indonesia. We must protect and promote it. Angklung should be developed as extracurricular in schools. In Jakarta, kids play angklung to guard their cooperation, discipline, and sense of harmony. The character of angklung is character of Indonesia." Then, foreshadowing the upcoming hands-on portion of the show, he concluded: "We will try angklung together soon."

Then, just as Hendropriyono promised, the event ended with an angklung workshop for the audience, directed by Tete Fitri from Saung Angklung Udjo. A video message from Ibu Mari Elka Pangestu, then the Minister of Tourism and Creative Economy of Indonesia, introduced the workshop. Tete taught hand signs for the different (diatonic) pitches. First, the audience was led through "Frere Jacques"; then "We are the World." Tete informed us that a new record will be broken next month in Beijing, China. Ten thousand people (tourists from around the world), she said, will play "We are the World" on angklung.[7]

When I commented to Bu about how much work and money this show required for a single performance, she commented that it would be simply too expensive to do more than once ... the food, the venue, the guest artists. It's impossible to know whether anybody calculated how much practical support the funds devoted to this one-night blowout might have provided for "protecting, maintaining, promoting, and preserving" the practice of angklung in lieu of this extravaganza.

Grand Symphony Angklung paid ample lip service to the indigenous ideology of gotong royong, and the importance of angklung to Indonesian heritage, but the event stressed more emphatically the values of celebrity, virtuosity, individuality, reinforcing the ideologies of globalism, neoliberal capitalism, and even (in the quest for "world's record" numbers of participants in mass performances) populism. In such contexts, angklung assumes its rightful place as a symbol of ... what, exactly? In fact, in the new order period, it has become a floating signifier, capable of linking to multiple, sometimes contradictory significations.

An event such as "Grand Symphony Angklung" exemplifies Rosemary J. Coombe's analysis that the kind of "heritage regimes" that created the event are neoliberal, and that it reflects a "dominance of market ideologies in heritage management and in its means of 'valuation' with an increasing emphasis on *investment* in cultural resources and human capital so as to yield economic returns, adding value to them" (Coombe 2013, 378).

Returning to Hodding's affordance/abstraction/resonance model of entanglement, and to the various approaches to care: the creative forces behind the "Grand Symphony Angklung" clearly care about employing an abstraction of angklung as a symbol of localized values, but quite effectively dampen any resonance those values might convey as representative of a uniquely Sundanese approach to music and culture. The goal here, rather, is to demonstrate that "tradition" (no matter how tenuously evoked) has both symbolic and economic currency in a globalized, modern, neoliberal world.

Entanglements 129

"Leuleus jeujeur liat tali"—*Galengan Sora Awi*

This proverb suggests that true wisdom is like good fishing gear—it requires both the flexibility of a bamboo fishing rod and the constancy of unbreakable fishing line. In Chapter 3, I recounted how the Dago-based group, Galengan Sora Awi (GSA), mobilizes bamboo's affordances as a flexible sound-producing material to create instruments capable of accompanying a range of modern Sundanese musical expressions, each of which would ordinarily require a specific instrumental ensemble. GSA cares about the abstractions and metaphors of bamboo's deep links in Sundanese history; they deploy them to democratize the contemporary Sundanese music repertory, which blends elements of folk, aristocratic, and global approaches to music. It is the bamboo-ness of their instruments that gives their instruments the credibility to cover all these bases.

The ethnomusicologist and instrument builder, Endo Suanda (b. 1947),[8] also relies on bamboo-ness to achieve a different kind of reconciliation of different genres. Since the mid-2000s, Endo Suanda has experimented with using bamboo in luthiery—the construction of fine (mostly plucked) string instruments. Although he has experimented with a variety of instruments, he focuses most of his efforts on perfecting his techniques for building guitars and *kacapi* (Sundanese zithers) out of laminated bamboo boards.

By any standard, Endo Suanda is a remarkable man. While growing up in a village near Majalengka, he learned various forms of traditional music and dance. He studied music and dance more formally at the Akademi Seni Tari Indonesia (Indonesian Academy of Dance, ASTI), first in Bandung, then in Yogyakarta.[9] He made a splash in the late 1970s as an experimental choreographer at national dance festivals at Taman Ismail Marzuki in Jakarta, and at events elsewhere in Indonesia, and abroad. He studied *topeng Cirebon* (a form of village masked dance from the rural areas around the north coast Javanese city of Cirebon), which became the topic of his master's thesis in ethnomusicology at Wesleyan University (1983). He also pursued doctoral studies at the University of Washington, helped establish an ethnomusicology program at Universitas Sumatera Utara (USU), taught at a variety of educational institutions in Indonesia and abroad, and has worked on a variety of Indonesian educational and cultural initiatives, in part funded by the US-based Ford Foundation.

Full disclosure: I have known Endo Suanda since the late 1980s, and our interests—and paths—have intersected in surprising and serendipitous ways ever since. Still, I was astonished to learn, in 2013, when I contacted him regarding my upcoming trip to investigate bamboo music revivals in Bandung, that he himself had been devoting considerable energy to building musical instruments from bamboo.

Endo Suanda first began to investigate making musical instruments of bamboo as a part of his efforts to reimagine a music education curriculum

130 *Entanglements*

for Indonesian children. As a firm believer in the educational value of doing rather than merely being preached to, he landed on bamboo as an inexpensive, easy-to-work material for children's musical instrument building projects.

During a trip to Portland, OR, Endo Suanda visited Bamboo Revolution,[10] a company dedicated to creating quality building materials from bamboo. He was impressed by the variety of products the firm had developed, as well as the uncompromising quality of these products—they shed their rustic bamboo qualities in favor of sleek, modern looks and feels. He told me that this experience made him a little bit frustrated; Indonesia, he said, is home to more bamboo varieties (not to mention a greater volume of bamboo), and bamboo is a common raw material in many Indonesian artefacts (see Chapter 1), yet Indonesians had fallen far behind American innovators (who must even import most of their raw materials) in creating bamboo products for the modern world.

He researched techniques for laminating wood and digested quite a bit of literature on the acoustics of wooden instruments (especially guitars). He also imported a quantity of glue and a variety of woodworking clamps from the USA and experimented with creating boards by laminating strips of bamboo. He also researched methods for bracing guitar soundboards to achieve the optimum thinness and strength for bamboo. He learned that the favorite wood of guitar makers is spruce, which is valued for musical instruments because—like bamboo—it has a very straight grain. At one point, he settled on using *bitung* (*betung*) bamboo, which has a large diameter; by laminating 5-cm strips together, he produced raw boards from which to fashion his instruments. He established a workshop in Bogor (about 180 km from Bandung). As of this writing (2021), he continues to experiment with technique for selecting bamboo boards and optimizing their resonant qualities.

Endo Suanda had just finished building a prototype bamboo guitar when I arrived in Bandung in late March 2013. I had the opportunity to hear several musicians, representing a variety of musical genres, play the guitar in public concerts. Most of these performers were excited to try out a bamboo guitar because they viewed bamboo as a material that could "localize"—Sundanize—their otherwise global musical expressions. At one of these concerts, Endo Suanda told the audience he focused on building guitars because there were many opportunities to compare the quality of his bamboo guitars to wooden ones (pc, April 10, 2013).

At another concert, a young man sitting next to me commented that the bamboo guitar had a unique, special voice (pc, Andika, May 29, 2013). Endo Suanda later related to me that the artist performing at that concert had requested to borrow the bamboo guitar because it was especially suitable for his acoustic songs—presumably a "bamboo" quality that somehow distinguished it from ordinary wooden guitars.

In 2021, Endo Suanda explained to me that his bamboo guitars tend to resonate high frequencies better than low frequencies—a quality that appeals to both musicians and producers for some (but not all) purposes. He is justifiably proud that popular recording artists, including Iwan Fals and Sony Surendra, along with their producers, have used his guitars for prominent projects. He has made about thirty guitars (including electric guitars and basses) over the past decade.

Endo Suanda also applies his knowledge and skill of guitar luthiery to the construction of kacapi (see Figure 5.5). In West Java, kacapi is a generic term for a wooden boat zither. It is associated with tembang Sunda (a.k.a. *Cianjuran*), an aristocratic genre of sung poetry that was refined in the nineteenth century by the bupati of Cianjur (about 56 km from Bandung), and repurposed in post-Independence West Java as a symbol of Sundanese identity (see Chapter 1).

To get some frank feedback on the quality of his first attempts at making a kacapi, he invited some fine tembang musicians and singers to his home for a *buka puasa* party (breaking the fast during the month of Ramadan).[11] I was fortunate to get an invitation as well. The first problem the musicians encountered was tuning. Typical kacapi have two sets of tuning pegs: (1) large, wooden friction pegs, around which the strings are wrapped, in the body of the instrument, and (2) small metal pins near the nut to which the strings are attached, and which can be adjusted with a key. In addition,

Figure 5.5 A collection of Endo Suanda's musical instruments made from boards of laminated bamboo. From top to bottom: kacapi indung; *gambus*; guitar; *tarawangsa*.

Source: photo: Henry Spiller.

132 *Entanglements*

the strings can be fine-tuned by adjusting movable bridges. Musicians typically do a rough tuning by adjusting the large wooden pegs, and fine tuning with the metal pins. They adjust tuning during performances with the movable bridges.

In contrast, Endo Suanda's first bamboo kacapi had only one set of tuning pegs—stubby little things, in three overlapping rows, behind the nut, which required a special gripping tool to adjust (visible on the right-side end of the kacapi in Figure 5.5). These were not only difficult to tune, the player pointed out, but also got in the way of his hands when playing.[12]

The musicians provided other criticisms of the kacapi: the string spacing was too narrow, and the instrument's bass strings did not have a rich enough timbre. One of the players speculated that bamboo is a harder material than wood and does not produce the rich resonant sound he prefers. It did, however, sound like a wooden kacapi.

In contrast to the bamboo instruments that Mang Akim created for GSA, which are for the most part idiophones, for which the actual sound-producing elements are made from bamboo, Endo Suanda's creations are almost exclusively chordophones, in which the sound-producing elements are metal strings, and the bamboo parts serve only as resonators. Endo Suanda was committed to the idea that the sound of bamboo resonators lent a special quality to his instruments—that there must be an audible bamboo signature from his instruments (pc, August 6, 2013). At the same time, he is adamant that his instruments should be equal in quality to—and indistinguishable from—the best instruments made from wood (pc, August 4, 2013). After considerable thought, he formulated the compromise that (1) his instruments should conform to the norms of regular instruments, but (2) still have something that sounds uniquely "bamboo" about them (pc, August 6, 2013).

Another musician, Jimbot,[13] a fan of Endo Suanda's bamboo instruments, provided a more colorful metaphor to understand the difference. He riffed on the widespread notion that the relationship of a (usually male) kacapi player to his instrument is like that of a husband and wife (see Zanten 2008). The bamboo kacapi, he told me, is like a pretty girl who grew up in the city, with Internet, and other modern conveniences. She might be just as pretty as a girl from the kampung (village), but she lives a faster lifestyle, is more social (*bergaul*), and a little bit less mellow than a country girl. That country girl, Jimbot told me, is like the wooden kacapi, with a slower approach to life. Neither is necessarily better than the other, he stressed, but there is a qualitative difference—one he can distinguish just by experiencing it.

GSA's instruments mobilize bamboo's affordances as a flexible sound-producing material to create instruments capable of accompanying a range of modern Sundanese musical expressions. Endo Suanda's bamboo guitars and kacapi, on the other hand, rely not on bamboo's affordance, or even its abstractions, but on its *resonance*—not only in the literal sense of the word, but in Hodder's sense as well: in which "coherence occurs

Entanglements 133

across domains in historically specific contexts" (2012, 126). It is primarily bamboo's status as an index of Sundaneseness that makes sense of Endo Suanda's instruments.

To make this resonance work, it is important that the instruments' bamboo-ness be evident—if not through any sonic signature, then through context (e.g., announcements, stage patter, program notes). It's worth noting that kacapi are typically painted black (or brown). But Endo Suanda often leaves his bamboo instruments unfinished, so that at least the color and grain of the bamboo remain visible. The ultimate goal of his products, I have concluded, is to prove that bamboo is not only a link to the Sundanese past, but it is a vibrant and ecologically sustainable material for modern Sundanese music—whether that music is traditional (like tembang Sunda) or global (like guitar music).

Kudu kawas awi jeung gawirna—Karinding Attack

"We should be like bamboo and its cliff"—bamboo quite literally holds the soil together, preventing erosion, and the soil nourishes the bamboo. Chapter 4's proverb emphasizes bamboo's ability to stabilize the earth, to provide a secure and predictable environment for human habitation. The current revival of karinding in Bandung and environs harnesses bamboo's capacity to literally hold things together and extends it to an entirely new musical milieu. Playing karinding in modern contexts invites resonances (in Hodder's sense) of *Sunda wiwitan* (old Sundanese) values (e.g., yakin, sadar, sabar ["confident, conscious, patient"]), and translates these values onto new expressions.

The members of Karinding Attack and their young fans have resurrected the Sundanese karinding and other archaic Sundanese bamboo instruments to compose and perform new music—music that is more global in nature than Sundanese. Karinding Attack's death metal-inspired songs, and the simple songs their young fans play and sing in similar bands, are rooted in Sundanese culture not by their genre, or their style, but rather by their performance on bamboo instruments. Like the bamboo on the cliff, the bamboo in these ensembles enables the musicians to cling to the Sundanese landscape, even while participating in a global music scene.

The ethnomusicologist and karinding innovator Asep Nata has taken the development of karinding in very different directions than the Karinding Attack musicians and their followers. A native of Bandung, Asep Nata studied ethnomusicology at Universitas Sumatera Utara (University of North Sumatra) in Medan (graduating in 1994[14]). He has taught at various institutions in the Bandung area while maintaining his own experimental practice of instrument building, which includes making ocarinas from mango seeds (Pramono 2017) and gamelan instruments from ceramics and aluminum (pc, April 30, 2013).

According to Tomy Suwandi, Asep Nata first encountered metal guimbardes when he was in college (in the late 1980s). It was while

134 *Entanglements*

demonstrating his guimbardes on a talk show in 2001 that he noticed his mouth had gone numb from a long period of playing. Recalling that the old players he had met in the past generally had lost their teeth, he resolved to look for an alternative that would allow him to keep his mouth intact. Drawing from information he gathered on a trip to Lombok, he experimented with wood and bamboo as raw materials for various forms of guimbardes (Suwandi 2013, 30–31). He settled on *awi surat* (another name for *bambu gombong* [*Gigantochloa verticillate*; Maradjo et al. 1976, 26]) as his favorite material, not only because of its qualities as a environmentally "green" material (it is fast-growing, non-invasive, and produces edible shoots), its strength and flexibility, its ready availability, and its versatility, but also because the word surat has positive connotations.[15]

Asep Nata told me that his musical training is primarily "western," and that salendro and pelog tunings are essentially "foreign" to him (pc, April 30, 2013). One of his goals is to produce sets of karinding with which a single performer can render pentatonic, diatonic, even chromatic melodies. When asked directly, he does not want to overemphasize the importance of "pitch" as a necessary musical parameter for karinding music; on the other hand, he was mildly critical of Karinding Attack in their approach to collaborating with musicians from more melodically oriented musical traditions; he suggests that the other musical styles are allowed to dominate while the karinding players merely *"jaga beat"* ("keep the beat").

His most successful experiments rely on special karinding on which a diligent performer can reliably and clearly bring out the 3rd, 4th, and 5th overtones (e.g., on a karinding with a fundamental of c2, the player can produce c4, e4, and g4). He binds several of these karinding together into a sort of fan; the additional karinding have fundamentals that are related to the first karinding by the interval of a 4th or 5th, so that a performer can produce additional pitches: (on g1) g3, b3, and d4 and (on f2) f4 a4, and c5. It may be possible to produce the remaining note (b4) as the 7th overtone. By adjusting the fan to place one or another karinding in front of the mouth, the player can quickly switch to the karinding with the desired note. Nevertheless, it takes considerable dexterity and skill to isolate the correct harmonic. These "fans" might include two, three, or more component karinding, depending on how many pitches a given performance requires; adjacent karinding's fundamentals are typically a 2nd or a 5th apart (see Figure 5.6).

Asep Nata calls his approach *karinding toél* (or *towel*), abbreviated *karto*. The term toél suggests that the karinding's tongue is set to vibrating by plucking it rather than hitting it. Many people agree that this technique is slightly easier than the striking technique conventionally used for Sundanese karinding; furthermore, it allows Asep Nata more accuracy in fine-tuning the fundamental pitch of each karinding. He advocates using multiple fingers (including the thumb) to pluck the karinding, which may facilitate the playing of melodies as well. The plucking technique also

Figure 5.6 One of Asep Nata's karinding toél.
Source: photo: Henry Spiller.

allows forward-backward motions, allowing for a single finger to pluck more rapidly.

Much of Asep Nata's research and innovations are promulgated via his Facebook page (www.facebook.com/nataasep), through which he meets other guimbarde aficionados from around the world, shares his research and wisdom, and tries to debunk some of the more dubious myths that circulate about karinding history and technique (see Chapter 4). Like Karinding Attack, Asep Nata has brought karinding into the modern world—in his case, via social media (Cook et al., 2017, 74). It was via Asep Nata's Facebook page that I learned about a karinding-making workshop in 2013. The leaders of the workshop were individuals who completed a training program that Asep Nata conducts, for which the final exercise is making thirteen karinding, each tuned to a different note in the chromatic scale.

I would say that Asep Nata focuses his matters of care more on "karinding" than on bamboo. His promotion of *karinding kartu*—the making of karinding from old credit cards, or from the plastic cards on which mobile phone SIMs are sold[16]—speaks to his primary motivations, namely (1) empowering ordinary people to make instruments and music, and (2) do so in an environmentally sustainable way. His projects rely, nevertheless, on the bamboo karinding's resonance (in Hodder's sense of the word) as something rooted in Sundanese locations, history, and values.

136 *Entanglements*

Conclusion—Awi

Ajining
Wiwitan
Ingsun

This final (I promise!) epigraph embodies all of Sundanese culture and philosophy in the acronym *awi*, which is the Sundanese word for bamboo. The component words comprise the phrase "self-knowledge born into the world (i.e., instinctive, indigenous Sundanese knowledge)" or "mantra of ancient wisdom," which are metaphorically encapsulated into the word for bamboo.[17] Indonesians often take inventory of a word's philosophical implications by use of a *kirata*—a retroactive acronymic etymology (see Zimmer 1999; Rosidi 1984, 157–158). By slyly presenting current notions about a word/concept as etymology, rather than as an exegesis, such "backronyms" (to use a recently coined English term) "lend the weight of history and precedence to modern interpretations of labels" (Spiller 2010, 34). This kirata presents bamboo as primal, as the source of instinctive, natural, local knowledge.

Bamboo links different musical expressions to a common fount of a Sundanese way of knowing the world. The sound of bamboo is the voice of the Sundanese landscape, and the musical characteristics afforded by bamboo—free-rhythm melodies and interlocking accompaniments—are characteristic of Sundanese music (see Chapter 1). Although diatonic angklung orchestras are far removed from their antecedents in ceremonial ensembles, they provide a durable, flexible, versatile medium for promoting Sundanese values of cooperation (see Chapter 2), or even surreptitiously challenging them (e.g., "Grand Symphony Angklung" described in this chapter). Galengan Sora Awi's renditions of many different genres of Sundanese music on homemade bamboo instruments demonstrate how the primary, secondary, and tertiary retentions (à la Bernard Stiegler [1998]) of bamboo tools perpetuate a Sundanese connection to the land through bamboo; their very name, Galengan Sora Awi ("the footpath of bamboo's voice") speaks directly to a metaphor of landscape through which they move (via the footpath) according to the sounds made by bamboo (see Chapter 3). The same holds true for modern karinding ensembles as well (see Chapter 4).

Sundanese music is profoundly entangled in bamboo. Bamboo affordances have shaped the musical materials—tunings, timbres, textures—that characterize traditional and modern Sundanese musical expressions. Its abstractions—notably gotong royong (the spirit of cooperation)—are key characteristics of Sundanese musical styles. Bamboo provides a means to broaden the scope of Sundanese culture; with bamboo, traditional Sundanese genres, heavy metal music, and sentimental pop can all be blended into a truly modern, yet uniquely Sundanese, culture. Bamboo's

Entanglements 137

resonance—both literal and in Hodder's sense of the word—continue to provide clear markers of Sundaneseness, as it has for generations.

Notes

1 For this chapter, I would like to rethink slightly the Sundanese proverb. In the spirit of Karinding Attack's "happy bamboo," I would like to see the irony and the justice in the mutually beneficial relationship of humans to bamboo among Sundanese people in Bandung. In its modern sense, "hoist" means "lift up"; to Shakespeare, it meant "explode" ... but let's deliberately misinterpret the word in its more modern sense of "lift up."

2 Note: pelog degung is distinct from the seven-pitch *pélog* tuning system of Central Javanese gamelan in that it is a five-pitch tuning system with one salendro interval. While there are gamelan tuned to seven-pitch pelog in West Java, the five-pitch pelog degung tuning is uniquely Sundanese, and is used for characteristic Sundanese genres such as tembang Sunda and [gamelan] degung.

3 According to Suwarna's report, for a six-hole suling, the maker uses bamboo that is 1.5 – 1.6 cm in diameter and 50 – 58 cm long (depending on the preferences of the buyer). The diameter is 1.7–2.0 for 60 – 64 cm suling (Suwarna 1999, 35).

4 Although Ellis was not alive to respond to the theory of blown fifths, Amrit Gomperts insists that "Ellis would have rejected Von Hornbostel's and Kunst's theory of blown fifths from the scientific point of view of vibrational acoustics of musical instruments and psychoacoustics" (Gomperts 1995, 174).

5 "Menyajikan karya dan apresiasi seni angklung, yang mencangkup tradisional, modern dan digital. Memainkan lagu-lagu dari seluruh penjuru dunia: Lagu Pop Nasional, Lagu Daerah, Lagu Barat, dan Lagu China."

6 Namely: Yulia Wibowo (married to Prabianto Mukti Wibowo, in 2019 Assistant Deputy Minister for Forestry, Ministry for Economic Affairs); Nora Ryamizard Ryacudu (daughter of former vice president Try Sutrisno and wife of General Ryamizard Ryacudu, who served in various government positions, including as Minister of Defense 2014–2019); Sally Sudrajat: wife of Sudrajat, former general, ambassador to China 2005–2009, and CEO of Susi Airlines; Tati Hendropriyono, wife of Abdullah Mahmud Hendropriyono, a retired honorary general and former head of Indonesia's State Intelligence Agency (BIN); Hani Diah Benny; Ratna Kiki Syanati; and Lisa Raf(f)ael.

7 The final total was 5,393, according to http://www.chinadaily.com.cn/china/2013-07/01/content_16698339_2.htm. The assembled masses also played a Chinese song, "The Moon is my witness," according to http://en.people.cn/90782/8306070.html. Subsequent events involved even bigger, but unofficially recorded, crowds: for example, 20,000 in Bandung (24 April 2015), according to https://www.globalindonesianvoices.com/20405/new-world-record-sets-as-20000-people-played-angklung-in-harmony/.

8 https://m2indonesia.com/tokoh/sastrawan/endo-suanda.htm

9 The former ASTI Bandung is now called Institut Seni Budaya Indonesia (ISBI; Indonesian Institute of Art and Culture); the former ASTI Yogyakarta is now called Institut Seni Indonesia (ISI; Indonesia Institute of the Arts).

10 https://www.bamboorevolution.com/

11 The instrumentalists were Mamat Rupiandi (*kacapi indung*), suling player Iwan Mulyana, and Iwan's son, Egi Redika, who played the small *kacapi rincik*.

138 *Entanglements*

Mamat's wife, Mae Nurhayati, and Rina Oesman, another guest, were the singers.

12 Especially, he said, when executing the technique he calls *suara karinding* ("karinding voice," which involves plucking close to the nut, like the classical harp technique known as *près de la table*), revealing yet another notable reference to bamboo technology.

13 a.k.a. Zimbot, a.k.a. Iman Rochman. He is a member of Karinding Attack (see Chapter 4).

14 Asep Nata is #120 in a list of Alumni of University of North Sumatra ethnomusicology program (see https://www.etnomusikologiusu.com/skripsi-satu.html)

15 According to Tomy Suwandi, because *surat* means "message," Asep Nata hopes the karinding's positive message will get through (2013, 34). Asep Nata told me that *surat* means "refined" (although my Sundanese dictionaries do not confirm this sense), and he thinks that association will help remove some of the negative associations of karinding with black magic or backwardness (pc, April 30, 2013).

16 See, for example, Asep Nata's step-by-step instructional video for making a karinding kartu at https://www.youtube.com/watch?v=6S9bNM2E1K0&list=PLTWxMAMq8X32-9ZBaDGe8sany4nZvFJOC

17 In a similar vein, Kimung also told me that awi is a singkatan for Asal WIwitan (source of traditional knowledge; pc, August 19, 2013).

References

Abdilah, Sukron. 2007. "Glokalisasi Urang Sunda." Blog posting, October 23, 2007, https://sukronabdilah.wordpress.com/2007/10/23/glokalisasi-urang-sunda/

Abdulgani-Knapp, Retnowati. 2007. *Soeharto: The life and legacy of Indonesia's second president: An Authorised Biography*. Singapore: Marshall Cavendish Editions.

Abdullah, Muhammad Irfan Nugraha Kamil. 2014. "The Main Function of Music: Muslim Headbanger: Konsep Karya Film Dokumenter." Diploma Empat (D4) thesis, Prodi Studi Televisi dan Film, Sekolah Tinggi Seni Indonesia (STSI) Bandung.

Adie, Bailey Ashton. 2017. "Franchising our heritage: The UNESCO World Heritage brand," *Tourism Management Perspectives* 24: 48–53. ISSN 2211-9736, https://doi.org/10.1016/j.tmp.2017.07.002.

Adkins, C. J. 1974. "Investigation of the sound-producing mechanism of the jew's harp," *The Journal of the Acoustical Society of America* 55(3): 667–670. doi: 10.1121/1.1914580.

Admin Inilahkoran. 2014. "Galengan Sora Awi, Inovasi Instrumen Tradisional," InilahKoran, December 19, 2014. Online resource.

Admin Inilahkoran. 2015. "Vitalnya Bulu Bebek," InilahKoran, January 23, 2015. Online resource.

Al-Kassimi. Khaled. 2018. "ALBA: A decolonial delinking performance towards (western) modernity—An alternative to development project," *Cogent Social Sciences* 4(1): 1546418. https://doi.org/10.1080/23311886.2018.1546418

Ali, Muhamad. 2004. "Islam and Economic Development in New Order's Indonesia (1967–1998)," paper presented at 3-d East-West Center International Graduate Student Conference, February 19–21, Honolulu, HI. www.eastwestcenter.org/system/tdf/private/IGSCwp012.pdf?file=1&type=node&id=32045.

Amelinda, Roswita. 2016. "The Urgency for the Innovative Design of Angklung Music Score." In *Proceedings of the 2nd International Music and Performing Arts Conference (IMPAC2016), 22–24 November 2016*, Faculty of Music and Performing Arts, eds. Mohd Kipli Abdul Rahman, Clare Chan Suet Ching, Zaharul Lailiddin Saidon, Christine Augustine, and Muhammad Fazli Taib Saearani, Universiti Pendidikan Sultan Idris, Malaysia, pp. 294–302.

Amilia, Aam. 2001. *Bintang Panggung: Biografi Tati Saleh*. Bandung: Granesia.

Amor Patria, Teguh. 2014. *Telusur Bandung*. Jakarta: Jakarta: PT Elex Media Komputindo.

140   *References*

Anderson, Benedict R. O'G. 2018. *Language and Power: Exploring Political Cultures in Indonesia*. Ithaca, NY: Cornell University Press.

anon. 2008. "Panitia Konser AACC Dituntut 3 Tahun," *Pikiran Rakyat*, Thursday, August 7.

Aprianti, Yenti. 2007. Bambu: Dari kelahiran hingga kematian urang Sunda, *Kompas* (July 28, 2007).

Arinda, Puspita. 2016. Blogs on Karinding. https://summervibes365.wordpress.com/author/puspitaarinda/.

Art Etsa Logam. 2013. "Sejarah karinding versi karinding attack," online resource, www.facebook.com/notes/komunitas-karinding-sagala-awi-/sejarah-karinding-versi-karinding-attack/1424557031094829.

Atmadibrata, Enoch, Nang Hendi K. Dunumiharja, and Yuli Sunarya. 2006. *Khazanah Seni Pertunjukan Jawa Barat*. Bandung: Dinas Kebudayaan dan Pariwisata Jawa Barat.

Baier, Randall. 1985. "The Angklung ensemble of West Java: Continuity of an agricultural tradition," *Balungan* 2(1–2): 8–16.

Bates, Eliot. 2012. "The Social Life of Musical Instruments," *Ethnomusicology* 56(3): 363–395.

Baulch, Emma. 2003. "Gesturing Elsewhere: The Identity Politics of the Balinese Death/Thrash Metal Scene," *Popular Music* 22: 195–215.

Becker, Judith. 1979. "Time and Tune in Java." In *The Imagination of Reality*, ed. A. Becker and A.A. Yengoyan, pp. 197–210. Norwood, NJ: Ablex.

Becker, Judith. 1980. *Traditional Music in Modern Java*. Honolulu: University of Hawaii Press.

Becker, Judith. 1988. "Earth, Fire, *Sakti*, and the Javanese Gamelan," *Ethnomusicology* 32(3): 385–391.

Bell, Albert. 2011. "Metal in a Micro Island State: An Insider's Perspective." In *Metal Rules the Globe: Heavy Metal Music around the World*, eds. Jeremy Wallach, Harris M. Berger, and Paul D. Greene. Durham, NC: Duke University Press, pp. 271–293.

Bendix, Regina F., Aditya Eggert, and Arnika Peselmann. 2013. "Introduction: Heritage Regimes and the State." In Bendix, Regina F., Eggert, Aditya, and Peselmann, Arnika (Eds.), *Heritage Regimes and the State*. Göttingen: Göttingen University Press, pp. 11–20.

Bennett, James. 2019. "'Ilm or fashion? The question of identity in the batik designs of Java." In *Ilm: Science, Religion and Art in Islam*, ed. Samer Akkach. Adelaide: University of Adelaide Press, pp. 157–180.

Bolman, B. C. 2006. "Wet Rice Cultivation in Indonesia: A Comparative Research on Differences in Modernization Trends." Master's thesis, Wageningen University.

Bourchier, David, and Hadiz, Vedi R. Hadiz. 2014. "Introduction," in *Indonesian Politics and Society: A Reader*, eds. David Bourchier and Vedi R. Hadiz. London and New York: RoutledgeCurzon, pp. 1–24.

Bourchier, David. 1998. "Indonesianising Indonesia: Conservative indigenism in an age of globalisation," *Social Semiotics*, 8(2–3): 203–214. doi: 10.1080/10350339809360408.

Bourchier, David. 2020. "Organicism in Indonesian Political Thought." In *The Oxford Handbook of Comparative Political Theory*, eds. Leigh K. Jenco, Megan C. Thomas, and Murad Idris. Oxford: Oxford University Press, pp. 598–617.

References 141

Brinner, Benjamin. 1993. "Freedom and Formulaity in the 'Suling' Playing of Bapak Tarnopangrawit," *Asian Music* 24(2): 1–37.

Bukofzer, Manfred. 1937. "Kann die 'Blasquintentheorie' zur Erklarung exotischer beitragen?" *Anthropos* 32(3/4): 402–418.

Bukofzer, Manfred. 1939. "The Evolution of Javanese Tone-Systems," *Papers Read by Members of the American Musicological Society at the Annual Meeting (September 11th to 16th, 1939)*. Berkeley, CA: University of California Press, pp. 241–250.

Byerly, Ken. 1964. "Party's Over—Until Next Year," *Newsday*, Oct 19, 1964, p. 4. https://search.proquest.com/hnpnewsday/docview/964452455/D97879D 143034171PQ/14?accountid=14505.

Bystriakova, Nadia, Valerie Kapos, Chris Stapleton, and Igor Lysenko. 2003a. "Bamboo Biodiversity: Information for Planning Conservation and Management in the Asia-Pacific Region." INBAR. Beijing: International Network for Bamboo and Rattan; Cambridge: UNEP World Conservation Monitoring Centre.

Bystriakova, Nadia, Valerie Kapos, Chris Stapleton, and Igor Lysenko. 2003b. "Distribution and Conservation Status of Forest Bamboo Biodiversity in the Asia-Pacific Region," *Biodiversity and Conservation* 12: 1833–1841.

Caro, Robert A. 1965. "Indo Blows Top at Fair At High Cost to Rip Down," *Newsday*, June 7, 1965.

Caturwati, Endang. 2017. "Angklung and Local Wisdom Values," *Research on Humanities and Social Sciences* 7(10): 7–11.

Chong, Jinn Winn. 2012. "'Mine, Yours or Ours?': The Indonesia-Malaysia Disputes over Shared Cultural Heritage," *Sojourn: Journal of Social Issues in Southeast Asia* 27(1): 1–53.

Christanty, L., D. Mailly, and J.P. Kimmins. 1996. "'Without Bamboo, the land dies': Biomass, litterfall, and soil organic matter dynamics of a Javanese bamboo talun-kebun system," *Forest Ecology and Management* 87(1–3): 75–88.

Clark, James. 2021. "Bandung Urban Transit System," *Future Southeast Asia*. https://futuresoutheastasia.com/bandung-urban-transit-system/.

Clark, Marshall. 2013. "The Politics of Heritage," *Indonesia and the Malay World* 41(121): 396–417. doi: 10.1080/13639811.2013.804979.

Clarke, Adele E., and Susan Leigh Star. 2008. "5: The Social Worlds Framework: A Theory/Methods Package," in *The Handbook of Science and Technology Studies*, eds. Edward J. Hackett, Olga Amsterdamska, Michael Lynch, and Judy Wajcman. Cambridge, MA: MIT Press, pp. 113–137.

Clinton, Esther, and Jeremy Wallach. 2015. "Recoloring the Metal Map: Metal and Race in Global Perspective." In *Conference Proceedings: Modern heavy metal: Markets, practices and cultures: International Academic Research Conference, June 8–12 2015, Helsinki, Finland*, eds. Karjalainen, Toni-Matti and Kimi Kärki. Helsinki: Aalto University, pp. 274–282.

Cook, Rosie H., and Luqmanul Chakim, Sa'id Abdulloh, Nicole Tse, and Margaret Kartomi. 2017. "Bundengan: Social Media as a Space for Collaboration in the Conservation and Revival of an Endangered Musical Instrument." In *Proceedings The 2nd Annual of International and Interdisciplinary Conference on Arts Creation and Studies*, ed. Donie Fadjar Kurnaiwan. Institute Seni Indonesia (ISI), Solo, Indonesia, pp. 63–79.

142   References

Coolsma, S. 1891. *Kitab Soetji. Hartosna sadajana kitab anoe kasĕbat Pĕrdjangdjian Lawas sarĕng Perdjangdjian Anjar.* Amsterdam: Nederlandsch Bijbelgenootschap.

Coolsma, Sierk. 1884. *Soendaneesch-Hollandsch woordenboek.* Leiden: Sijthoff.

Coombe, Rosemary J. 2013. "Managing Cultural Heritage as Neoliberal Governmentality." In Bendix, R. F., Eggert, A., and Peselmann, A. (eds.), *Heritage Regimes and the State.* Göttingen University Press, pp. 375–388.

Cotter, Bill, and Bill Young. 2014. *The 1964–1965 New York World's Fair.* Arcadia Publishing.

Crescenti, Peter. 1976. "Indonesian Nightmare Strikes Deep Purple," *Rolling Stone Magazine,* January 29.

Cribb, Robert. 2010. *Digital Atlas of Indonesian History.* Copenhagen: NIAS Press.

Daryana, Hinhin Agung. 2017. "The Popularity of Karinding among Bandung Society," *Panggung* (ISBI) 27(4): 353–363.

Daryana, Hinhin Agung. n.d. Sundanese Metal: The Symbolic Movements of Cultural Identity. Unpublished paper posted on researchgate. www.researchg ate.nct/profile/Hinhin_Daryana/publication/326752532_SUNDANESE_ METAL_The_Symbolic_Movements_Of_Cultural_Identity/links/5b61f819a 6fdccf0b206b8ea/SUNDANESE-METAL-The-Symbolic-Movements-Of-Cultural-Identity.

Dean, Gary. 1999. "The New Order State and the Tempo Affair: A conflict of values." Blog post, November 1, 1999. https://garydean.id/works/tempo

Deleuze, Gilles, and Félix Guattari. 2004. *A thousand plateaus: capitalism and schizophrenia.* London: Continuum.

Devi S. 2019. "Karinding dan Celempung Abah Olot, Diapresiasi Camat Cimanggung," Kapol.id, July 18, 2019. https://kapol.id/karinding-dan-celemp ung-abah-olot-diapresiasi-camat-cimanggung/.

Dijk, Henk Mak van. 2007. *De oostenwind waait naar het westen: Indische componisten, Indische composities, 1898– 1945.* Leiden: KITLV.

Diliyanto, Yoega. 2008. "Kronologis tragedy Konser Beside di AACC Bandung," blogpost dated February 11, 2008. https://yoega.wordpress.com/2008/02/11/kro nologis-tragedi-konser-beside-di-aacc-bandung/.

Dim, Herry. 2017. "Taka ada lagi 'Awi jeung Gawirna,'" Banjir dan Longsor pun Berdatangan," UniversArts (blog), arts-and-universe.blogspot.com, January 15, 2017. arts-and-universe.bogspot.com/2017/tak-ada-lagi-awi-jeung-gawirna-banjir.html.

Diratmasasmita, Handiman. 2005. "Angklung Padaeng" (web document). http:// angklung-web-institute.com/content/view/86/74/lang_en/.

Dransfield, S., and E.A. Widjaja. 1995. *Bamboos. Plant Resources of South-East Asia No. 7.* Leiden: Backhuys Publishers.

Durban Arjo, Irawati. 1989. "Women's Dance among the Sundanese of West Java, Indonesia," *Asian Theatre Journal* 6(2): 168–178.

Dwiyono, Abdurochman. 2012. Analisis Keputusan Berkunjung Wisatawan Domestik Di Saung Angklung Udjo. Thesis, UPI Bandung.

Ekadjati, Edi S. 1995. *Kebudayaan Sunda (Suatu Pendekatan Sejarah).* Jakarta: Pustaka Jaya.

Ellis, Alexander J. 1885. "On the Musical Scales of Various Nations," *Journal of the Society of Arts* 33(1): 485–527.

Eringa, F.S. 1984. *Soendaas-Nederlands woordenboek.* Dordrecht: Foris Publications.

References 143

Faisal, Budi, and Putri Kinasih. 2010. "Experimenting Bamboo as an Architectural and Socio-Cultural Feature. Case Study: The Bamboo House at Eco-Pestantren Daarut Tauhiid, West Bandung, West-Java, Indonesia." In *Proceedings: Arte Polis 3 International Conference—Creative Collaboration and the Making of Place, Bandung, 22–24 July 2010*, Vol. 1, pp. 323–342.

Fern, Ken. n.d. Tropical Plants Database, tropical.theferns.info. 2021-12-07. tropical.theferns.info/viewtropical.php?id=Schizostachyum+blumei.

Fisher, Berenice, and Joan Tronto. 1990. "Toward a Feminist Theory of Caring." In *Circles of Care: Work and Identity in Women's Lives*, eds. Emily K. Abel and Margaret K. Nelson. New York: SUNY Press, pp. 35–62.

Foley, Kathy. 1985. "The Dancer and the Danced: Trance Dance and Theatrical Performance in West Java," *Asian Theatre Journal* 2(1): 28–49.

Foster, Michael Dylan. 2015. "UNESCO on the Ground." *Journal of Folklore Research* 52(2–3): 143–156.

Frakking, Roel. 2017. "'Gathered on the Point of a Bayonet': The Negara Pasundan and the Colonial Defence of Indonesia, 1946–50," *The International History Review* 39(1): 30–47.

Gathen Constanze, Wilhelm Skoglund, and Daniel Laven. 2021. "The UNESCO Creative Cities Network: A Case Study of City Branding." In *New Metropolitan Perspectives. NMP 2020. Smart Innovation, Systems and Technologies* 178, eds. Bevilacqua C., Calabrò F. and L. Della Spina (eds.). Cham: Springer, pp. 727–737.

Giles, Ray. 1974. "Ombak in the Style of the Javanese Gongs," *Selected Reports in Ethnomusicology* 2(1): 158–165.

Gomperts, Amrit. 1995. "Tunings, Tone Systems and Psychoacoustics of Sundanese, Javanese and Balinese Music." In *Oiedeion: The Performing Arts World-Wide*," ed. Wim van Zanten. Leiden: Centre of Non-Western Studies, Leiden University), pp. 173–207.

Grame, Theodore C. 1962. "Bamboo and Music: A New approach to organology," *Ethnomusicology* 6(1): 8–14.

Groneman, I. (Isaac), and J.P.N. (Jan Pieter Nicolaas) Land. 1890. *De Gamĕlan Te Jogjåkartå*. Amsterdam: Koninklijke Akademie van Wetenschappen.

Haas, H.W.M. de. 1964. "Oud bamboe schud-instrument maakt furore in Indonesië," *De Tijd-Maasbode*, December 14, 1964, p. 5.

Hakim, Amalia Ayuni, Elvinaro Ardianto, and Hanny Hafiar. 2012. "Konservasi Kesenian Karinding oleh Komunitas Karinding Attack (Karat) dalam Upaya Pelestarian Budaya Seni Sunda," *eJurnal Mahasiswa Universitas Padjadjaran* 1(1): 1–14.

Hall, Kenneth R. 1985. "Maritime Trade and State Development in Fourteenth-Century Java," In *Maritime Trade and State Development in Early Southeast Asia*. Honolulu: University of Hawai'i Press, pp. 250–281.

Hall, Kenneth R. 2001. "The Roots of ASEAN: Regional Identities in the Strait of Melaka Region Circa 1500 C.E." *Asian Journal of Social Science* 29(1): 87–119.

Hanafi, Taufiq. 2014. "Engineered Narrative: Writing/Righting History in *Sang Mokteng Bubat*." In *Proceeding [sic]: Literary Studies Conference 2014, Universitas Sanata Dharma, Yogyakarta, 16–17 October 2014*. Eds. B. Alip, F.X. Siswadi, et al. Universitas Sanata Dharma Press, pp. 1–7.

Haraway, Donna. 2015. "Anthropocene, Capitalocene, Plantationocene, Chthulucene: Making Kin," *Environmental Humanities* 6: 159–165.

Harris, Keith. 2000. "'Roots'?: The relationship between the global and the local within the Extreme Metal scene," *Popular Music* 19: 13–30.

144 References

Heins, Ernst. 1968. Liner notes for Musiques populaires d'Indonesie: Folk music from West-Java (Ocora OCR 46). Series: International Folk Music Council, Anthologie De La Musique Populaire, recorded by Ernst Heins.

Heins, Ernst. 1977. Goong Renteng: Aspects of Orchestral Music in a Sundanese Village. PhD dissertation (music), University of Amsterdam.

Helmholtz, H. 1863. *On the Sensation of Tone* (A.J. Ellis, Trans., 2nd English ed.). New York: Dover.

Hendrik, A.P., Cace. 2009. *Karinding Ciramagirang di desa Ciramagirang Kecamatan Cikalong Kulon Kabupaten Cianjur, Suatu Tinjauan Awal.* Thesis: Sekolah Tinggi Seni Indonesia (STSI), Bandung.

Herdiani, Een. 2017. "Dynamics of Jaipongan on West Java from 1980 to 2010," *Asian Theatre Journal* 34(2): 455–473.

Herlina Lubis, Nina. 2000. *Sejarah Kota-Kota Lama Di Jawa Barat.* Sumedang, Indonesia: Alqaprint Jatinangor.

Herlina, Nina, and Obsatar Sinaga, Mumuh Muhsin Z, and Miftahul Falah. 2019. "Reorganization of Region and Traditional Political Structure in Priangan after the fall of The Sunda Kingdom," *International Journal of Innovation, Creativity and Change* (www.ijicc.net) 5(2), 1517–1533.

Herlinawati, Lina. 2009. "Fungsi Karinding Bagi Masyarakat Cikalongkulon, Kabupaten Cianjur," *Patanjala* 1(1): 96–110.

Hermawan, Deni, Abun Somawijaya, Dinda Satya Upaja Budi, Ucu Mulya Santosa, and Iyon Supiono. 2012. *Angklung Sunda Sebagai Wahana Industri Kreatif Dan Pembentukan Karakter Bangsa (Sundanese Angklung as a Vehicle for Creative Industries and the formation of a National Character).* Unpublished manuscript.

Hodder, Ian. 2012. *Entangled: An Archaeology of the Relationships between Humans and Things.* Malden, MA: Wiley-Blackwell.

Hoffman, Stanley. 1978. "Epistemology and music: A Javanese example," *Ethnomusicology* 22(1): 69–88.

Hornbostel, Erich M. von, and Curt Sachs. 1961 [1914]. "Classification of Musical Instruments: Translated from the Original German by Anthony Baines and Klaus P. Wachsmann," *The Galpin Society Journal* 14: 3–29.

Hutagalung, Ridwan. 2006. *Features of World Music.* Mustika: Bandung.

Hynson, Meghan. 2016. "Indonesian Angklung: Intersections of Music Education and Cultural Diplomacy." In *Performing Indonesia*, eds. Andy McGraw and Sumarsam. Washington D.C.: Smithsonian Institution. https://asia.si.edu/ess ays/article-hynson/

Imran, Ahda, Miftahul Malik, et al. 2011. *5 Dasa Warsa Irawati* Menari. Bandung: Pusbitari Press.

Indrawati. 2006. "Sistem Pewarisan Seni Karinding di Lingkung Seni Sekar Komara Sunda Kampung Citamiang Desa Pasir Mukti Kecamatan Cineam Kabupaten Tasikmalaya," Thesis, UPI.

Iskandar, Rudi. 2003. "Calung Renteng Gaya Gandari Sebagai Inovasi Dalam Perkembangan Seni Calung di Jawa Barat," Thesis, UPI.

Jack, Homer A. 1955. *Bandung: An On-the-Spot Description of the Asian-African Conference, Bandung, Indonesia, April 1955.* Chicago, IL: Forward Freedom.

James, Kieran, and Rex Walsh. 2015. "Bandung Rocks, Cibinong Shakes: Economics and Applied Ethics within the Indonesian Death-metal Community," *Musicology Australia* 37(1): 28–46. doi: 10.1080/08145857. 2015.1021438

References 145

Kahn, Douglas. 2013. E*arth Sound Earth Signal: Energies and Earth Magnitude in the Arts.* Berkeley, CA: University of California Press.

Kartomi, Margaret J. 1973a. "Music and Trance in Central Java," *Ethnomusicology* 17(2): 163–208

Kartomi, Margaret J. 1973b. "Jaran Kepang and Kuda Lumping: Trance Dancing in Java," *Hemisphere* 17: 20–27.

Karyawanto, Harpang Yudha. 2018. "Bentuk lagu dan ambitus nada pada orkestrasi mars unesa," *VIRTUOSO (Jurnal Pengkajian Dan Penciptaan Musik)* 1(1): 8–14.

Kimung. 2010. "Jurnal Karat #3," *Kimun666's Weblog*, https://kimung666.wordpr ess.com/page/2/.

Kimung. 2011a. *Jurnal Karat: Karinding Attack, Ujungberung Rebels.* Bandung: Minor Books.

Kimung. 2011b. "Karinding, Alat Musik Karuhun Nan Unik." Facebook post, July 4, 2011. www.facebook.com/notes/dunia-pengen-tahu/karinding-alat-musik-karuhun-nan-unik/128942463858549/.

Kimung. 2013. "Kelas Karinding: Sejarah Karinding Klasik (Hingga 2010)." Blog post, January 10, 2013, https://kelaskarinding-blog.tumblr.com/post/40163943 562/sejarah-karinding-klasik-hingga-2010.

Kimung. 2016. "Filosofi Karinding Sunda," *Extension Course Filsafat (ECF)* vol. 2. Bandung: Universitas Parahyangan. Online resource: http://journal.unpar. ac.id/index.php/ECF/article/view/2298.

Kimung. 2019. "Sasakala Karinding #9 Giri Underground," Pangauban Karinding (online resource), https://pangaubankarinding.com/sasakala-karinding-9-giri-underground/.

Knight, Edward H. 1878. "The Paris Exposition of 1878 (Part II)," *Lippincott's Monthly Magazine* 22: 403–417.

Koizumi, Fumio, Yoshihiko Tokumaru, and Osamu Yamaguchi. 1977. *Asian musics in an Asian perspective: Report of Asian Traditional Performing Arts 1976.* Tokyo: Heibonsha.

Kubarsah, Ubun. 1996. *Waditra: Mengenal alat-alat kesenia daerah Jawa Barat.* Bandung: CV Beringin Sakti.

Kunst, Jaap, and R. T. A. Wiranatakoesoema. 1921. "Een en Ander Over Soendaneesche Muziek," *Djawa* 1: 235–252.

Kunst, Jaap. 1948. *Around Von Hornbostel's theory of the cycle of blown fifths.* Amsterdam: Indisch Instituut [Mededeling no. LXXVI, afd. Volkenkunde 27.].

Kunst, Jaap. 1973. *Music in Java.* 3rd enlarged ed. 2 vols. The Hague: Martinus Nijhoff.

Kurz, Sulpiz. 1876. "Bamboo and its Use," *The Indian Forester* 1(3 & 4): 219–269, 335–362.

Kusnadi. 2006. "Seni singiran dalam ritual tahlilan pada masyarakat Islam tradisional Jawa," *Imaji* 4(2): 218–231.

Kustiasih, Rini. 2010. "Abah Olot Melestarikan Karinding," Komaps.com, July 7, 2010.

Latour, Bruno. 2005. *Reassembling the Social: An Introduction to Actor-Network-Theory.* Oxford: Oxford University Press.

Ledang, Ola Kai. 1972. "On the Acoustics and the Systematic Classification of the Jaw's Harp," *Yearbook of the International Folk Music Council* 4, 95–103.

Lee, Dorothy Sara, ed. 1984. *The Federal Cylinder Project, Volume 8: Early Anthologies.* Washington: Library of Congress.

146 References

Lindsay, Jennifer. 2012. "Performing Indonesia Abroad," in *Heirs to World Culture: Being Indonesian, 1950–1965.* Eds. Jennifer Lindsay and Maya H. T. Liem. Leiden: Brill, pp. 191–220.

Lippit, Takuro Mizuta. 2016. "Ensembles Asia: Mapping experimental practices in music in Asia," *Organised Sound* 21(1): 72–82. doi:10.1017/S1355771815000394

Lubis Nugroho, Ratna. 2017. "Towards Ecopreneurial Society in Bandung City Indonesia: A Case Study from Rw-05 Cihampelas Street," *Academic Journal of Science*, CD-ROM ISSN: 2165-6282:: 07(03): 513–554.

Lyra, H.M., D. Indira, and T. Muhtadin. 2019. "The expression of cultural values in Sundanese manuscripts of the *Mandala* period." In *Urban Studies: Border and Mobility (Proceedings of The 4th International Conference on Urban Studies (ICUS 2017), Universitas Airlangga, Surabaya, Indonesia, 8–9 December 2017)*, eds. Kerr, Thor, and Bekisizwe Ndimande, Jan Van der Putten, Daniel F. Johnson- Mardones, Diah Ariani Arimbi, and Yuni Sari Amalia. London and New York: Routledge / Taylor & Francis Group, pp. 61–66.

Maceda, José. 1979. "A Search for an Old and a New Music in Southeast Asia," *Acta Musicologica* 51(1): 160–168.

Maceda, José. 1990. "In Search of a Source of Pentatonic Hemitonic and Anhemitonic Scales in Southeast Asia," *Acta Musicologica* 62(2/3): 192–223.

Maceda, José. 1998. *Gongs & Bamboo: A Panorama of Philippine Music Instruments.* Dilman, Quezon City: University of the Philippines Press.

Majid, Rida Fadilah Husni. 2013. Pembelajaran arumba pada kelompok arumba cilik usia 10–14 tahun di saung angklung Udjo. Thesis: UPI Bandung.

Maradjo, Marah, et al., eds. 1976. *Tanaman Bambu.* Jakarta: PT Karya Nusantara.

Martin-Iverson, Sean. 2014. "Running in Circles: Performing Values in the Bandung 'Do It Yourself' Hardcore Scene," *Ethnomusicology Forum* 23(2): 184–207.

Martin, Aryn, Natasha Myers, and Ana Viseu. 2015. "The politics of care in technoscience," *Social Studies of Science* 45(5): 625–641.

Masunah, Juju, Rita Milyartini, Oya Yukarya, Uus Karwati, and Deni Hermawan. 2003. *Angklung di Jawa Barat: Sebuah perbandingan.* Jakarta: Pusat Penelitian dan Pengembangan Pendidikan Seni Tradisional.

Mignolo, Walter D., and Catherine E. Walsh. 2018. *On Decoloniality: Concepts, Analytics, Praxis.* Durham, NC: Duke University Press.

Milyartini, Rita. 2012. "Transformasi Nilai Budaya Melalui Pembinaan Seni Angklung: Studi Kasus Di Saung Angklung Udjo," unpublished manuscript, http://file.upi.edu/Direktori/FPSD/JUR._PEND._SENI_MUSIK/131760 819%20-%20Rita%20Milyartini%20Dra%20Msi/makalah/TRANSFORM ASI%20NILAI%20BUDAYA%20MELALUI%20PEMBINAAN%20S ENI%20ANGKLUNG.docx.

Moriyama, Mikihiro. 2005. *Sundanese Print Culture and Modernity in Nineteenth-century West Java.* Singapore: Singapore University Press.

Muljadji, Yusar 2016. "The Folk Underground Music as Culture Revivalism: Mixing The Sundanese Traditional Musical Instruments And Underground Music As The Struggle For Culture Sovereignty." In *Keep It Simple Make, It Fast!: An Approach to Underground Music Scenes*, eds. Paula Guerra and Tania Moreira. DIY Cultures, Spaces and Places Programme. Porto: University of Porto, pp. 15–22.

Musthofa, Budiman Mahmud. 2018. Transformasi Angklung Sunda Dan Dampaknya Bagi Masyarakat: Studi Kasus Kretivitas Angklung Di Saung

References 147

Angklung Udjo. *Seminar Nasional Teknologi Terapan Berbasis Kearifan Lokal* 1(1): 546–554.

Natapradja, Iwan D. 1972. Review: *Musiques populaires d'Indonesie; Folk Music from West-Java* by Ernst Heins. *Ethnomusicology* 16(2): 313–316.

Noorduyn, J., and A. Teeuw. 2006. *Three Old Sundanese Poems*. Leiden: KITLV Press.

Nugraha, Asep. 2015. "Angklung Tradisional Sunda: Intangible, Cultural Heritage of Humanity, Penerapannya dan Pengkontribusiannya Terhadap Kelahiran Angklung Indonesia," *Jurnal Awi Laras* 2(1): 1–23.

Oktavia, Fitri, and Kusmawardi, Suwardi. 2013. "Pembelajaran Karinding di Kelas Karinding (Kekardi Komunitas Musik Metal Jl.Muara Rajeun No. 15, Bandung)," *Pembelajaran Karinding* 1(3): 1–6.

"On the Midway Plaisance." 1893. *Current Literature* 13 (May– August): 172–175.

Ortner, Sherry B. 2016. "Dark anthropology and its others," *Hau: Journal of Ethnographic Theory* 6(1): 47–73. doi: http://dx.doi.org/10.14318/hau6.1.004.

"P." 1921. "Het eerste Congres van het Javainstituut te Bandoeng (17–20 Juni 1921)," *Indië* 5(20): 328–332.

Pasmandas. 2011. "Angklung," blog post dated February 23, 2011, http://pasman das-sman12plg.blogspot.com/2011/02/angklung.html.

Paulus, Erick, and Riki Nawawi, Mira Suryani, Undang A. Darsa, and Setiawan Hadi. 2018. "Upaya Revitalisasi Cagar Budaya Kabuyutan Ciburuy Melalui Rancang Bangun Aplikasi Bernama Mandala, *Jurnal Sosioteknologi* 17(1): 39–52.

Paxling, L. 2020. Exploring technology design among mobile entrepreneurs in Kampala: An open space workshop. *E J Info Sys Dev Countries*. 86:e12116.

Permata, Nadya Asri. 2021. "Pemahaman siswa tentang nilai karakter yang terkandung dalam lagu nasional di kelas V SD Negeri 84 Kota Bengkulu." Thesis: Institut Agama Islam Negeri Bengkulu, Benkulu, Indonesia.

Perris, Arnold B. 1971. "The Rebirth of the Javanese Angklung," *Ethnomusicology* 15 (3): 403–407.

Poetry, Haeranie Antania Riesta. 2011. Analisis daya tarik wisata Saung Angklung Udjo di kota Bandung. Thesis: UPI Bandung.

Pramono, Arditya. 2017. "Menengok Pembuatan Alat Musik Tiup dari Biji Mangga." Ayobandung.com. https://ayobandung.com/read/2017/01/20/15412/ menengok-pembuatan-alat-musik-tiup-dari-biji-mangga.

Pramudya, Windy Eka 2019. "Kelas Literasi: Sejarah Karinding Priangan," *Pikirin Rakyat*, Saturday, October 19, 2019.

Pramudya, Windy Eka. 2018. "Satu Dekade Tragedi AACC, Merancang Masa Depan Panggung Metal Bandung," *Pikiran Rakyat*, Saturday, February 10, 2018.

Price, Percival, and Joan Shull. "Handbell." *Grove Music Online*. Oxford University Press.

Puig de la Bellacasa , Maria. 2011. "Matters of Care in Technoscience: Assembling Neglected Things," *Social Studies of Science* 41(1): 85–106.

Purwanti, Indah., and Widiastuti, Indah. 2015. Creative Empowerment in Nonformal Education Institution. Case Study: Education System in Rumah Musik Harry Roesli (RMHR). *Procedia-Social and Behavioral Sciences* 184: 63–70.

Raffles, Thomas Stamford. 1817. *The History of Java*. Two volumes. London: Black, Parbury, and Allen.

148 References

Reerink, Gustaaf. 2015. "From Autonomous Village to 'Informal Slum': Kampong Development and State Control in Bandung (1930–1960)." In *Cars, Conduits, and Kampongs: The Modernization of the Indonesian City, 1920–1960*, eds. Freek Colombijn and Joost Coté. Leiden: Brill, pp. 193–212.

Reid, Anthony. 1988. *Southeast Asia in the Age of Commerce, 1450–1680*. Vol. 1. New Haven, CT.: Yale University Press.

Ridwan, Indra. 2014. *The art of the arranger in Pop Sunda, Sundanese Popular Music of West Java, Indonesia*. PhD dissertation (music), University of Pittsburgh.

Rigg, Jonathan. 1862. *A Dictionary of the Sunda Language*. Batavia: Lange & Co.

Riyadi, Armand. 2011. *Analysis Lagu Hampura Ema karya grup kesenian Karinding Attack Commonroom*. Thesis, Universitas Pendidikan Indonesia, Bandung.

Roberts, Brian Russell and Keith Foulcher, eds. 2016. *Indonesian notebook: a sourcebook on Richard Wright and the Bandung Conference*. Durham, NC: Duke University Press.

Roelcke, Gottfried, and Gary Crabb. 1994. *All Around Bandung: Exploring the West Java Highlands*. Bandung: Bandung Society for Heritage Conservation.

Rogers, W. A. 1894. "The Little People from Java," *St. Nicholas: An Illustrated Magazine for Young Folks* 21: 275–278

Rosidi, Ajip. 1984. Ciri-ciri Manusia dan Kebudayaan Sunda. In *Masyarakat Sunda dan Kebudayaanya*, ed. by E. Ekadjati. Jakarta: Girimukti Pasaka, pp. 125–161.

Rosidi, Ajip. 2003. *Apa Siapa Orang Sunda*. Bandung: PT Kiblat Buku Utama.

Ross, Laurie Margot. 2016. *The Encoded Cirebon Mask: Materiality, Flow, and Meaning along Java's Islamic Northwest Coast*. Leiden: Brill.

Rosyadi. 2012. "Angklung: Dari Angklung Tradisional Ke Angklung Modern," *Patanjala* 4(1): 26–40.

Rusnandar, Nandang. 2009. "Awi," blog post on *Padjadjaran Anyar*, November 16, 2009. http://sundasamanggaran.blogspot.com/2009_11_01_archive.html.

Sachs, Curt. 2006 (1940). *The History of Musical Instruments*. Mineola, NY: Dover Publications.

Sadikin, Syaeful Husni. 2009. Proses Pembelejaran Arumba di Saung Angklung Udjo Bandung. Thesis: UPI Bandung.

Sanui Edia S. 2007. "Karena Jiwa Kependidikannya Alm. Daeng Soetigna Berhasil Mewujudkan Karya Musik Angklungnya." In *Membela Kehormatan Angklung: Sebuah biografi dan bunga rampai Daeng Soetigna* (Defending Angklung's Honor: A Biography and Anthology of Daeng Soetigan) eds. Sumarsono, Tatang, and Erna Garnasih Pirous, Bandung: Yayasan Serambi Pirous, pp. 285–309.

Satya Upaja Budi, Dinda. 2015. Angklung Dogdog Lojor pada Masyarakat Kasépuhan Ciptagélar Kasatuan Adat Banten Kidul. Dissertation, Universitas Gadjah Mada (Yogyakarta, Indonesia).

Schafer, R. Murray. 1977. *The Tuning of the world*. New York: Knopf.

Seeger, Anthony. 2015. "Understanding UNESCO: A Complex Organization with Many Parts and Many Actors," *Journal of Folklore Research* 52(2–3): 269–280

Semedi, P. 2011. "Padvinders, Pandu, Pramuka: Youth and State in the 20th Century Indonesia," *Africa Development* 36(3&4): 19–38.

Setiadijaya, Barlan. 1996. "Keunikan sejarah lagu 'Hallo Bandung,'" *Kompas Online*, March 4, 1996.

Shimazu, Naoko. 2011. "Diplomacy as Theatre: Recasting the Bandung Conference of 1955 as Cultural History," Asia Research Institute, Working Paper Series No. 164, October, 2011. https://eprints.bbk.ac.uk/4914/2/4914.pdf

References 149

Shimazu, Naoko. 2014. "Diplomacy as Theatre: Staging the Bandung Conference of 1955," *Modern Asian Studies* 48(1): 225–252.

Simon, Artur. 1985. "The Terminology of Batak Instrumental Music in Northern Sumatra," *Yearbook for Traditional Music* 17: 113–145.

Simon, Artur. 2010. Southeast Asia: Musical Syncretism and Cultural Identity. *Fontes Artis Musicae* 57(1): 23–34, p. 25.

Siswantara, Yusuf. 2015. *Kritik Teks Atas Naskah Sewaka Darma*. Thesis, Universitas Katolik Parahyangan.

Sjamsuddin, Helius, Hidayat Winitasasmita, and Proyek Inventarisasi dan Dokumentasi Sejarah Nasional (Indonesia). 1986. *Daeng Soetigna, Bapak Angklung Indonesia*. Jakarta: Departemen Pendidikan dan Kebudayaan. Direktorat Sejarah dan Nilai Tradisional, Proyek Inventarisasi dan Dokumentasi Sejarah Nasional.

Sjukur, Slamet A. 2007. "Angklung, Dunia Kebetulan." In Sumarsono, Tatang, and Erna Garnasih Pirous, eds, *Membela Kehormatan Angklung: Sebuah biografi dan bunga rampai Daeng Soetigna* (Defending Angklung's Honor: A Biography and Anthology of Daeng Soetigan) eds. Sumarsono, Tatang, and Erna Garnasih Pirous, Bandung: Yayasan Serambi Pirous, pp. 268–270.

Slimmens, Ebenezer (a.k.a. A. J. Dockarty). 1894. *The Midway Plaisance: The Experience of an Innocent Boy from Vermont in the Famous Midway*. Chicago: Chicago World Book Co.

Soedarsono, R.M. 2002. *Seni pertunjukan Indonesia di era globalisasi*, 3rd ed. Yogyakarta: Gadjah Mada University Press.

Spiller, Henry. 2004. *Gamelan: The traditional sounds of Indonesia*. World Music Series. Santa Barbara, CA: ABC-CLIO.

Spiller, Henry. 2009. "Tunes that bind: Paul J. Seelig, Eva Gauthier, Charles T. Griffes, and the Javanese other," *Journal of the Society for American Music* 3(2): 129–154.

Spiller, Henry. 2010. *Erotic Triangles: Sundanese Dance and Masculinity in West Java*. Chicago: University of Chicago.

Spiller, Henry. 2015. *Javaphilia: American Love Affairs with Javanese Music and Dance*. Honolulu: University of Hawai`i Press.

Spiller, Henry. 2018. "From the Rice Harvest to 'Bohemian Rhapsody': Diachronic Modernity in Angklung Performance." In *Making Waves: Traveling Musics in Hawai`i, Asia, and the Pacific*, eds. Frederick Lau and Christine R. Yano. Honolulu: University of Hawai`i Press, pp. 19–38.

Stevens, Mrs. Mark. 1895. *Six months at the World's Fair*. Detroit, MI: Detroit Free Press.

Stiegler, Bernard. 1998. *Technics and time: The fault of Epimetheus* (Vol. 1). Stanford: Stanford University Press.

Stiegler, Bernard. 2014. "Organology of Dreams and Archi-Cinema," trans. Daniel Ross, *The Nordic Journal of Aesthetics* 47: 7–37.

Sukma, Agustika Harini. 2013. Studi organologi instrumen angklung diatonis buatan handiman diratmasasmita. Thesis: UPI Bandung.

Sumardjo, Jakob. 2011. "Pengantar: Sejarah Kota Bandung" in *200 Tahun Seni di Bandung*, edited by Irawati Durban Ardjo, Bandung: Pusbitari Press, pp. x–xxxvi.

Sumarsono, Tatang, and Erna Garnasih Pirous, eds. 2007. *Membela Kehormatan Angklung: Sebuah biografi dan bunga rampai Daeng Soetigna* (Defending Angklung's Honor: A Biography and Anthology of Daeng Soetigan). Bandung: Yayasan Serambi Pirous.

150 References

Surono, Seno Jotio. 2005. "Sebuah Hotel yang Dilupakan," *Tempo* 34(7–12): 88–90.

Sutherland, Heather. 1975. "The Priyayi," *Indonesia* 19: 57–78.

Suwandi, Tomy. 2013. "Perkembangan Nada-Nada dan Bentuk Alat Musik Karinding Towel di Daerah Buah Batu Bandung, Jawa Barat." Thesis: Universitas Negeri Jakarta.

Suwarna, Cici. 1999. *Proses Pembuatan Alat Tiup Suling oleh Endang Toto* (Endang Toto's process of making a Suling), Laporan Penelitian (Research Report), STSI Bandung.

Trimillos, Ricardo D. 1983. "The Sound of a Bell: Aesthetics and World Music," *Music Educators Journal (MEJ)* 69: 44–46.

Tronto, Joan. 1993. *Moral Boundaries: A Political Argument for an Ethic of Care.* New York: Routledge.

Tryana, Tino. 2011. Pertunjukan Angklung Buncis Dalam Acara Seren Taun di Kecamatan Cigugur Kabupaten Kuningan. Thesis: UPI.

Tucker, Joshua. 2016. "The machine of sonorous indigeneity: craftsmanship and sound ecology in an Andean instrument workshop," *Ethnomusicology Forum* 25(3): 326–344.

UNESCO. 2020. *Basic Texts of the 2003 Convention for the Safeguarding of the Intangible Cultural Heritage.* Paris: UNESCO. https://ich.unesco.org/doc/src/2003_Convention_Basic_Texts-_2020_version-EN.pdf.

Wahl, Uli. n.d. "The Famous 'Weeping Bamboo' or the Bamboo Aeolian Organ." Online resource: www.windmusik.com/html/bamborgl.htm.

Wallach, Jeremy. 2005. "Underground Rock Music and Democratization in Indonesia," *World Literature Today*. September–December: 16–20.

Wead, Charles Kasson. 1902. *Contributions to the history of musical scales.* Washington, DC: Government Printing Office.

Weinstein, Deena. 2011. "The Globalization of Metal." In *Metal Rules the Globe: Heavy Metal Music around the World*, eds. Jeremy Wallach, Harris M. Berger, and Paul D. Greene. Durham, NC: Duke University Press, pp. 34–62.

Weintraub, Andrew N. 1990. "The Music of Pantun Sunda: An Epic Narrative Tradition of West Java, Indonesia." M.A. thesis (music), University of Hawai'i.

Weintraub, Andrew N. 1993. "Creative Musical Practices in the Performance of Pantun Sunda," *Balungan* 5(2): 2–7.

Weintraub, Andrew N. 1994/1995. "Tune, Text, and the Function of Lagu in Pantun Sunda, A Sundanese Oral Narrative Tradition," *Asian Music* 24(1): 175–211.

Weintraub, Andrew N. 2006. "Dangdut Soul: Who are 'the People' in Indonesian Popular Music?" *Asian Journal of Communication* 16(4):411–431.

Wessing, Robert. 1977. "The Position of the Baduj in the Larger West Javanese Society," *Man (New Series)* 12(2): 293–303.

Wessing, Robert. 1998. "Bamboo, rice, and water." In *The Garland Encyclopedia of World Music, Volume 4: Southeast Asia*, eds. T.E. Miller and S. Williams. New York: Garland.

Westfall, Sammy. 2022. "Indonesia passes law to move capital from Jakarta to Borneo," *Washington Post*, January 18, 2022. www.washingtonpost.com/world/2022/01/18/indonesia-capital-city-jakarta-borneo/

References   151

Wilken, G.A. 1912. "Het Animisme bij de volken van den Indischen archipel." In *De Verspreide geschriften van Prof. Dr. G. A. Wilken*, ed. F.D.E. v. Ossenbruggen. Semarang: G.C.T. van Dorp.

Williams, Sean. 2001. *The Sound of the Ancestral Ship: Highland Music of West Java*. Oxford: Oxford University Press.

Wilson, Wilfrid G., and Steve Coleman. 2001. "Change ringing." *Grove Music Online*. Accessed September 1, 2022. www.oxfordmusiconline.com/grovemu sic/view/10.1093/gmo/9781561592630.001.0001/omo-9781561592630-e-000 0005399.

Winitasasmita, Mohd. Hidaya and Drs. Budiaman. 1978. *Angklung: Petunjuk Praktis* (Angklung: Practice Hints). Jakarta: PN Balai Pustaka.

Wiradiredja, Mohamad Yusuf. 2012. "Peranan R. A. A. Wiranatakusumah V Dalam Penyebaran Tembang Sunda Cianjuran," *Jurnal Seni & Budaya Panggung* 22(3): 225–250.

Wiramihardja, Obby A.R. 2007. *Sejarah Angklung (Angklung History)*. Jakarta: Masyarakat Musik Angklung (MMA). Online resource: https://angklungmusic society.wordpress.com/sejarah-angklung/.

Wiramihardja, Obby A.R. 2011. *Panduan Bermain Angklung* (A Guide for Playing Angklung). Jakarta: Masyarakat Musik Angklung.

Wolf, Eric R. 1982. *Europe and the people without history*. Berkeley, CA: University of California Press.

World Bank. 2012. "Indonesia: Clean rivers needed to promote water and food security," blog post, www.worldbank.org/en/news/feature/2012/03/22/clean-riv ers-needed-to-promote-water-and-food-security.

Wright, John. 2001. "Jew's harp." *Grove Music Online*. Oxford: Oxford University Press.

Yampolsky, Philip, Sumarsam, Lisa Gold, Tilman Seebass, Benjamin Brinner, Michael Crawford, et al. 2001. "Indonesia." *Grove Music Online*.

Yonatan, Stevanus. 2010. *Menyosialisasikan Karinding Kepada Generasi Muda Jawa Barat*. Undergraduate thesis, Universitas Kristen Maranatha.

Yulianti, Tya Eka. 2015. "Cerita Angklung yang Dimainkan pada KAA Tahun 1955," detikNews. (April 17, 2015). https://news.detik.com/berita/2890585/cer ita-angklung-yang-dimainkan-pada-kaa-tahun-1955.

Zainal, Mohd Ridzuwary Mohd, Salina Abdul Samad, Aini Hussain, and Che Husna Azhari. 2009. "Pitch and Timbre Determination of the Angklung," *American Journal of Applied Sciences* 6(1): 24–29.

Zanten, Wim van. 1989. *Sundanese Music in the Cianjuran Style: Anthropological and Musicological Aspects of Tembang Sunda*. Dordrecht: Foris.

Zanten, Wim van. 1995. "Aspects of Baduy Music in its Sociocultural Context, with Special Reference to Singing and Angklung," *Bijdragen tot de taal-, land- en volkenkunde* 151(4): 516–543.

Zanten, Wim van. 2008. "The Marriage Relationship between Player and Kacapi Zither in West Java," *Ethnomusicology Forum* 17 (1): 41–65.

Zanten, Wim van. 2014. "Musical Aspects of Popular Music and Pop Sunda in West Java." In *Sonic Modernities in the Malay World: A History of Popular Music, Social Distinction and Novel Lifestyles (1930s–2000s)*, ed. Bart Barendregt. Leiden: Brill, pp. 323–352.

152 References

Zanten, Wim van. 2021. *Music of the Baduy People of Western Java: Singing is a Medicine*. Verhandelingen van het Koninklijk Instituut voor Taal-, Land- en Volkenkunde, Volume 313. Leiden: Brill.

Zimmer, Benjamin G. 1999. "Unpacking the word: the ethnolexicological art of Sundanese kirata." In: *SALSA VI: Proceedings of the Sixth Annual Symposium about Language and Society—Austin, Texas Linguistic Forum* No. 42. Austin, TX: University of Texas Department of Linguistics, pp. 275–84.

Zubillaga-Pow, Jun. 2014. "The Dialectics of Capitalist Reclamation, or Traditional Malay Music in fin de siècle Singapore," *South East Asia Research* 22(1): 123–139. doi:10.5367/sear.2014.0195.

Index

Abah Olot 69, 89, 90, 91, 94, 96, 101–2, 113n15, 114n18
abstraction *see* entanglement
affordance *see* entanglement
Agus I. P. Wiryapraja 77, 79, 84n7
"Akang Haji" ("Sorban Palid") 79–80; historical recordings of 80
Akim Tarkim 67–9, *67*, 70–2, *70*, *71*, 73–7, 79, 117, 132
aksara Sunda kuno 87
angklung 2, 10, 12, 23–6, 28, 33–59; breaking world records 128; care and 124–8; ceremonial ensembles 38–9; construction of *23*, 37; cooperative nature 33; diatonic 10, 39–41, 49, 51–3, 136; diatonic, notation 42–3; diatonic, range 42–3, 60n11; diplomacy 46, 53, 127, 59n2; as education tool 53; as flexible representation of different economic systems 58–9; historical records 37–9; massal 51; performance practice 25–6, *26*, 31, 37, 53, 55; popularity of in Bandung schools 57; precursors of 37; sustainability 38
angklung badeng 38, 39
angklung Badud 39
angklung buncis 39
angklung diatonik *see* angklung, diatonic
angklung gubrag 39
angklung interaktif 48–50, 61n20, 62n26
angklung modern Sunda 49
angklung orchestra 50
angklung padaeng 3, 49, 52, 58, 59, 62n38

angklung paduan 54–9, 62n38
angklung pentatonik 49
angklung toél (angklung towel) 55–6, *56*, 126, 127
Angklung Web Institute (AWI) 58
arumba 127
Asep Bobeng 77, 80–2
Asep Nata 90, 95, 98, 113n9
Asep Nugraha 63n43
Asia-Africa Conference (Bandung 1955) 6, 11; *see also* Konperensi Asia-Afrika
assemblages 122–3
Atmadibrata xii; Enoch 5
awi buluh *see Schiostachyum brachycladium*
awi hideung *see Gigantochloa atroviolacea*
awi temen *see Gigantochloa atter*

backronym 136
Badan Koordinasi Musik Angklung (BKMA) 51–3
Baduy 38
bamboo 1–3, 65; affordances of 132, 136–7; assemblages and 122–3; biology 1; distinctive appearance 9, 133; distribution of 2, 17; as index of Sundanese-ness 19–23; musical sounds of 31; musical tunings derived from 116–22; resonance of 132–3; as producer of sound without human intervention 21; sonorous qualities of 2, 8; species/ varieties of 2; Sundanese place names and 21; as symbol/emblem of Sundanese landscape 1–3, 8, 11, 12, 22, 30, 79, 133, 136; uses of 2; *see also* bambu

154 *Index*

bamboo musical instruments, care and 129–33
bamboo retentions *see* retentions, bamboo
bamboo vs bronze 19–20, 92
bambu ater *see Gigantochloa atter*
bambu betung *see Dendrocalamus asper*
bambu gombong *see Gigantochloa verticillate*
bambu hitam *see Gigantochloa atroviolacea*
bambu perling 2
bambu talang *see Schiostachyum brachycladium*
bambu tamiang *see* tamiang
Bandung 1, 3–8; as capital city 5, 86; as cosmopolitan city 6; death metal in 99–100; history 85–7; population 5, 11n3; public transportation in 6
Bandung Death Metal Sindikat (BDMS) 100
"Bangbung Hideung" 80
Bandung Lautan Api (BLA) 42
Banten 14
"Banodari" 80
Batavia 4; *see also* Jakarta
batik patterns 18
BDMS *see* Bandung Death Metal Sindikat
"Besame Mucho" 54
"Beungong Jumpa" (Ibrahim Abduh) 78
Bhinneka Tunggal Ika ("Unity in Diversity") 14–15, 126
"Blue Danube Waltz" 41, 54
bitung (betung) 130; *see also Dendrocalamus asper*
blasquintentheorie *see* cycle of blown fifths
"Botol Kecap" 79
bronze 1, 17, 19–20, 122
Bubat War 12–15
Budi, Dinda Satya Upaja 56, 57
Budi Supardiman *see* Supardiman, Budi
Bukofzer, Manfred 121
bupati 17, 26, 85, 131; *see also* regent
Burhan Sukarma *see* Sukarma, Burhan

calung 2, 48
capitalism *see* economic systems
care 122–3; angklung and 123–8; bamboo musical instruments and 129–33; karinding and 133–5

Car Free Day 81
Cavalera, Max 103, 114n28
celempung 3, 7, 33, 67–9, *70*, 99, 103, *106*, 109, 111, 112; construction 70–2, *71*
celempungan 68–9
celempung renteng 71–2, 103, *72*, *107*, 108
Cianjuran 26–7, *28*, 131; *see also* tembang Sunda
CIHOG *see* Cikapundung Hiking Orienteering Games
Cika Cika 82
Cikapundung Hiking Orienteering Games (CIHOG) 66, *66*, 77–82
Cikapundung river 11, 64, *65*, 66, 79–82, 85
Cirebon 14, 39, 129
coherence 121–3, 132
colonialism *see* economic systems
colotomic 29, 72–3
Common Room 7, 102, 115n36; kelas karinding and 110
communism *see* economic systems
cycle of blown fifths 118–19; debunking of 121, 137n4

Daendels, Henrik Willem 85
Daeng Oktaviandi Udjo 48
Daeng Soetigna *see* Soetigna, Daeng
Dago 4, 10, 64, 66, 68, 81, 129; bamboo in 68
Dago Thee Huis 32n4, 64
dangdut 10, 30–1, 81
dasasila Bandung (ten resolutions) 35
Dayang Sumbi 85
death metal 3, 8, 98–101, 108–12, 133; in Bandung 99–100, 102; musical characteristics of 102
"Death of Citraresmi" 18–19
debus 100
Deep Purple 98, 114n20
degung *see* gamelan degung
Dendrocalamus asper 2, 11n1
Departemen Pendidikan dan Kebudayaan (Department of Education and Culture (Depdikbud) 51
Dewi Sri 2, 23; *see also* Nyi Pohaci
Dharmawan, Dwiki 125, 127
Dim, Herry 2, 3, 17
Dinda Satya Upaja Budi *see* Budi, Dinda Satya Upaja
Diratmasasmita, Handiman *see* Handiman Diratmasasmita

Index

DIY *see* do-it-yourself
Djaja 52, 59, 60n6
Djoko Nugroho 54
Doel Sumbang 98
dogdog lojor 38
do-it-yourself (DIY) 8, 100
dramatari 18
Dunham, Ann 126
Durban Ardjo, Irawati *see* Irawati
Durban Ardjo
Dutch East India Company *see*
Vereenigde Oostindische
Compagnie

economic systems 33; capitalism 28,
33, 45, 47, 50, 53, 55, 111, 124,
128; capitalism and angklung
55; colonialism 33, 41, 55, 124;
communism 33, 46, 53, 124;
egalitarianism 33; globalism 33;
neoliberalism 10, 33, 35, 55, 59, 123,
124, 128; socialism 10, 33
Edi Permadi 53
egalitarianism *see* economic systems
Endang Sugriwa *see* Abah Olot
Endang Toto *see* Toto, Endang
entanglement (musical) 116–23, 128,
137; abstraction and 116–17, 121–4,
128, 129, 132, 136; affordance and
116–17, 121–3, 128, 129, 132, 136;
resonance and 116–17, 121–4,
128, 132, 133, 135, 137; Sundanese
tunings and 121–2
equidistance 117–2
Ewing, Michael 5
expositions 1, 21; *see also* World's
Columbian Exposition (1893);
New York World's Fair (1963)

G30S *see* Gerakan 30 September
Gajah Mada 12–15
galengan 65
Galengan Sora Awi (GSA) 10,
65–83, *66*, *67*, 132, 136; approach to
arranging songs 80–2; repertory
81–2; status as amateurs 82–3
gambang 2
gambang awi 75–6, *76*, *78*
"Gambang Suling" *see* "Suara Suling"
gamelan 1, 19, 28, 29, 57, 72, 76, 77,
81, 122, 126, 137n2
gamelan degung 77, 82
gamelan salendro 29–30, *29*
Gedung Merdeka 35–7, *36*, 86
geger 3

Gerakan 30 September (September 30th
Movement, G30S) 47, 52
Gigantochloa atroviolacea 11n1
Gigantochloa atter 2, 11n1
Gigantochloa verticillate 2
Gilman, Benjamin Ives 93, 97
globalism *see* economic systems
glocalization 87–8
golok (Sundanese machete) 18
goong 29, *29*, 69, 73, 74
goong awi 73–4, *73*
gotong royong (spirit of mutual
cooperation) 10, 35, 47, 53, 124,
127
Grand Symphony Angklung 10, 125–8,
136
Grote Postweg 85, 112n1
guimbarde 88–9; other names for 88,
112n4
guitar 7, 29, 31, 76, 81, 127, 133;
Endo Suanda's bamboo 129–12, *131*;
in death metal 102–8, 111

"Hallo-Hallo Bandung" (Ismail
Marzuki) 41–5, 52; as decolonial
gesture 45; Daeng Soetigna's
angklung arrangement 42–5, *42*, *43*;
musical analysis 45
handbell choirs 60n8
Handiman Diratmasasmita 51–3, 57,
59n2
Hari Roesli *see* Roesli, Hari
Hayam Wuruk 12–15, 18
Helmholtz, Hermann von 118
heritage regime 128
Hermawan, Deni 57
Hety Udjo 48
history: Sundanese 12–18
Ho Chi Minh 52
Hodder, Ian 10, 116–17, 121–3, 133
Hornbostel, Erich M. von 118–20

ibing keurseus 19
ICHH *see* UNESCO List of Intangible
Cultural Heritage of Humanity
(ICHH)
Ichsan, Sony M. 54
iket 18, 87, 95, 102
"Imagine" (John Lennon) 127
Iman Rahman Angga Kusuma *see*
Kimung
industri kreatif 57
Institut Seni Budaya Indonesia (ISBI)
7, 63n42; *see also* Sekolah Tinggi
Seni Indonesia

156   Index

Institut Teknologi Bandung (Bandung Institute of Technology, ITB) 54; diatonic angklung groups *see* Keluarga Paduan Angklung ITB
Intangible Cultural Heritage of Humanity (ICHH) *see* UNESCO List of Intangible Cultural Heritage of Humanity (ICHH)
Irawati Durban Ardjo 60n13, 98
Ismail Marzuki 42
ITB *see* Institut Teknologi Bandung

jaipongan 10, 48, 80, 81
Jakarta 4, 6, 30, 41, 42, 96, 125, 128, 129
Javanese, population 14
Java, topographic map of *16*; *see also* West Java
Jawa Barat *see* West Java
jaw's harp *see* guimbarde
Jaya *see* Djaja
jengglong 29
jew's harp *see* guimbarde
Jimbot 32n9, 114n26, 132, 138n13

kabupaten 17
kacapi 69, 129; Endo Suanda's bamboo 131–3, *131*
kakawen 80
Kalimantan, plans for new Indonesian capital 4
karéng 90
karinding 3, 7, 10, 33, 76–7, 87–93, *88*, *91*; at 1893 Chicago Exposition 93; bamboo microphone stands for 91, *91*; bamboo resonator for 90–3; care and 133–5; construction of 88–9; courtship and 92, 94, 98; death metal and 98–102; decline of 97–8; etymologies 92; as fashion item 95, *95*; functions of 93–4; historical references to 92–3; history of 93–6; learning to play 110–11; LEKRA and 94, 97; part names 88–9, *89*; as pest control 95–6; repertory 96–7; standard patterns (pirigan) of 96–7; Sundanese values and 111–12
Karinding Attack 10, 102–11, 133, 135; personnel of 114n25, 114n26
karinding kartu 135
karinding toél (karto) 90, 134
karinding towel *see* karinding toél
karto *see* karinding toél
Kasur 52, 62n33

kekeluargaan ("family-ism") 47, 48, 50–1
kelas karinding (KEKAR) 97, 110, 115n36
Keluarga Paduan Angklung ITB (KPA-ITB) 54
"Kembang Gadung" 79
"Kembang Tanjung" 80
kendang 7, *29*, 68, 69, 74–5; construction of 74–5, *74*
kendang awi 74–6, *75*
kenong 29, *29*, 72
keris (Javanese knife) 18, *19*
ketuk tilu 72, 79, 80
Ki Amenk *91*, 101, 114n25, 114n26
Kimung (Iman Rahman Angga Kusuma) 87, 94, 96, 97, 100, 102, 109, 110, 114n25, 114n26
kirata 136
Konperensi Asia-Afrika 11, 33–7, 41, 45, 51, 54; angklung performances at 36–7, 60n3, 60n4; as decolonial gesture 41; twenty-fifth anniversary celebration of 54; *see also* Asia-Africa Conference
"Kuda Lumping" (Rhoma Irama) 30–1
kujang (Sundanese weapon) 18, *19*, 87
kulanter 74
Kunst, Jaap 7, 29, 38, 68, 69, 72, 90–4, 96, 118–20, 137n4

lagu mars 43–4
lagu monumental 54
lamella 88–90
"Lapar Ma" (Karinding Attack) 108, 114–15n32
latihan 82
LEKRA *see* Lembaga Kebudayaan Rakyat
Lembaga Kebudayaan Rakyat (LEKRA) 52, 95, 97; karinding and 95, 97
lesung 126
Lingga Buana 12–15
Linggajati agreement 41

"Maaf" (Karinding Attack) 108–9, *109*
Maceda, José 117
Majapahit 12–15, *13*, 28
Mang Engkus 101
Man (Jasad) 101, 109–10, 114n25
mars *see* lagu mars
Mashudi, General Dr. H.C. 37, 57, 60n5
massal *see* angklung massal

Masyarakat Musik Angklung (Angklung Music Community, MMA) 55, 57, 58
Mataram 14, 17, 28, 37
mataraman 79
menak 4, 17–19; personal names 17
MMA *see* Masyarakat Musik Angklung
modernity, modernities 7, 8, 41, 87, 88, 123
Mohd. Hidayat Winitasasmita, 53
mouth harp *see* guimbarde

Nalan, Arthur S. 81–2
Nan Udjo 48
Narohardjo (Naroharjo), Oyon *see* Oyon Naroharjo
Nata, Asep 11, 90, 95, 98, 133–5, 138n14–16; as builder of bamboo musical instruments 134–5; biographical information 133–4
Negara Pasundan 14, 41
neoliberalism *see* economic systems
New Order 3, 35, 47, 50–1, 53, 87, 95, 97, 99, 100, 128, 111
New York World's Fair (1963) 45–7; angklung at 46; location of Indonesian pavilion at 46; Sundanese delegation to 46, 60n13; USSR and 46
ngabungbang 82, 94
Ngalagena, Udjo *see* Udjo Ngalagena
non-aligned movement 34, 35, 41, 124
No Car Day 10
Nugraha, Asep *see* Asep Nugraha
Nugroho, Djoko *see* Djoko Nugroho
"Nusantara Medley" (Galengan Sora Awi) 77–9, 81
Nyi Kentring Manuk 85
Nyi Pohaci 2, 23; *see also* Dewi Sri

Obama, Barack 126
Obama Ndesanjo, Mark Okot 126–7
Obby Wiramihardja *see* Wiramihardja, Obby A.R.
Old Order 47, 53, 111
Olot, Abah *see* Abah Olot
Orde Baru *see* New Order
Orde Lama *see* Old Order
Oteng Sutisna *see* Sutisna, Oteng
Oyon Naroharjo *89*, 90, 94, 97

Padasuka 47, 49, 51
paduan 54, 58, 59, 62n38
Pajajaran 4, 12–15, *13*, 17, 38, 58
"Pajajaran" (degung piece) 82

pangsi 87
Parahyangan 4, 17
Partai Komunis Indonesia (PKI) 47, 52, 95, 97
partitur 40, 44
pathet lima 78
pelog degung 79, 117, 120–1, 137n2
penca silat 18, 19, 77, 81, 93, 100
Pengurus Guru Republik Indonesia (Teachers Association of the Republic of Indonesia, PGRI) 52
pirigan 110, 96–7, *106*, 110, 113n15
PKI *see* Partai Komunis Indonesia
pop Sunda 10, 76, 77, 79, 81, 122
Postweg *see* Grote Postweg
Preanger 4, 17
Preanger Hotel 35, 36
Priangan 4, 17
Program Studi (Prodi) Angklung dan Musik Bambu (STSI) 57
proverbs, Sundanese 1, 9–10, 33, 86, 87, 111, 116, 118, 122, 123, 129, 133
Puig de la Bellacasa, Maria 122–3

Radio Parahyangan 69, 84n5
Raffles, Sir Thomas Stamford 20, 38
rakyat 17–19, 26, 100; personal names for 17
Rasta, Otong 5
rebab 29, *29*, 68, 79
reformasi 3, 8, 55, 58, 98–100, 111
"Refuse/Resist" (Sepultura) 103–8, *104–5*; Karinding Attack's cover 103–8, *106–7*
regent 14, 17, 26, 93; *see also* bupati
renewable resources 8
rengkong 126
resonance *see* entanglement
retentions (Stiegler), bamboo 66–8, 81, 83, 136; primary 66, 68, 83; secondary 66, 68, 83; tertiary 66–8, 83
revival: bamboo musical instruments 7–8, 10, 31, 33, 83; karinding 77, 95, 111, 133
Rhoma Irama 30–1
rice cultivation 3, 37, 39
Roesli, Hari 6, 98
ronggeng 79
Ruchimat, Ismet 7, *118*

Saleh, Tati *see* Tati Saleh
salendro 49, 76, 110, 117, 119–21; equidistance and 120; *see also* gamelan; gamelan salendro

158   *Index*

Sambasunda 7
Samin 69
Sam Udjo 48, 49
Sangkuriang 85
Sanu'i Edia S. 52, 53, 61n17, 62n37
Saung Angklung Udjo (SAU) 39,
   47–51, 128; afternoon performance
   at 48–50, *50*, 61n21; Bandung
   tourism and 48, 61n23; as reflection
   of New Order 50–1; training
   program 49
scales, musical 30, 59, 117–22
Schiostachyum blumei 2; *see also*
   tamiang
Schiostachyum brachycladium 2
Schoemaker, Charles Prosper Wolff 35,
   59n1, 86
Sekolah Menengah Atas Negeri 3
   (SMAN 3) 54, 55, 58
Sekolah Tinggi Seni Indonesia (College-
   level School of Indonesian Arts,
   STSI) 32, 54, 57; *see also* Institut Seni
   Bandung Indonesia (ISBI)
September 30th Movement *see* Gerakan
   30 September
Sepultura 100, 103, *104*, *106*
siter 69
SMAN 3 *see* Sekolah Menengah Atas
   Negeri 3
"Sorban Palid" *see* "Akang Haji"
Soeharto 3, 15, 35, 47, 51, 52, 55, 57,
   63, 97, 99, 100, 111
Soetigna, Daeng 36, 39–41, 46–8, 58,
   126; arrangements 55
Somawijaya, Abun 57
Sony M. Icsan *see* Ichsan, Sony M.
soundmarks 9, 11, 12, 22, 27–31, 45,
   83, 117
"Spanish Eyes" 54
Stiegler, Bernard 66–8, 83, 84n1, 136;
   see also retentions
STSI *see* Sekolah Tinggi Seni
   Indonesia
Suanda, Endo 10, 97, 129–33; as
   bamboo musical instrument builder
   129–33; biographical information
   129–30
"Suara Suling" (Nartosabdho) 78
Subardja, Abay xii, 5
Suharto *see* Soeharto
Sugriwa, Endang *see* Abah Olot
Sukarma, Burhan 27, 97
Sukarno 12, 14, 15, 34–6, 41, 45–7,
   50, 85, 111; vision of Indonesian
   governance 42, 46

suling 12, 19, 26–8, *78*, *118*, *119*; as
   index of rakyat 19; construction of
   26, *27*; equidistance of fingerholes
   117–21, *118*, *119*; panjang 117,
   118–20, 121, *121*
Sumarna, Undang xii, 5
Sumbang, Doel *see* Doel
   Sumbang
Sumiati, Uum *see* Uum Sumiati
Sunda wiwitan 88, 131, 133
Sundanese music, basic texture 12,
   28–31, 79, 117; basic texture of and
   bamboo 136; gamelan salendro
   and 29–30; tembang Sunda and 30;
   tunings 117
Supardiman, Budi 24, 54, 57, 58
Supiono, Iyon 57
Sutisna, Oteng 51, 62n29

taleot 77, 117
Taman Budaya 64, 67
tamiang 2, 9; entanglements and
   116–22; *see also Schiostachyum
   blumei*
tampian (rustic bathing shelter) 33, *34*,
   124
Tangkuban Perahu 85, *86*
Tarkim, Akim *see* Akim Tarkim
tarompet 77, *78*
Tati Saleh 46, 60n15
Taufik Hidayat Udjo 48, 56
Teddy Kusmayadi 77, *88*, 90
tembang Sunda 26–7, *28*; *see also*
   Cianjuran
things *see* assemblages
tonggeret 96, *105*, 110, 113n12
Toto, Endang 32n9, 117, *118*
Touch of Seven 126, 127, 137n6
Tragedi AACC 101, 102, 111
trisula 18
trump *see* guimbarde
Tucker, Joshua 67, 84n1, 123
tunings, bamboo-derived
   116–22

Udjo Ngalagena 47–8, 52, 53, 61n18,
   127; background of 48; children of
   48, 61n20
UNESCO List of Intangible Cultural
   Heritage of Humanity (ICHH) 1, 57,
   124–5, 127
Universitas Pasundan (UNPAS) 7
University of California, Santa
   Cruz 5
Uum Sumiati 47–8

Index 159

Vereenigde Oostindische Compagnie (VOC; Dutch East India Company) 14

VOC *see* Vereenigde Oostindische Compagnie

wayang 48, 57, 78, 80, 81, 90, 125
"We are the World" (Michael Jackson and Lionel Richie) 128
Wead, Charles 117, 120
West Java 1–5; bamboo and 20; geography 15–18; historical names 4, 17; history 12; population 14;

see also Pasundan, Parahyangan, Preanger, Priangan
Wiramihardja, Obby A.R. 51–4, 58
Wiranatakusumah II 85
Wiryapraja, Agus I. P. *see* Agus I. P. Wiryapraja
Wisnu *91*
World's Columbian Exposition (1893), Java Village 21–2, *22*

yanggun 126, 127
Yayan Muliana Udjo 48, 55–7
Yayan Udjo 126

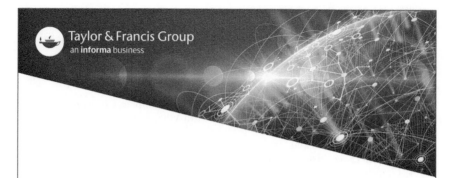